The Daemonolater's Guide To Daemonic Magick

S. Connolly
Valerie Corban
Brid Delaney

Also with articles written by and with Anjie Anon, M. Delaney, Selinda T. Dukante, Darrek Mallory, Brad Morlan, Lisa P., Ellen Purswell, and Kelly & Nicholas (GoeticNick) Schneider

The Daemonolater's Guide To Daemonic Magick

S. Connolly
Valerie Corban
Brid Delaney

Also with articles written by and with Anjie Anon, M. Delaney, Selinda T. Dukante, Darrek Mallory, Brad Morlan, Lisa P., Ellen Purswell, and Kelly & Nicholas (GoeticNick) Schneider

DB Publishing
United States of America

DB Publishing is an imprint of Darkerwood Publishing Group, PO Box 2011, Arvada, CO 80001. Contact the publisher for bulk purchases and discounts or contact ofs.admin@gmail.com for online wholesale purchase links.

Parts of this book were first published in:
The Complete Book of Demonolatry, DB Publishing, 2006 by S. Connolly and The Art of Creative Magick, 2007 by S. Connolly.

Library of Congress-in-Publication Data

Connolly, S. ; Corban, Valerie ; Delaney, Brid 2009
    The Daemonolater's Guide to Daemonic Magick
    I. Occult, II. Demonology, III. Demonolatry
        Indexed
ISBN: 978-0-9788975-1-2

Book Design by DB Publishing, Adrianna.
Cover Design: Adrianna
Sigil Art & Pineapple God Art: Donated by Kenneth Betts
Printed in the United States of America

Warning: No incenses, tinctures, or oleums contained in this book should be taken internally. DB Publishing and the authors are not responsible for any person using the incenses or oleums improperly in a way that might cause personal injury, illness, or death. Poisonous herbs used in some of the traditional recipes included are clearly marked and should not be taken internally. *DISCLAIMER:* The information in this book is provided for information purposes only. The authors and publisher are not responsible for any person who uses the information in this book for illegal activities or if any person is injured or harmed by use of the information contained herein. No warranties are expressed or implied by publication of this material.

About This Book

There are several ways in which you can read this book. First, you can read it cover to cover. However, each little section was written on its own as a separate essay. Therefore you can skip around and read on topics individually as your interest dictates. This is also why the order of the book may seem somewhat strange or chaotic. We attempted to keep like topics with like topics, but it didn't always pan out. It's all interconnected, after all…

Dedication & Acknowledgements

We would like to dedicate this work to all of the Daemonolaters out there who inspired this book. Without your encouragement and support, we may never have pulled it all together. We'd also like to thank those authors who only penned a section or two, and those Daemonolaters who merely looked things over and offered input or a fresh eye. This book wouldn't have happened without you.

Brid Delaney and Valerie Corban (along with all the other writers) would like to personally thank S. Connolly for editing and formatting this work in its entirety. The reader should also be aware that Ms. Connolly did the largest majority of writing for this book and helped us put into words what we could not. She is a most accomplished magician as she was able to turn us into writers. She also did all the indexing. This is clearly a tome she could have written herself and we feel honored she asked us to co-author this work with her. This is why we insisted her name appear most prominently as the main author of this work.

S. Connolly would like to personally thank Jeremy Carroll for transcribing and typing up the formulary section of the book, J. Caven for lending a fresh eye during editing, and Kenneth Betts for his work in re-making and scanning all the Dukante and Warding sigil graphics and other sigils as needed. To learn more about all the authors and contributors to this book, see the back of the book. While I may have been the one to pull it all together, the whole is only as strong as the sum of its parts. Even those who contributed an opinion are greatly appreciated. You know who you are.

CONTENTS

Introduction to Daemonic Magick

Daemonic magick is the practice of invoking Daemons, from the original root words meaning divine intelligences replete with wisdom, to aid change in conformity with your will. In Daemonolatry, this is accomplished through respectful invocation and modification of what already exists within the three great pillars of magick and beyond. The process of Daemonic Magick can take many forms from simple kitchen witchery to complex ritual and ceremony. Daemons work with an individual's energy in tandem and harmony to amplify personal power through focus and direction of energy. Many also believe there is a direct transference of energy from Daemon to practitioner. You share your energy with them, and them with you in natural balance.

Some also believe you do not have to be a religious Daemonolater to practice Daemonolatry. All of us sat down and discussed this. While we agree that someone who does not worship Daemons can work Daemonic Magick as prescribed in this book, we wonder if perhaps some of what we'll discuss in this book will be of any use to non-Daemonolaters. I suppose the saying, "Take what works and leave the rest" would apply.

1

This book is not meant to be the gospel of anything or the beginning or end all of Daemonic Magick. Perhaps you'll find some of the methods in this book do not work for you or that you disagree. That's okay. We'd be surprised to learn that any off the shelf magick worked for *everyone* "as is".

We'd also like to dispel the myth straight away that invocation of a Daemonic entity to physical manifestation is always desirable and that if you aren't invoking (or evoking or summoning ::cringe::) Daemons to physical manifestation you're doing something wrong and your rituals aren't effective. This common misconception is not true and is the fantasy of dabblers. Daemons don't always appear or respond in bright flashes of light and plenty of fan faire. To those naysayers who believe otherwise we say, "Show us and prove it." We're open-minded to be sure and none of us who helped pen this book are all knowing. We still have plenty to learn. But we would guess that with over 85 years of experience between the three of us main authors and the additional 100+ years of experience of the people we consulted for additional information and articles in this book, if we haven't found a sure-fire way of causing Daemonic entities to physically manifest (barring any use of drugs, smoke and mirrors) every single time that there likely isn't one. If there were, there would be obvious discretion in sharing something so potent anyway.

For those who know better know that the Daemonic is physically manifested always within ourselves. We are the physical manifestations of the Divine, after all.

Please note that this book is just a *starting point*. You aren't going to be able to read this book and be an all-knowing magician afterward. This book is gold for the beginner and a good primer and grimoire for the more advanced Daemonolatry Magician. Also be aware that everything we know (individually or collectively) is not contained in this book. To share every ounce of knowledge

2

we all possess would require volumes and volumes of material. Instead, what we have collected here is foundational, general know how, and a reference work for the Daemonolatry student and the adept.

This book will make more sense in the context of TG (Traditional Generational of the Khemetic/Canaanite variety) Daemonolatry. If you would like to learn more about the religious and magickal aspects of this particular type of Daemonolatry pick up a copy of *The Complete Book of Demonolatry* by S. Connolly.

We would also like to make clear that this book does not share any "sacred" rituals not meant for the non-initiated or sell out our belief system by "giving away all its secrets." This is a practical modern grimoire of Daemonic Magick, written, published and released to the general public to make Daemonolatry style magick accessible to those magicians who wish to utilize it. Nothing less, nothing more.

The Courtesies

From Ellen Purswell's Goetic Daemonolatry and reprinted here with permission.

· The magician who hath a supposed greater knowledge of magick and contradicts knowledge of another magician of greater or lesser rank will never excel in his studies. [*This basically means keep your ego in check. You are still only mortal and arrogance on your behalf will only hold you back.*]

· The powerful magician doth not boast of power or greater knowledge. He shall excel. [*A little humility goes a long way.*]

· The rank of one magician compared to that of another should not be viewed as competition. [*You are not in competition with others of your faith, you are brethren and should help one another.*]

· A magician of lesser rank is not inferior and should not view another of greater rank as a threat, but as an equal and one to be learned from. [*Those more experienced can help you achieve your goals.*]

· A magician of greater rank is not superior and should not view another of lower rank as weak or inferior, but as an equal and one to be learned from. [*The experience of the magician should not be used to pull rank even though there are times it is tempting. I think we all have had experiences where we broke this courtesy to put a young, arrogant magician in his/her place. We just need to try NOT to do this regardless the temptation.*]

· What one magician sees as the best or only way of magick, another may not. We are all individuals. [*There are many ways to perform the same magickal operation and no one way is the best way. What works for one person may not work for another.*]

· As in everything, each individual has an area within magick where he is most adept and will excel rapidly. [*We all have different strengths and weaknesses. It's up to us to find out where we excel and where we could use practice. Know thyself.*]

· Each magician is given at least one gift from the universe. This gift may be one that another magician might possess, but another will lack in to where excelling is almost impossible. This is because a gift is a natural extension of something the magician is born with. [*Don't beat yourself up if divination (for example) comes easier to others than it does to you otherwise your self-confidence will duly suffer. You might pack a wallop when it comes to sending and directing energy whereas those who excel at divination might not.*]

I should also go into more specific reasons why these Courtesies have been put in place. It seems that when it comes to magick [especially *rare* group operations], many practitioners allow things such as jealousy to stand in the way of their own personal growth. This happens often between people who, at one time, were good friends. From a personal standpoint I've seen a good number of sects and friendships fall apart because of this. Humans are naturally competitive due to our egos. Therefore the courtesies are in place to keep the magician humble. It helps to remind him that just because he is at odds with another magician, that he should take pause before pulling out the black candles and throwing a curse, which is usually how these ego-wars turn out.

More often than not, those magicians who do get caught up in their egos end up underestimating their opponents. The magician's natural gift may be focusing and throwing energy, but their opponent may also have the same gift, or could be someone who easily fends off the negative energy, sending it back to it's source. So if you've done a rite to curse someone and have not thought it through, don't be surprised when you are the one who falls ill while the victim remains untouched.

Remember always that knowledge comes to us easier when we can admit to ourselves, and others, that we do not know or that we are not superior to anyone because of what we know. That is one of the keys to knowing the self.

Other Ground Rules
(from the authors)

There are a few ground rules for magick.

◊ **Do not throw curses indiscriminately**. Seriously consider whether or not you want to waste your energy on the person. **Make sure you will have NO REGRETS whatsoever** or you can inadvertently pull that negativity back on yourself. Also remember that some people curse themselves by default. Don't waste your energy on those people.

◊ Remember that **for every action there is a reaction**. Be fully aware of all consequences that can arise from **any** magickal operation and **be willing to take full responsibility for ALL of your magickal actions**.

◊ **Let it go.** Once you've performed a magickal operation (especially where you're attempting to effect someone else's will), it will be most effective if you let it go. Don't brag on it, talk to everyone about it, or obsess over it. Don't constantly lift the lid on your cursing or healing pots. Don't revisit the graves of worked magick. Now, sometimes letting a cursed person know they're cursed will speed the curse along. On the other hand, if that person is a magician as well – you're giving them opportunity to defend themselves and possibly curse you in return. On the flip side of that, sometimes it's more effective to tell a person you're working healing magick for them so they can open themselves to it. Sometimes they'll be more resistant. **Part of the wisdom of magick is knowing when to keep silent and when to speak up.**

◊ **To Know, To Will, To Dare, To Keep Silent** – that is the ancient wisdom. Take it as you will.

◊ **Intention is everything**. Ultimately, it's your will that directs the path your magick takes once you send it out into the universe. Sometimes when magick doesn't work or falls short, it's because your will, focus, and direction weren't on the same page as your emotions. You can say all you want that you want to make more money, but if deep down you fear a higher position or taking a chance on a new career, or you have low self esteem and don't think you really deserve the raise, the likelihood of magick along that vein manifesting to its full potential, or even at all, diminishes.

◊ **Follow up and follow through**. Not all magick works without a little help. Sure, cursing and healing and magicks that influence others can't always be followed up on or followed through with. However, magick having to do with your own situation can be. For example, if you seek to lose weight, you still have to eat right and exercise. If you want a better job, you have to go looking for one. If you want to attract a mate, you can't hide at home and never go out to meet people. That's just not how it works. You still need to do some follow up legwork to improve the chances that your magick will be successful.

◊ **Sometimes it will take more than one working**, depending on the difficulty level of what you're trying to achieve and how talented a magician you are. For some, practice (doing things over and over again) is necessary. For others it isn't. **Be realistic with your magickal goals** and your will, and you'll get realistic results.

◊ Kitchen witches will tell you that magickal timing and various correspondences aren't too big of a deal. Other magicians swear on precise timing and exact corresponding colors, stones, herbs, etc... The authors of this book are all of the belief that **the more specific and detail oriented you are with your ritual magick, the more likely you are to be able to manifest your true will effectively and to the fullest extent**. More will be discussed about this in other sections.

◊ **Learn foundation**. Behind every good magician is a strong foundational knowledge of magick (of various schools of occult thought), correspondences, ritual structure, purposes behind ritual actions, methods employed and the reasoning/symbolism behind each tool, action, color, planet, etc… Once you have this foundational knowledge – then experiment. If you experiment before you have foundation, we feel you're missing out on your full potential as a magician.

◊ **Feel free to experiment (once you have foundation)** and you'll find what works for you and what doesn't and you'll soon be able to modify rituals to their most potent form for you and your work.

The Types of Magicians
By S. Connolly

The Types of Magicians

Arm Chair Theorists: These are the types of magicians who read a lot about magick, may have tried one or two things, but who don't really practice. These people are ones who merely "theorize" about how things should work and love talking about magick. Talk is great until you want to really discuss real experience. I think Arm Chair Theorists really miss out.

Astral Magicians: These are people who do a lot of meditation, but not much else for whatever reason. They have great, vivid imaginations and amazing minds, and are often very effective magicians. These are people who often don't prepare for ritual work so they miss out on the valuable lessons preparation teaches. Not to mention they miss out on a completely different aspect of ritual work, in my humble opinion, that can be deeply satisfying and balancing.

Kitchen Witches: These are folks who are into spells, formulas, charms, candle magick, color magick, stone magick, folk magicks, and kitchen witchery. They do magick to make stuff happen, but they aren't into ritual or ceremonial magick or more complex techniques or methods. Many of these people often see the power outside themselves and spend their time tapping external sources. They may or may not look within

Whatever Works, Works, Magicians (WWWM): These are folks who make it up as they go along and it works for them. They may use magick for life transformation or self work, but they have little to no foundational knowledge in other systems. Unfortunately (or fortunately depending on your perspective) I've come to believe that a lot of foundational knowledge is really important. For Whatever Works, Works people - you really need to understand why things work - and that comes from having a foundation. It's after you have the foundation that you can progress to "Whatever Works, Works". **WWW is NOT a starting point** (though numerous new magicians start here because it's easier than taking the time to learn foundation). It's my humble opinion that people who start here are simply holding themselves back from their full potential.

High Magicians Who Want Stuff: These are the people who will get into more complex systems of ritual or ceremonial magick, but who only graze the surface. They don't use magick to its full potential. Instead, they often use it to get stuff or change cosmetic life situations, but rarely go any deeper than that. They may or may not combine their love of high magick with kitchen witchery, astral magick, and armchair theorism. I've known a few of these folks who sadly got into CM for the sex magick.

High Magicians Learning About Themselves: These are the people who will get into more complex systems of ritual or ceremonial magick, but who only use it to explore

11

themselves deeply. While this is not a bad thing – some of these folks may not use magick to its full potential. They concentrate on the Great Work, but some get lost in their own egos along the way and consequently - miss a great deal.

Dabblers: These are folks who get their feet wet in everything but never really delve deep enough to really transform much of anything except the aesthetics (if even that). Unfortunately a great number of "theistic" and "spiritual" Satanists and groups fall into this area.

Magicians: Finally, and I'm making a huge leap here in suggesting this - there are the few magicians who have been dabblers, theorists, astral magicians, kitchen witches, WWWM's, high magicians of both varieties, and who are eventually transformed into real, honest to goodness magicians over time. They've been all of the above and combined it all into something so complex that one couldn't just write a book about it, let people read it, and create more folks like themselves. Most of what anyone needs to know (basic foundational knowledge) about magick is already written somewhere.

The problem is that in order to become a magician you need genuine working experience and you need strong foundation. Most people are too lazy or unmotivated to bother. Very few are nimble enough to take what they've learned and pull it all together in such a way that it's balanced and becomes such a part of everyday life that living without magick is like trying to breathe under water. It just can't happen. Most people "specialize". While there are benefits to specializing, it's really impossible to do with magick because ultimately -- **it's all interconnected**. Magicians are the ones who see that connection. They're the ones who, not out of snobbery - but rather in dismay and sadness, have learned that there really are few true Adepts (with regards to Magick) in this world.

I have not created this category system to minimize anyone else's experience or to knock anyone – or even to pigeonhole anyone with a label they don't want. I'm just pointing out that this last category obviously isn't for everyone and there are many types of magicians. It's food for thought anyway and hopefully my thoughts on the matter will make the serious magician ask him/herself, "*What kind of magician am I and what kind of magician would I like to be?*" Or even, "*What kind of magician do I need to be at this very moment for my own growth and edification?*"

What is an Adept?
By S. Connolly

A magickal adept is a lot different from someone who is spiritually adept. Spiritual adeptness suggests one is able to take responsibility for his or her own spiritual growth and progress. This means they can guide themselves without a lot of help or constantly having to contact their spiritual leaders to help them along the way. So oftentimes in Daemonolatry when we're discussing the "Adept" we're actually talking about spiritual adeptness. There is a huge difference in being magically adept vs. spiritually adept. A spiritually adept person may not be an adept magician. However, I've never met an adept magician who wasn't spiritually adept. This section is going to discuss what being an adept magician really means.

Some books will give you lists of what adept magicians can or should be able to allegedly do while including some really interesting "skill" sets. Most of them metaphoric and including, but not limited to, levitation, invisibility, flying, and turning rocks into gold. Instead of repeating the more archaic lists here I am going to give you a practical list of what we (the authors collectively) ultimately felt someone must reasonably be able to do to consider him or herself an adept Daemonolatry magician.

1. **Know thyself.**
2. **Be able to physically manifest the Daemonic Divine.** Think about this carefully I'm not being facetious, just purposefully archaic.
3. **Manifest His/Her Will effectively and successfully at least 95% of the time.**
4. **Live comfortably**. This doesn't mean you have to rich or famous. Very few people actually aspire to fame and excessive wealth anyway. Just comfortable. That means, you have everything you want, or you are able to get for yourself everything you want. If you're living on the street, constantly moving, never able to keep a job, or constantly struggling to make ends meet, you're not an adept magician.
5. **Keep Chaos at bay**. Adept magicians do not have chaotic lives that they cannot control. They're not experiencing upheaval at every turn and they're not slaves to turbulent emotions.
6. **Find and Maintain Healthy Relationships**. The magician whose personal relationships are constantly a mess – not an adept magician.
7. **Be psychologically balanced and healthy**. Adept magicians have mastered emotional intelligence and while they may slip once in awhile (don't we all), they're not constant emotional wrecks who are medicated, addicts, constantly being thrown into psyche wards, or threatening to commit suicide at every turn.
8. **Obtain at least basic knowledge and have _working_ experience in most areas of magick and the occult** including high and low magick, various methods, and have practiced magick for every

purpose you can possibly fathom. This means you don't just sit around reading about magick and committing Agrippa (or whoever) to memory so you can show up your online pals. This means not only do you actually know what you're talking about (for the most part) – but also you've successfully **practiced it!** Sure – you're not going to know everything and you'll be a student until the day you die, but at least don't be an armchair theorist, or one of those memorize, regurgitate, repeat type people. The Adept Magician isn't afraid to get his/her hands dirty and actually jump into the magick circle.

9. **The Adept Magician LIVES magick and it's a huge part of his/her life.** It's not a weekend hobby.

10. **The Adept Magician has FOUNDATION and knows how to use it.** This means the magician understands the reasons behind why fire rules passion, anger, love, lust, creativity, and action. He understands why some traditions might use a black candle to absorb negativity and white to shield. He knows when to use a spell vs. a ritual. He knows , for example, how to properly use a Heptameron ritual construct (and other ritual space constructs) for his purposes, and he can effectively substitute so that others who have foundation will go, "Oh, okay. I get it." Basically – he understands there are some basic rules that most magicians agree upon. It's not always just whatever works, works. *You don't invoke Amducius and Verrine using brown candles, and roses at the hour of Pluto during a full moon so you can get a new job and then expect others to think you know what you're doing.* There are a lot of reasons that scenario may not work.

This isn't to say the Adept Magician won't have his/her problems. Life is a series of moments – some of those moments are obstacles. It's how we navigate the problems that matters. If every little problem destroys us or sends our lives into cataclysmic chaos, or if we can't even manifest healthy relationships or sound minds for ourselves, then how can we seriously call ourselves adept magicians?

Grimoires & Magickal Texts of Note

Everyone is fascinated with grimoires and magickal texts. They allegedly hold all the secrets to creation, life, death, our desires and the secrets of the cosmos. Most of us start out with a healthy interest in some grimoire we found on a local bookstore bookshelf. Here's a list of some of the most readily available and mildly interesting grimoires for your reference and reading pleasure. By all means – every magician should have copies of these in their library and most can be found online in PDF. This is by no means a complete list of all the Grimoires or books about Magick in existence either. All of it is modifiable. Remember, *books are collections of ideas*, not gospel.

To modify, generally one would replace "Angel" or "Spirit" names with Daemonic names one was comfortable with and use corresponding symbols, invocations, enns, sigils, and the like in place of the offending sigils, names, or evocations. It's also perfectly reasonable for a Demonolater to work Enochian Magick, or Planetary Magick, or any other type of magick by the book as is. Your own personal definition of a Demon is what comes into play during such modification.

--CLAVICULA SALOMONIS REGIS, which has five
sections. Goetia, Theurgia-Goetia, The Pauline Art,
Almadel, and finally Ars Nova or the Notary Art (Ars
Notoria)
-Grimorium Verum (based on The Key of Solomon)
-Grimoire of Honorius or also called the Grimoire of Pope
Honious
-The Book of Sacred Magic of Abra-Melin the Mage
-The Book of Black Magic and of Pacts
-Grand Grimoire (or Red Dragon)
-The Magus by Francis Barrett
-The Black Pullet (or Treasure of the Old Man of the
Pyramids or Black Screech Owl)
-Verus Jesuitarum Libellus (or True Magical Works of the
Jesuits)
-Mysteria Magica
-The Grimoire of Armadel - Ars Armadel
-The Sixth and Seventh Books of Moses
-The Necronomicon
-The Heptameron of Peter de Abano
-The Golden Dawn by Isreal Regardie
-The Grimoire of Pope Leo French Grinmoire - Enchiridion
Leonis Papae
-The Sword of Moses
-The Secret Grimoire of Turiel
-Three Books of Occult Philosophy Cornelius Agrippa
-The Fourth Book of Occult Philosophy Cornelius Agrippa
-The Book of Dagon
-Codex Decium
-Codex Tenebrarum
-Grimorium Imperium
-The Demotic Magical Papyris of London and Leiden
-Papyri Graecae Magicae
-The Book of Protection 1912

-The Book of Going Forth By Day (i.e. Egyptian Book of the Dead – there are allegedly over 200 spells in that manuscript)

There are also numerous modern grimoires and magickal texts that are wonderful as well. Keep your eyes open. Also remember while book shopping that just because you find something current does not make it invalid. There is a certain school of occult thought out there that nothing is valid unless it's at least 100 years (or more) old. Think about magick as a subjective topic and we are sure you'll realize that the theory of "older = more valid" completely falls flat. Sure, embrace history and tradition and realize the old predecessors influenced all modern magick, but also remember that someone somewhere was the first to write it down. 100 years from now – the book published in 2010 could be considered sacred historical text to someone else.

Modifying Other Magickal Systems:
by S. Connolly

One important thing to remember is that the three great pillars of magick can all be traced back to Ancient Egypt, Canaan, Sumer, and Babylon. There is nothing unique or original in Kabbalah, Hermeticism, or even Enochian really. Not at a base philosophical or magickal level.

I don't say this to downplay the importance of each system of magick. Each has its merits and its own unique style that has contributed a great deal to modern magickal practice as a whole. I'm merely saying that since the foundations of most Western magickal systems seem to be Hermetic and Hermeticism actually equals Khemeticism, that they are all derived from older sources. So the whole idea of, for example, the Enochian entities being angels seems more to me like a modern interpretation of Hermetics which is really just Ancient Egyptian philosophy repackaged by the Greeks. Even the Qabbalah (tree of life etc) can be traced back through Canaanite and to Khemetic origins. Since Daemonolatry is Hermetic and thus Khemetic and in some cases has later Canaanite origin at its foundation, Demonolaters tend to modify Enochian and Qabbalah workings by looking back to the available source

21

material surviving from its time and removing the "church clothes". That isn't to say you need to go visit museums and translate rare and original manuscripts. Many wonderful modern occult scholars have done that work for you. Please see the work in particular of David Rankine, Joseph Peterson, Lon Milo DuQuette, Christopher Hyatt, and Stephen Skinner – among some of the most scholarly magicians and teachers of our time.

Enochian tablets can also be modified for Daemonolatry (see the Daemonolatry Tablets section of this book for more). Hermetic theorems were first written down by the Ancient Egyptians, and the tree of life has both Ancient Egyptian and Ancient Canaanite predecessors (that have been found carved in temple walls etc..).

Sadly, what the average and largely uneducated modern Western ceremonial magician has done, in my humble opinion, is taken all the magickal systems and put wedges between them. Only the true adepts of Ceremonial Magick see that it's all interconnected that that method is merely a means to the manifestation of the will. With the high magickal arts, the act of magick is to discover the will of the Self, and manifest change in the Self - thus changing the external world. The Hermetic philosophy is that in discovering the Self, one discovers the universe both within and outside the Self.

In Daemonolatry magick it is no different. We seek to discover ourselves, the universe, and our place within. It is from that which the physical changes of magick manifest. The Daemons are our guides and teachers to that end.

So the general rule of thumb when modifying Western magickal practices, in my mind at least, is to go back to the source material when possible and realize that the Abrahamic context of most "Jesus Magick" is oftentimes a metaphoric smoke screen. The actual "God" in whose name the magick is worked is, in truth, not the same

22

manifestation of deity the fundamentalist Christian or Modern Catholic worships today. Adept Ceremonial Magicians know this and the God(s) of their understanding are individual to them. The same applies to you. Your relationship and understanding of the divine is your own and no one can change that or take it away from you.

So when modifying, also make sure you understand completely why what was done where, all symbolism, all correspondences, and in some instances the history of what you're doing and why can lend some insight into the work as well. To not have a personal understanding of the source material or the foundation is just lazy on the part of the magician and screams *dabbler*. Please note that doesn't mean your understanding or personal opinion or beliefs about the material needs to match anyone else's. Magick is a very subjective topic and each (wo)man's magick is her/his own.

The Power of Words
by S. Connolly

In the beginning, Heka (magick) *was the word, and the word was sacred.* It was the word that brought all things into being. (The universe is mental. Words are the physical connection and expression of thought and spirit.)

Over and over again I keep running across magicians, even those who claim to understand what modern Western magick teaches, who believe in the power of words, but who don't take it a step further to explain *why* there is power behind words. The end result being a bunch of untrained magicians who think the power is in the "words" only - thus without the magick words - magick won't work.

It's great to say that any one word, for example, *Abracadabra*, holds some sort of "secret power" all its own just by it's mere utterance. What is often not taught the magician (which we all eventually figure out) is that the power in the word is not there until our understanding of the word **puts** it there.

In the Daemonic language, for example, each word is not merely a vocal sound expressing meaning. It's a sound, a vibration, a feeling, and an image all in one. In some instances a logical verbal translation (into human

24

language) accompanies the sound. Knowing this - the magician has made an enn, for example, more powerful.

Otherwise they're just sounds without meaning unless meaning, and an understanding of that meaning, is *put* into them. Yes, this means that I do believe that the magician can use nonsense words in magick. She just needs to put meaning into them.

The same applies to all "words of power". Words of power are, in fact, reliant on the magician putting meaning into the words and putting feeling behind them when they are spoken or vibrated - as well as associating images with them. Words have power because we give words power. Another consideration: a word may have more power if you understand its gematriac value. For example, in Demonolatry the number nine is often considered the number of balance and foundation. So if you wanted to balance yourself, you could realistically chant the word 'nine' over and over again and it could be a word of power for you. Why? Because you've given it a concrete feeling, meaning, image, and you've imposed your will and intent onto it. Many talismans and magick squares work much the same way.

The Gods gave Heka to men, the Heka that is sacred. So the word itself does not have power until the magician gives it power. The same often goes for objects, books, and people. Unless an object itself has been enchanted with the residual energy of someone else's will and you are in a position to be dissuaded by someone else's will, then objects themselves have no power. Again - **we** give them power.

Eventually, every magician will embark on experiments in vibration and sound. This is ultimately energy work (you can see the chapter about energy manipulation for more). For example, one of my recent vibrational experiments was done at the nursing home my grandmother was at. Before going in, I would choose an emotion and set my "*frequency*" to that particular emotion. Then I would go in and observe how people reacted to me. By setting my vibration to anger or sadness, I noticed people would stay away from me and not make eye contact. Compassion and happiness vibrations caused people to reach out for me and look at me. For me, it lent to the credibility of the theory that when visiting sick people (or in this case, the elderly) -- the energy you bring with you into their space really does effect them either positively or negatively.

To learn to set mood vibrations I picked sounds that set my own vibrational frequency to match a mood. Then I'd sit and chant that particular sound until I felt the frequency change and my mood adjust. You can change your mood using the sounds at will with a little self-training. So for myself, when I'm really pissed off, for example, if I just sit and chant OM (my sound choice for peace and tranquility), I can literally effect my mood.

I paid close attention to the types of words I use (especially sounds) when I'm experiencing certain emotions. From that - I pulled out the sounds that embodied certain emotions. For example, when I'm angry- GA! or KA! are excellent. Irritation – ER. Happiness - AYE!

But it's not just the word - each of these sounds evokes (for me anyway) a certain emotional response. And I've been using these sounds (and ultimately conditioning myself to them) during meditation as a tool to explore certain aspects of myself.

For the Daemonolater choosing to work with vibrations and words - it helps to pick an enn, any enn, and vibrate it. See how it makes you feel, and note it. Then - when reciting enns, add that emotion to it (along with any visual images you get) and so on -- to get the full effect of the enn because ultimately you'll change the entire vibration. Saying something is one thing, but feeling it as you say it takes it to a whole different level. Writing it can further solidify the intent behind it (as the written word is just as important as a visual stimulus)

One particular exercise I enjoy is to pick up an object, feel it's vibrational frequency, then add a sound to the object (like identifying a sound with the *feel* of the object). For example: one of my cats feels like a Nya. I have a knife that feels like "Set". And note that when I choose a sound - it's the vibrated version of it. So Nya is Nnnnnnyaaaaaaaaaaaaaaaaaaaa.   Likewise,   Set   is Ssssseeeeeeeeeeeeeeeeeeeeeet.

It's also safe to say that each of us vibrates at our own frequency, too. So my Errrrrrr sound may vibrate at a slightly different frequency than your Errrrr sound. Especially since our voices also have different pitch. You'd have to vibrate at the exact frequency I've conditioned myself to in order to effect me and vice versa. Just some food for thought.

Vibration & Music In Magick
By S. Connolly

Some people suggest low vibrations are depressing, foreboding, or connected to more negative emotions and energies whereas higher vibrational frequencies are equated with positive emotions and energies.

Some traditions, like Golden Dawn or Thelema will give you specific instructions on how you should stand and move during vibration. Our philosophy on this is that the magician should experiment and take notes, ultimately deciding how vibration works into their magick and for which situations it works best. That is not to say prescribed methods don't work. They certainly do. But going beyond what is tried and true is the hallmark of a good magician because you might find something that works better for *you*.

Ultimately, vibration lends a great deal to magick by evoking or arousing certain emotional responses (and hence intent) within the magician.

Music during ritual works much the same way. Those who work with music during ritual do it to evoke atmosphere and a specific emotional response conducive to the work being performed. So, for example, if country music or rap makes you extremely angry - perhaps it can be used during execration magicks or dispelling negativity magicks in order to evoke that emotional response from within yourself. It's certainly one option. Also consider that different types of music may appeal to different people simply because of pitch, tempo, and vibrational qualities that may harmonize with a person's personal vibrations.

Physical Manifestation
by S. Connolly

I know this is repetitive, but I feel this is very important to reiterate. There are some people involved with Daemonolatry and magick in general who seriously believe there is only one way to skin a cat.

Again, quite recently in fact, I heard the interesting (albeit archaic) B.S. that unless you're evoking, invoking, or summoning (these "critics" see no difference between these words when they are actually quite different in meaning) Daemons to physical manifestation, evidently you aren't doing "*it*" right.

Considering the source - I find this amusing. I also, obviously, disagree.

Of course I've also heard this claim from several magicians I have some (at least a tiny bit) respect for. Naturally my reply, defensive, always comes out, "Well, I've had physical, full bodied manifestations come out of my magick before -- but not from your allegedly only one true way. Explain that." To which no one has yet produced a realistic explanation.

But, allegedly, there are claims that there is a sure fire way to produce physical manifestations of Daemons with *every* working utilizing the Heptameron in conjunction with any of the old grimoires (without *any* modification whatsoever, or with only certain modifications only special people are privy to). The process of this is often referred to as old magick. This is no secret. The same group of *old school* magicians boasting having learned the oral traditions of old magick have been running around suggesting physical manifestation of spirits is possible with **every** ritual for years. Some of them clearly traumatized by a zealous Catholic upbringing.

Having been taught via the oral tradition and from (what I consider) fairly old school traditions myself - I know there's a catch. There always is because old school magicians *love* being archaic.

See – beginners into magick all begin by taking it literally. Just as I took a ritual to evoke Asmodeus literally all those years ago. I cut the tree branch from the right species of tree at the stroke of three a.m.. I collected water from a running river. I carried a loadstone in my pocket for weeks. I performed the meditations and magickal exercises and when it was all said and done -- Asmodeus never materialized and neither did the wealth of treasure I was *supposed* to receive.

But my own willpower, dedication, and devotion to the task rose above that of other students and my teacher took me on as a student.

So did I really fail? No. Asmodeus manifested **within** me and I did gain an incredible wealth. The wealth I received came from gaining a teacher and the experience and information that teacher could impart.

Now when you ask these magicians if they're speaking of actual manifestation of the Daemonic (in a physical form as in – a guy with horns standing in front of you as solid as you or I) as opposed to an internal manifestation -- often what you'll get is a smile. After all, a Daemon is a divine intelligence and can dwell within as well as externally. Can it not? I mean - magick entirely within is magick without and magick entirely external is also without. Both internal and external magick can manifest and from my view - one without the other makes for a half-assed magician. Not to mention haphazard magick.

From what I've learned in my own twenty-five years (as of the publication of this book) of practice, manifestation does not always happen outside the self. If we're talking figurative manifestation - then yes, I would agree that one should be able to produce a physical manifestation with *each and every* ritual. Whether that manifestation be within the self, an external result (including magickal results that **manifest**) or even a Daemon appearing to the practitioner. But one of these people in particular is saying specifically that a spirit (whether it be Daemon or whatnot) should manifest physically into a corporeal being during *every* ritual. I think the critics (most of who brag about their magickal ability but who are never specific) actually believe that a physical, no nonsense, full bodied Daemon should emerge from the ether.

Behind the coy smiles, narrowed eyes, and "*knowing*" looks without spoken confirmation one way or the other - I am left to believe that these magicians who speak so adamantly of physical manifestation of Daemons are simply talking smoke and mirrors and quite frankly -- metaphor. And I'm not so sure Daemonolatry's harshest critics understand this necessarily - but I suspect the elder magicians do know this (and if they don't - well then maybe I'm in error and someone needs to educate me - point me in the right direction), including the authors of the books our harshest critics seem to think no one but they possess.

So I sent out a challenge to our critics who get angry when myself and other Daemonolaters say that physical manifestation {as in corporeal Daemonic entities} is not a requirement for effective magick. Of course the biggest critic spoke in no uncertain terms and was too afraid to even give us the method by which this alleged constant physical manifestation of the Daemonic was to be attained. A little research from his clues took me right back to my bookshelf with a book by Lisiewski. One of those old school, don't modify type magicians who has his own way of doing things. I've read Lisiewski, I personally don't agree with his conclusions. That isn't to say some of the things he says aren't useful. I do respect him as a magician. I merely disagree with him.

My own experiments with traditional, by-the-book magick (yes, I have practiced straight forward evocation and grimoiric magick folks! Imagine that.) has led me to uncover more smoke and mirrors and archaic nonsense not appealing to the practical magician such as myself. Most of us old school Daemonolaters are not ineffective magicians as some have asserted. We are not ignorant of other schools of occult thought. Evidently our critics simply had no luck with our (Daemonolatry Specific) methods in their own magick. Nothing wrong with that. Not every technique is going to work for every person, especially if they don't identify with it.

I do think it's safe to say those who think Daemons should manifest to **physical** manifestation with EVERY ritual -- need to stand up, put their money where their mouth is, and prove it to the rest of us (leaving the smoke and mirrors outside their Heptameron circle).

I still assert that a full-bodied, physical, visible Daemonic manifestation is not required for effective Daemonic Magick. Rituals can be 'well attended' without it. Not to mention I see no practical purpose for invoking to physical manifestation anyway. I have been told there are sure-fire Daemonolatry rituals that will make it happen. These rituals are kept under lock and key and even I have never seen them. Yes, I have personally witnessed a full-bodied physical Daemonic manifestation. I still see no *practical* reason for such rituals (except sheer curiosity on the part of the magician). I think it's a safe bet that if Daemons need to manifest, they will - whether you want them to or not. Work with the Daemonic long enough and you're going to eventually get a Daemonic manifestation (as in a full bodied physical being – or in the very least a shadow and palpable energy). That's simply the way it is.

The Power of Daemons
by S. Connolly

I have heard inexperienced and beginner Daemonolatry magicians claim time and time again that the power of Demonic/Daemonic (however you wish to spell it) Magick comes from the Daemons. As if the magician is simply a groveling servant hoping to be thrown a bone every now and again. While there may be a positive exchange of energy (the Daemonic energy amplifying your own) between practitioner and Daemon, this isn't about groveling or the Daemon having ALL the power. There is a flaw with this logic because it doesn't mesh with a Traditional Daemonolatry philosophy or belief system. *A Daemon does not a Magician make.*

Remember that in Daemonolatry, the individual is also seen as being a part of the divine. We all come from the same source as the Daemonic. They're just larger bits, while we're smaller parts of that whole. That means that, yes, we too have our own personal power. Technically, the invocation of the Daemonic is not necessarily a prerequisite for effective magick in general. However – for the purpose of Daemonic magick, obviously Daemons are involved otherwise we wouldn't call it Daemonic Magick.

35

Think of Daemons as being helpful in amplifying your own personal power and helping you to direct your will. They are also beneficial through the impartment of wisdoms and revelations about your Self and your magick that make your magick more effective. It's all interconnected. There are instances in Daemonic Magick where we send energy to the divine (Daemonic) and allow them to choose what to do with it. An example of this is a ritual for Leviathan to Judge if Someone Has Wronged You (see *The Complete Book of Demonolatry*). Once again, the type and method of magick and how the Daemonic plays a role in that magic is often up to the wisdom of the Magician and the "want to help" of the Daemonic.

So about now you're asking why you just can't force the Daemonic to help. After all, Ceremonial Magicians (CMs) hold sigils over fire to coerce and force Daemons to comply and to do their bidding. Here's the real secret there: if you truly intend to perform the magick and the result is honestly desired by your true will, the Daemonic *will* help out each and every time. Many CMs see the Daemonic as forces completely *within themselves* as opposed to being *both* internal and external. So the method they use is really meant to force their will and intent into submission. I suppose there is a valid argument there that some people feel they need to kick their own ass to get what they want from life.

However, from a Daemonolatry stance, Daemons are not only internal forces, but they are singular external energies/entities (depends who you talk to) as well. Thus you can seek the Daemonic within, but if you're going to use evocation, we believe you should apologize afterward. After all, most Daemonic names were the names of deities prior to Abrahamic perversion.

Proper Invocation & Additional Considerations

If you own any DB Publishing titles, some of the information on the following pages will seem repetitive. However, it is worth repeating for easy reference.

When calling the demons into your ritual circle, the traditional way to do it is to use the enn, or an invocation of your own devise, and use the ritual dagger or your hand to draw the following in the air in front of you (kind of diagonal to the sky if that makes sense), starting at the arrow and ending at the dot:

The invocation symbol above is often referred to as the ZD or DZ sigil (because of the shape – not because an actual letter z or d has any significance). It is also used as a sigil representing Satan. Within the ZD are nine points representing the nine demonic divinities. The nine divinities from the Dukante Hierarchy are: Satan, Lucifer, Flereous, Leviathan, Belial, Verrine, Amducious, Unsere, and Eurynomous. For the Goetic Hierarchy these points would represent Satan, Oriens, Amaymon, Paymon, Egyn, Adromolech, Astaroth, Belphegor and Lilith. The symbol is one fluid motion and is encircled as a sigil to represent the whole encircling all its parts. The ZD is also employed to invoke each Demon, no matter which one, with respect to the nine.

Some common courtesies (to avoid disrespect toward the Demons) when invoking:

- Don't command or be aggressive with the demons.
- Don't stab the ritual blade into the air.

Circle Construction

Circle construction can be performed in a variety of ways. However, for **foundational** reference we'll start with a simple elemental circle construct. This creates a balanced ritual space that keeps the practitioner balanced and your Daemonic guests comfortable.

Start at the East point of the circle, draw the DZ in the air with the ritual dagger (without thrusting it) and recite the enn for Lucifer or your equivalent Air Daemon (*Renich Tasa Uberaca Biasa Icar Lucifer*).

Walk to the South point of the circle, draw the DZ in the air and recite the enn for Flereous or your equivalent Fire Daemon (*Ganic Tasa Fubin Flereous*).

West is Leviathan or equivalent water Daemon (or Belial if you prefer Earth West) (*Jedan Tasa Hoet Naca Leviathan*), and North is Belial or equivalent earth Daemon (or Leviathan if you prefer Water North) (*Lirach Tasa Vefa Welhc Belial*).

Then, Satan (*Tasa Raimi Laris Satan*) or the head of your pantheon is invoked from the center.

It is okay to use different elementals. Remember - the entire point of the ritual circle is not for protection, but rather balance.

Daemonic Magick worked within a balanced ritual space keeps the practitioner balanced and freed from having to perform all sorts of cleansings, banishings and balancings, and it creates a comfortable atmosphere for the Daemonic. This doesn't mean you can't construct different types of circles (or spaces of other shapes) within which to work.

Advanced magicians will often find the standard elemental circle too limiting. Many rituals in this book will deviate from the elemental circle. You'll find this is also the case with Heptameron circle construction. The Heptameron circle is one of those constructs that is always changing. More on that later.

Invocation vs. Evocation
by S. Connolly

It's out of simple respect that Daemonolaters use invocation instead of evocation. Ultimately this is because many Demonolaters believe that numerous Daemonic names are the names of the Old Gods, devilized by Abrahamic mythology. Evocation suggests forcing the Daemon against its will by use of threats. For example, "I command you to come here!" Daemons are not our pets or servants. Daemonolatry means "Daemon Worship". If you worship (revere, respect, hold in high regard) something or someone, you do not treat it/them poorly. If your Daemons are actually Gods devilized by Abrahamic faiths and you respect those God Forms (as the Authors of this book do), it is really disrespectful and egotistical to command them.

Invocation is a prayer request. Some people have said we use invocation because we can't make a connection any other way. This isn't so. Many Daemonolaters have found invocation and treating the Daemons with proper respect makes for stronger results. I think a polite prayer when inviting them to a rite, giving offerings, or some sort of positive exchange as in prayers of thanks are appropriate if you're a practicing Daemonolater regardless if you have a close connection or not.

41

Otherwise I believe we risk taking the Daemons for granted. Like any friendship or personal relationship, both parties have to give and take and treat one another with respect. It's no different with Daemons. Many Daemonolaters also believe that what you put out is what you get back. If you put nothing out - you get nothing back. If you put out ego and aggression, guess what you're getting back?

Many of the regular rituals I perform are in celebration of holy days, at which time I ask the Daemons be present so that I may honor them. I've have never had an instance where at least one of the Daemons invoked didn't show. They seem to enjoy attending.

With regards to rituals for magickal work - it is always polite to invoke if you are wanting a Daemon's influence whether it be to ask for strength, wisdom, or a positive outcome because you should never assume the Daemons will help or expect that they should even though they probably will.

So overall, it's not so much that people invoke because they can't make the connection. We invoke because it's polite, respectful, and considerate. Remember that Daemonolatry means **DAEMON WORSHIP**. That means we hold Daemons in high regard and respect them as teachers and guides. For more information about the spiritual side of Daemonolatry, read my book *The Complete Book of Demonolatry*.

Daemonolaters also frown upon the use of "protective circles" (as in protecting yourself from what you are calling up), spiritual/magickal condoms of any kind, or attempting to bind Daemons into triangles or vessels of any kind for the simple reason that we respect them. **While I agree there is a time and place for protection and banishment**, I think that banishing your deities or protecting yourself against them is a bit odd. That's all we're saying. That isn't to say that I (or any of the other authors) think all Daemonic forces are friendly and cuddly either. Far from it. I'll be the first to admit everything's a shade of gray. When I'm invoking Focalor I don't expect a big hug and warm fuzzy feelings. We construct ritual spaces conducive to the magick being worked and take into considering that which keeps the magician BALANCED. We also take full responsibility for what we invoke with our magick, even if that Daemonic force decides to kick our asses in some way.

Myself and the other authors are of the firm belief that the Daemonic reacts to you based on your approach to it. This means if you're terrified of the Daemonic and view it/them from a Judeo-Christian perspective, you are opening the door to scaring yourself senseless. If you approach a Daemonic force with fear or anger, don't be surprised if they don't make it come true. After all – if your intentions are to invoke an angry Daemon or a scary Daemon, and those intentions are strong enough—you're going to get exactly what you expect.

I am sure numerous ceremonial magicians will pick up this book and disagree with the Daemonolatry view of Daemons and with our non-spiritual condom method most vehemently. That's fine. I don't expect everyone will agree with a Traditional Daemonolatry philosophy of the manner in which we choose to work with the Daemonic. That's fine. Do what works for you. Even among Daemonolaters there are still those who use Solomonic ritual space construction.

Some people will tell you they use a Triangle of Art as a focal point for manifestation of the Daemonic (rather than a standard binding). Others will tell you that such methods are too restricting and disrespectful. It really depends on the magician and how they've modified specific rituals for their personal needs. Just remember that for Daemonolaters (i.e. Daemon Worshipers) Daemonic Magick is always a respectful "working with" the

Daemonic regardless how you choose to create your ritual space or if you choose to clear/banish the space, or stay inside your own little protective energy bubble.

If you don't see the subtle differences between the words invoke, evoke, or summon – you can use them interchangeably. I guess the difference between myself and others is that I see the differences in the meanings of these words. Some people don't and feel that people like me are merely mincing semantics. And perhaps they're right.

Take it as you will.

For those who view the Daemonic as nasty parts of our psyche that must be pushed around and bullied by us - just know that for *most* (notice how I never say all) Daemonolaters that's not the case either. Self-love and self-acceptance and ultimately self-knowledge means integrating and accepting those parts of our being that society has labeled "evil" and "bad" and learning to respect and manifest changes within ourselves to minimize our negative traits and tendencies rather than just bully them, then pretend like they don't exist (and bury them). If you respect yourself as a part of the Divine – and you view the Daemonic as part of the self – then shouldn't you still treat the Daemonic (i.e. your Self) with respect rather than disdain and arrogance? Think about it.

Non-Elemental Circles and Other Configurations
by S. Connolly

You'll find that as you become more experienced, you'll start to experiment. Circles can feel differently built clockwise or counterclockwise or using different Daemons, or invoking nine divinities vs. four elementals, vs. all death Daemons. I generally start at Lucifer and end at Belial (or Leviathan depending who I put North, which I do for more Khemetic workings) for most generic rituals (often of the offering, worship variety). I will close counterclockwise. However, If I'm doing a ritual for creative work meant to generate income, for example – I may choose to invoke South, North, West, East. If I'm doing a work that deals with some sort of emotional work I'll start West, perhaps move South, and then to North or East depending on the priorities of the attributes of a direction (or Daemonic force) to the working. I've also experimented with construction from indirect compass points. Such as invoking from Southwest, Northwest, Northeast, Southeast (for alchemical combination attribution). Also, you can assign polar genders to the Daemonic and the directions for additional balancing effects. For example: West being feminine, East being masculine. Likewise, North being feminine, and South being Masculine. If I'm performing a ritual for long term stability I might go with more feminine Daemons corresponding to the elements. If I'm looking for more immediate, direct results - I might go for more masculine Daemonic energies. Planetary, hour, and day rulerships may also be considerations.

This can become very complex and each of a million combinations can give your ritual a different energy source/feeling. I may invoke creativity Daemons of each different element if I'm doing a working (instead of generic elementals) dealing with that. Or - if I'm doing a working for business, perhaps more goal/stability oriented Daemons of the different elements.

Personally, I do not recommend beginners experiment with various constructions until they have a strong foundation and can effectively balance themselves (because many non-generic constructions can and will imbalance the magician). Some configurations can literally cause nausea, fainting or weakness. It is because of imbalance in the magician that most Western schools of occult thought teach constant banishing and "protective" circle creation. We teach balancing in place of this. Use whatever you're more comfortable with.

See the following pages for more information on various non-elemental circle constructs.

Mandatory warning: I can't stress enough that people with emotional problems (or diagnosed psychological disorders) should be very careful when practicing any form of ritual, magick, or meditation because it can increase symptoms. I've actually watched friends with depression become suicidal and people with bi-polar disorder go over the edge due to excessive ritual and meditation done without any regard to maintaining balance. Perhaps people with such imbalances should create protective circles and practice banishing. They seem to be the ones who need banishing rituals most often anyway*. So I recommend that anyone with bipolar or depression NOT experiment with alternate circle construction since they are often imbalanced very easily. People with clinical anxiety should be careful when working with fire Daemons. Also, those sensitive to the amplifications of certain stones or substances should be careful not to employ them in their magicks unless they know what they're doing and can effectively negate imbalances that might arise from their works. End mandatory warning.

---

*We've all had that one magickal friend who constantly thinks there's an evil spirit in their closet or that the astral sludge is closing in on them. It's probably true. People with mental disorders or emotional imbalance often attract that sort of thing to them.

Example Diagrams of Alternative Ritual Layouts

Pyramid (triangle):

Diagram of Altar Facing West

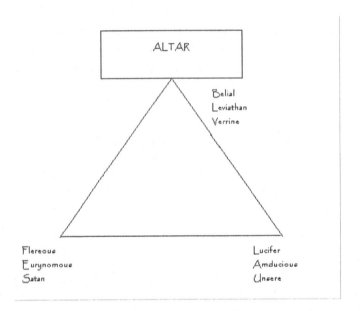

This is not the only configuration that can be used. For example, all of the more "destructive" Daemons can be put together (Amducious, Flereous, Eurynomous), the creation Daemons put together (Unsere, Verrine, Leviathan), and all the enlightenment Daemons put together (Lucifer, Belial, Satan).

Circles using the nine (the top being Earth):

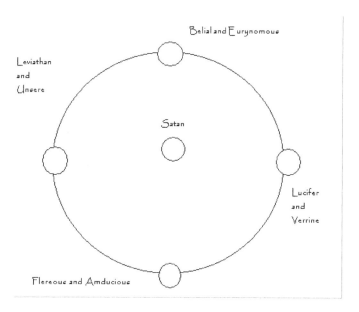

This particular circle is elemental. However, you can also choose polarity in which Lucifer and Leviathan would be in the East, Belial and Flereous in the North, Unsere and Amducious in the South, and Verrine and Eurynomous in the West. Or any combination thereof. In the case of Circles of Nine, Satan (or the head of your pantheon) is always invoked from the center OR He can be invoked at every elemental point.

Later in this book you'll see two different examples of hexagon constructs. You can work with pentagram constructions as well, or even Tree of Life constructions if you have the space. Feel free to experiment with this. Think in three (or four) dimensions. There is definitely more than one way to construct an effective ritual space.

Modifying the Heptameron Circle Construct
by S. Connolly and Nick Schneider

The Heptameron circle construct of Medieval magicians, we suspect, derives from an older source of ritual configuration (likely Egyptian and/or Canaanite sources both) and can be easily modified for Daemonolatry simply by tracing the roots of the God-names, and angel/spirit names back to ancient Canaan. In the Canaanite religion, the highest god (similar to Khemetic Atem / Atun / Aten / Amen) was called El. You'll find El added to most masculine God-forms in later Canaanite pantheons and later to the Judaic generic "*God*". This is similar to the use of Ba'al as Lord within certain Canaanite deity names (i.e. Ba'al Ial, Ba'al Berith, Ba'al Athim etc...). It can also be compared at Atem Ra or Amen Ra. Amen was the highest, hidden part of the deity, whereas Ra was the visible side (i.e. the Sun). Iah was generally a Canaanite signaling for feminine deities. So you'll find numerous "angel" names end in Iah or El (for masculine). On that note, Amen, a word generally said after prayer, started out as an Egyptian end to prayer (to send the prayer to the highest, hidden form of God) and was later adopted by Semitic peoples as a word that meant "So be it." So please – feel free to use Amen to your heart's content without feeling the need to modify any ritual that uses it.

As was stated in *Non-Elemental Circles and Other Configurations* earlier in this chapter, the basis for a Heptameron circle is that it changes according to the work. The spirits invoked, the hours, the planets, and other considerations change as your needs change – meaning the circle is never stagnant. It is always changing depending on the magical work. Again, the reason we often give new Daemonolaters the simple elemental circle construction is because it is the foundation that can always be gone back to as needed and it's the basic configuration for worship. However – if you are a Daemonolatry Magician, one size does not fit all with regards to circle construction.

With regards to the Heptameron circle, there are three circles, all oriented with the proper names of the spirits of the hours, days, planets etc… necessary for the work. The Daemonolater's job in modification is to decide which spirit names they're comfortable working with. Some Daemonolaters will happily use Angel names as well – choosing to view them as any Iah's being feminine "spirits" and El's being masculine. So instead of Michael, Mi cha El. Instead of Raphael, Ra pha El. This works for those for whom the "Christianization" of ancient poly/pantheistic practices can be undone with a simple space and capitalization. For those who seriously take issue with anything seemingly Christian or Judaic and who cannot see that the Abrahamic faiths ripped off almost everything from religions previous to them (perverting the ancient wisdom and God-forms), then you will have to change the spirit names to names you are more comfortable with.

51

Above see an example of the traditional Heptameron circle construction. Some believe that the crosses should be replaced with Ankh's, representing "the key" to eternal life, while the Alpha and the Omega should be represented with the actual Greek characters for Alpha and Omega. The equal armed cross in the center of the circle represents the four cardinal points and will help you situate your spirit names at the proper directional point relevant to the working and the aspects you wish to invoke. For Daemonolatry, place the main Daemonic names relevant to your working in the outer circle. In the second circle, situate the spirit or Daemonic names that suit the hour, day, and/or planetary correspondences. In the third circle, situate (in the proper cardinal direction for their importance of the work) the names of your highest deities. For example, instead of

Tetragrammaton, Adonai etc… use El, Ba'al, or Satan, or Lucifer, or even the name of your Matron/Patron or Mentor.

Students and Magicians alike should note that Heptameron is also an anagram for Promethean. Prometheus was the deity who stole fire from heaven and gave it to men. Sound familiar? Lucifer is the Daemon that corresponds to Prometheus. He was the first to give wisdom and knowledge to men, and was considered "fallen" for doing so. This is why he is often referred to as "The Light Bringer". Note that fire and light are obvious metaphors for knowledge and wisdom.

Magick

What is Magick?
By S. Connolly

Aleister Crowley defined magick as the art of causing change in conformity with one's will. The Daemonolater adds to that, Magick is the art of causing change in conformity with one's will as matter cannot be created or destroyed, it can only change form. Therefore, magick is all about transformation. It is an alchemical process by which we synthesize, distill, purify, and bring to the forefront the elements we desire in our lives and filter out those we don't.

Magick, the k being used to distinguish it from illusionary or stage magic (though you may find magicians who spell it magic or magik or majik or whatever), is so much more than mixing together potions and brews, or to create talismans or mojo bags to cultivate change. It goes beyond working with stones, colors, and the plethora of "things" that allegedly make magick work. Daemonic Magick goes beyond asking Daemons to help you or simply drawing a sigil. Magick, true magick in any form, incorporates pathwork and complex symbols, rituals, and tools meant to help change the individual (what many magicians call self-work or **The Great Work** as the highest goal is "*Man, know thyself and thou shalt know the Gods*"), thus changing the world around him or her. Some people incorporate angels into their pathwork. Others incorporate generic spirits. The Daemonolater incorporates the Daemonic, or the Divine Intelligences; beings with a higher knowledge and understanding about the universe and the alchemical process, and who will willingly impart this wisdom with those who truly seek it. Magick is not something you do to get stuff, nor is it a passive activity.

Getting stuff and causing things to change is simply the natural outcome of manifesting our true will, and is symptomatic of knowing one's self. If you know yourself, you learn what you want, you can then create a plan for change, you can manifest the change by following through, and then move onto the next thing or area in your life that requires work. Magick is simultaneously physical, mental, and spiritual. You mentally acknowledge the need for change and create a working plan, you spiritually and mentally prepare for the change, you physically work the magick and follow through to create the change, the change manifests and you find yourself in a better position physically, mentally, and spiritually. When one is content, the other two are nurtured.

This is why balance is stressed in Daemonolatry. You can't concentrate on the physical and ignore the mental and spiritual. Or concentrate on two and leave one out. They're all interconnected and each requires your acknowledgement.

Does Magick Work?
By S. Connolly

As a natural magician I admittedly have never had to worry about my magick *not* working. It always works, just not always in the manner I intend. My biggest obstacle with magick has been learning to control the magnitude of the energy I use, learning focus, how these things affect the results, and learning the wisdom to know when certain magick is warranted, and when it isn't. Some magicians will tell you that you have to practice magick over and over again to get it to work. This is true for some people to some degree. It depends on your skills and natural abilities and the resistance of that thing you are trying to change. Certain energy building, focusing, and projecting exercises are always going to be easier the more adept you are at navigating your energy, yourself and your own strengths and weaknesses. Some people will not be able to perform even the slightest magickal operation with good results. This seems to be because not everyone is suited to every type of magick (or magick at all sometimes). If you have erratic energy or a natal chart non-conducive to working magick that doesn't always mean you can't work magick. But it can mean you need a different approach. Chaos charts often work very well with chaos magick. See the chapter on astrology and magick for more.

Some argue that if you aren't rich, well then obviously magick is crap. What these people fail to realize is that people who are serious about magick often find things more valuable to go after. After all, money is only a temporary need for physical existence and you can't take it with you. Not all of us aspire to fame and excessive wealth.

Yet to some degree I actually agree. A successful magician will not have a chaotic life, will live comfortably, and can at least maintain relationships. They will not have mental problems and should, in the very least, be somewhat financially stable. If your magick can't at least help you make your life more comfortable and your physical existence bearable, then you're doing something wrong.

About now, someone brings up all those poor destitute magicians who left behind a legacy of magick, but whose lives were miserable. Does this mean we label them failures and discount all their work the occult world has labeled sacred? No. With power comes responsibility and sometimes power is great enough to throw people off their path and into their egos. So for those who argue that Crowley, Barrett, and numerous other magicians whose work is the staple for modern occultism died destitute, crazy, or alone and miserable – perhaps they lost their way, drunk with power. Or maybe they allowed themselves to get addicted to mind altering substances, which can surly knock someone off their spiritual and magickal path just as sure as it can cause them to make really bad financial decisions.

Finally – maybe they were after something bigger than money or fame.

Why Does Magick Work on Some People and Not on Others?

When you work magick on another person, or for their benefit (or detriment), you are directly attempting to manipulate **their** will. Not all people can be manipulated or coerced into doing your will. Some people are just too strong (mentally) for that. It is for this reason that some people cannot be cursed or healed (with standard magick anyway) and it's the same reason others can be. Certainly there are methods to break down these natural defenses in order to help (or hurt) another person. Duration ritual work is one method. Another method is simply to ask the person to be open to it (as in the case of healing).

Using Wisdom With Magick

Firstly, magick is not a quick fix for anything. Don't expect to perform a ritual, sit back, and wait to *get stuff*. Sometimes that may work, but not always. When possible, there does need to be some activity on your part as this will increase your chances of performing effective magick. Magick is not for spectators. This means, for example, that if you want the promotion at work, you must put in the extra effort and show your boss you're capable of handling the job. Use magick to make him/her notice you, or look upon you as the favorable choice. By now you're likely thinking, then why do magick at all? Because magick can help you mentally prepare to meet a goal and can influence others. I'm not saying magick cannot influence a situation or cause things to happen (without your direct help). I'm just saying that the more you show the Daemons and yourself how serious you are about wanting the outcome in your favor - the more likely it is to work. In magick, intention is everything. The stronger your intention - the stronger the magick.

The Science of How Magick Works
by S. Connolly

We would be lying to you if we told you we had the answers to how, scientifically, magick works. Some people speculate that quantum physics holds the answers to how energy is directed and applied to influence a situation at a quantum-molecular level. This theory relies on the possibility that thought has the ability to create changes we can't see. It works along with the Hermetic Principle, "The Universe is Mental." Basically – your life is what you make it. You create your own reality. That sort of thing.

Other people will tell you magick only works by intervention of otherworldly spirits or entities. Others still will tell you that magick is the state of mind of the individual and there's nothing supernatural involved and that all those spells/rituals you did to win the lottery were coincidence and luck. That magick is merely psychology.

In all honestly I am no expert in quantum physics, I'm not a psychologist, nor am a believer in coincidence, and I believe that magick can be performed successfully using self-power, just as much as borrowing on the energy and wisdom of the Daemonic. My experience has proven to me that Magick simply works. While I'm sure there is a perfectly reasonable, sound, and scientific explanation out there, I don't think we quite understand it completely yet. I mean, certainly some of it really is just psychology. But I've seen things psychology cannot explain. (I suspect some magick may be dependent on the ability of the human mind to affect the physical world molecule by molecule). I also imagine with the advancement of human technology and science, eventually (if we are so fortunate to not have destroyed ourselves or our environment) much of what we discover and apply 100 years from now would look like magick to people living today.

The Use of Blood in Magick
by S. Connolly and Valerie Corban

Blood rituals are a cornerstone in Daemonolatry practice. This is also true for Daemonic magick. It's the authors' opinions that a person who isn't willing to sacrifice (i.e. make sacred) a small drop of their own blood (nothing drastic here) during a working of extreme importance to the magician (in the very least) probably ought not be practicing Daemonic Magick. If you are not willing to suffer even the slightest pin prick for what you want, are you really serious about wanting it? It's something to consider.

There are alternatives for the squeamish and pacifists among us, of course. For women, menstrual blood is always a clear, simple choice and for others, nails, hair, saliva, and sexual fluids can alternatively be used in place of blood.

When it comes to blood, however, it is always taken in the LEAST destructive way possible and in the most sanitary way possible due to the plethora of modern blood borne diseases. The easiest method is by using a diabetic lancet device. These are relatively easy to come by at your local pharmacy and are inexpensive. They are also sanitary, virtually non-destructive and non-scarring, relatively painless, and really – you only need a drop or two for each magickal working. So buck up and stick out your finger. It will only hurt a little.

For group ritual, keep alcohol handy to clean the area to be lanced, and bandages at the ready for the occasional bleeder. The side of a finger often yields a good amount of blood.

The reason behind the use of blood in Daemonic Magick is very symbolic. Firstly, blood is the life force. It is the substance that courses through our veins and delivers nutrients to all the cells in our bodies. Without blood, we cease to function. So giving up something of ourselves, something so personal, the essence of ourselves (even a drop), is not only a respectful self sacrifice, but also a declaration that we are serious enough about the magickal working to make that small sacrifice.

Note how it is often said that Daemonolaters take blood in the least destructive manner possible. It used to be, back in the day, that people would use daggers to cut hands, legs, etc... But let's face it – that can be dangerous, especially if you don't know what you're doing. The point isn't to mutilate yourself, scar yourself, or hurt yourself, but rather to make a drop of your blood sacred as an offering of yourself to your will.

Not all magicians will see this as a necessary step and that's okay. For those of you who choose to practice blood offering in the practice of your magick, that's fine. If not, that's fine, too. Just know that most of the rituals and/or methods in this book will employ blood as an ingredient to the magick. See the more extensive section in this book about Blood Magick by B. Morlan for more.

Addiction, Magick and the Magician
by S. Connolly

I am not going to preach that one should never use mind-altering substances during ritual. After all, mind-altering substances and magick have been mixed before as surely as they will be again. However, I have learned a few things about Addiction and the Magician over the years.

This topic hits close to home because a lot of people I know struggle with an addiction. My own addiction use to be with cigarettes. I was thinking about how a lot of the old grimoires and essays written for the magician talk about abstaining from substance **abuse** (whether it be nicotine, alcohol, or drug use). It's one of the things all the great Mystery Schools seem to teach. When I was younger I used to scoff at the idea that my body was my temple. But as I get older the more I realize there might be something to that.

When you truly know yourself and truly care about your well being, you begin to care about what you put into your body. On my own quest for a more healthy lifestyle, I dropped the cigarettes. I've never really been one to drink and I am personally anti-drug, so my only remaining vice is coffee. Even then - I drink decaf most days, which almost defeats the purpose of drinking coffee altogether.

Ultimately, while I have noticed the health benefits of having quit smoking, I wondered if my quitting smoking had actually done something for my self-growth and my magick. To check this out, I poured through my journals and experiments to see how much had really changed since I quit. Imagine my own surprise when I discovered the answer to my question was not just yes, but YES, a lot had changed.

I discovered I was no longer as twitchy, irritable, and aggressive as I was when I smoked. My nicotine addiction seemed to have a negative effect on my personality. In one journal entry I noted, "Today, my co-worker mentioned that I've really calmed down in the past few months"

Quitting smoking also amplified my intuition and sensitivity to various energies and entities. So much in fact that I noticed a strange spidery energy sensation in my hands during ritual work. When it first started I thought maybe I'd pinched a nerve in my arm. But it only happened during magickal work, or when I was "feeling" something (person, object, or situation) out. It happened often during yoga or tai chi and sometimes during meditation. In my journal, I described it as, "*I feel like I've put my hand in a web. My arm hairs stand on end as if I'm touching a palpable energy that courses through my veins like a mild electrical currant. This energy rides up my arms, through my torso, and up through the back of my neck.*"

So is it true the magician should overcome addiction? I think that for most people, addiction is one of those obstacles in Da'ath. The Great Abyss the magician must cross in order to complete The Great Work. As a friend of mine put it - not everyone has to deconstruct him or herself while crossing Da'ath. Some need it more than others. It's Da'ath that is the great equalizer because it makes it apparent to your Self just how flawed and imperfect we all are, and the best we can do is attempt to fix those flaws in ourselves in order to calm the stormy waters of ourselves, and cross the river to emerge the other side wiser, stronger, and more knowledgeable about the Self.

In short – I believe the answer is yes. The magician who overcomes addiction is that much closer to understanding and wisdom. The magician who fails to overcome addiction may never be able to cross Da'ath whole. This basically means that the road to wisdom and understanding - or clarity and spiritual wholeness is NOT paved with Jack Daniels, marijuana, or Marlboros, or even Folgers. Perhaps not even chocolate.

That isn't to say we can't indulge in a cigar, or a drink, or a chocolate every now and again - but as with all things, *moderation* is key and the body truly is a temple. For on the great Egyptian temple walls it was writ, *"Man know thyself, and thou shalt know the gods."*

When Good Magick Goes Bad
By Nick Schneider (GoeticNick) & S. Connolly

There are many ways that magick can go terribly wrong. Sometimes it's just a simple ritual screw up such as you forget a ritual implement or say an Enn wrong, or forget a certain part of the ritual that goes undone. These infractions are minor and they're really not a big deal. Just forgive yourself and move on. Make a journal note to remember or fix those issues in subsequent rituals if necessary.

It's when the magick either comes back on you, works only partly, gives you what you want but requires a major sacrifice, hits the wrong target, or goes overboard in intensity that good magick goes bad. These are the bigger infractions that could have serious consequences. Oftentimes the main reason magick goes bad is lack of focus and intent on the part of the magician.

Intensity Issues: If your magick is too weak or too intense, you need to learn how to focus and control your intensity. If it's too weak, attempt energy raising exercises before performing magick. Making sure you're in optimal health before performing magick is also key. If your magick's results are too intense, try to balance and ground yourself before workings and practice only opening the "flood gate" of your energy about half way, and adjusting as needed.

You'll eventually get your intensity levels right with practice and experience.

Magick "Sling Shotting" or Coming Home to Roost: If you are not the intended target of your own magick, and you regret it in the slightest bit, what you send out can come straight back to you. Be wary of this especially when working negative and/or execration magicks. There must be **no guilt** over what you're doing. Guilt is the slayer of a good magician.

Magick Working, But Not as Intended: So you've done a ritual for money, and suddenly your favorite aunt dies in a horrible accident and you inherit some cash. Not exactly how you wanted to gain that "free" cash? Learn to be specific. The more specific you are and the more you focus on the specifics, the more likely your magick will work in ways you did intend.

Magick Hits the Wrong Target: You curse a co-worker and her three year old ends up in coma. Sounds to me like your magick hit the wrong target. Again, learning to be specific in what you want and who or what your target is makes this less likely to happen.

Magick Just Isn't Working: Sometimes magick doesn't work because the individual has no magickal talent whatsoever. There are people who have no natural talent. However, I believe that such a lack of talent is rare. Instead, I believe that sometimes magick just doesn't work because the magician isn't really serious in their intent. So you're pissed at your friend and you want to curse her? It doesn't work. Why? Either she naturally deflects external energy or it's more likely you really didn't want to hurt her. If you're not getting the lottery numbers you want, chances are it's because you really have no intention of getting them.

Sometimes belief and intent are closely related, meaning if you don't believe in what you're doing, your intention isn't on board with you. Intention is a tricky thing. You either want something with your entire being and are willing to sacrifice for it, or you are not. This is why you'll find that many magicians aren't asking for wealth, fame, or lottery numbers. Most of us really have no genuine desire to be wealthy, famous, or lottery winners.

Group Magick
by S. Connolly and M. Delaney

Many magicians will tell you that group magick is famous for rendering no results because too many people have different ideas of what will work. They're on the right track, but there's more to it than that. Group magick often fails because the different energies of the different individuals either work well together or they do not. Most magicians, if they look for it, are able to find one other person (or maybe a few, more than five is too many) with whom they can effectively work magick.

For effective group magick, several things need to be considered. First and most important, you need to know the strengths and weaknesses of ALL the magicians involved. You can't expect the group to be able to direct energy if one person continuously has a habit of causing energy to scatter. You also can't practice divination with people who have no talent for it because they'll end up blocking you. Some people naturally block external energy from people they don't care for. Others naturally bring on a lot of negativity. Some people can't practice effective magick to save their own lives.

Sometimes you have too many people of a certain element non-conducive to the ritual purpose itself. And, of course – sometimes not everyone is on the same page. The reasons against group magick are numerous and varied.

Some advice:

Keep the group small. The fewer people involved the better. It reduces the chances of not everyone having the same goals or being on the same page.

Make sure everyone knows their job and does it. Nothing is more annoying than too many cooks in the kitchen spoiling the soup. So give everyone a task they're best suited to and let them do it. Assign one person to build energy, one person to send it. Or assign specific people to work the divinatory devices. Make sure everyone's elemental make-ups and talents are conducive to the task they're assigned. For example, don't give the job of empathy to someone who has no water in their chart or who doesn't have an empathic bone in their body. Don't give the job of building energy to someone who has no fire. And so on.

Make sure everyone knows EXACTY what the goal is by being VERY specific in invocations, incantations, and actions. For example, if you're trying to heal someone, make sure everyone knows the person to be healed and has an image of that person in his/her head. You also need to make sure that everyone agrees on the Daemons being invoked for the task. If two people think you should be invoking Verrine and two people think you should be invoking Buer, you're going to have problems. If you're trying to get a law passed, make sure everyone has read the desired law, agrees with it, and badly wants it to pass.

If the magick you are performing is ceremonial and requires numerous ritual actions, implements, and very specific construction, **make sure you go over this thoroughly (including the reasoning behind each action if necessary) with everyone who is going to be involved.** You might even consider a "rehearsal" beforehand.

Remember that in Daemonolatry, group ritual proper is often about *worship* rather than magick. All Daemonolater Magicians do a lot of solitary work for this reason. However, in that rare instance where you find yourself in a group magick situation, consider these things and your magick will be better for it. And if the people you're working with refuse to heed these guidelines, you might as well tell them you'll pass because the chances of the magick working will be marginal at best. No sense wasting energy if you can help it.

On that note – there is one way in which you can work magick effectively with other people. That is to choose a time at which a specific work is to be performed and every person participating does his/her own ritual at the same time, but alone and at their own location. Participants can then get together after the work is done to compare notes. This ensures that only persons who truly want to participate do (because a person who doesn't care isn't going to take the time to perform the ritual) and no one's energy interferes with anyone else's.

Fasting for Magick
By S. Connolly

I wanted to include a brief section about fasting for magick since it's a question I get often. Firstly – some rituals will require you to fast. The reasoning behind this is three-fold. First, it is said to clear toxins from your system since you can still drink liquids. Second, it is symbolic of your dedication to your cause (your will). Third, fasting allegedly makes us more aware of the energy around us and can symptomatically invoke spiritual experiences (in the form of light headedness, fainting, and even hallucinations). I don't necessarily agree with this third reason for fasting.

There are some considerations for a proper fast.

1. Make sure you are healthy enough to perform a 24 hour fast.
2. If you are performing a longer fast, talk to your physician to make sure you are healthy enough to fast for longer durations.
3. If you are hypoglycemic or have other health issues that require you to eat something, consider ice cream, pudding, milk, juice, tea, broth, water, fruit

smoothies and Jell-O etc… Basically a liquid diet. It's the next best thing to a fast if your body won't tolerate a fast with just water.

4. For the day of your fast, make plans to take the day off. You don't want to exert too much energy so take it easy.

5. Drink water during your fast. You need to remain hydrated. Becoming dehydrated can be dangerous!

6. If you start feeling light headed or hallucinating, you might want to take in some liquid nourishment in the form of soup. Also, be realistic about your definition of a spiritual experience. Just because you're ready to pass out and feel light headed doesn't necessarily mean it's the Daemonic making contact. That's your body telling you it needs food.

7. After a fast you may want to ease back into eating solid foods by moving from liquids to soups to pastas to solids.

The Tools of Magick

By S. Connolly, Valerie Corban, and Brid Delaney

There are several tools all magicians who work in the physical realm will need. It is your choice to spare no expense for your tools as some people feel that their rituals should honor the Daemons in the highest way, or you can choose to keep it simple and just use what you have. The tools should all consist of styles and designs that you like and feel a personal connection to.

Each tool must be prepared, blessed, sanctified, and dedicated (explained later in this chapter) specifically to your practice of magick. This means that if you use a glass chalice or wine glass for ritual work, do not use it to drink from every day. Do not allow others to touch your tools unless they, too, are initiated into the artes. This is the way of Traditional Daemonolatry.

Chalices – You can find chalices made in everything from brass to silver to glass. We recommend glass because you can throw it into the dishwasher. For those of you who

75

don't mind polishing the silver or staving off tarnish, consider silver or brass.

Bowls – On any altar, most of us keep at least two bowls. One for burnt offerings and one for salt. Salt to purify and cleanse amulets or to bless water or earth. Some may choose to keep a third bowl on the altar for non-burnt offerings.

Thuribles/Incense Burners – We suggest keeping at least 2-3 different styles of incense burners at hand. A stick incense burner, a regular metal bowl for burning self-igniting charcoals, and a third for burning simple cone incenses. There are burners that can serve all three purposes if you can find them.

Ritual Blades – Every magician should have at least one sword, one dagger for invocation, and one utility (practical) knife for cutting things. A note to that: do not gift ritual blades to others. Always make them pay at least a penny lest your friendship be severed.

Staves / Wands – Not like in Harry Potter. Wands are often used for directing energy and will often have a crystal or stone at one end. It is believed by many that crystals in particular can help one channel or focus energy (i.e. direct it). Staves can be used in place of a sword to draw circles upon the ground. Both are very phallic. One of each should cover you for any needs that may arise. S. Connolly's Note: If you can make your staves and wands yourself – more power to you. Literally. See the recipe for the Blasting Rod/Wand in this book for instructions.

Blood Letting Device: Your diabetic lancet with fresh lancets and a sharps container to dispose of used lancets. Some people might use knives or razor blades. Remember that blood should be taken in the least destructive way possible and you should be fully aware of what you're doing (i.e. where vital tendons, veins, arteries, are) if you choose to use knives or razor blades to draw blood. Lancet devices are preferred.

Candle Holders – Various sizes here. Make sure you have taper, votive, tealight, and pillar holders.

Other Handy Items: An Altar Box, to keep all your ritual oils, blood letting devices, stones, etc... in. For those of us who like to be organized and have clean, neat altar – the box is a necessity.

Journal – You'll likely end up with a collection of these over your career as a magician. Use journals to keep rituals, thoughts, progress, results, etc... in. We tend to keep journals separate. For example, a formulary journal separate from a dream work journal. An energy work journal separate from a ritual construction journal. A ritual results journal separate from a group work journal and so on. It makes things easier to find. Of course most magicians' journals contain a little of everything.

Items Needed to Work Magick on Others *(taglocks and other personal items):* You will need something, a focal point if you will, to work magick on someone else. A sample of handwriting, a picture, some hair, nail clippings, skin, a personal item of the person, or something they've touched or had contact with will suffice. If you are working the ritual for yourself, your blood, hair, urine, spit, skin, nail clippings, pictures, personal symbols and words of power, etc... will do the job nicely.

Parchment – Parchment is one of those things called for in all sorts of ritual work. You can either make your own paper (see the section on execration magicks for more) or you can go to a paper store and buy a package of "parchment". Do not buy parchment at your local occult shop unless you're desperate for it and don't have time to make a run to your local office supply or paper store. Why? Because most places don't sell handmade parchments. They just buy a package of 500 sheets at the local paper or office store for $5-$7 and then turn around and charge you $0.50 - $1 a sheet (I've heard of them charging more). Little known secret, that.

A Final Word: You may find you need other tools based on the magick being worked. Some rituals will require certain sigils (more permanent made of specific materials like wax or wood), other rituals might require specific amulets or rings. Some rituals require specially prepared altars specific to the work being performed. All of these items should be prepared and made ready before you start your ritual. It's perfectly okay to make yourself a checklist to make sure you don't forget anything.

Prepare, Bless, Sanctify, and Dedicate the Tools:

Invoke the elemental Daemons. Have upon the altar the tools to be blessed, solar sea salt mixed with water (*Talot Pasa Oida Belial et Leviathan*), and an oleum of Delepitorae, Thoth, or other "Magician's" Daemon. Let there be present tools for etching, painting, or writing symbols upon each tool. Burn frankincense alone or a favorite incense blend containing frankincense.

Hold the tool above you: *"By the Daemons present this tool be blessed and sanctified for the magickal work it will be used to perform."*

Dip the item into the salt water (be careful and make sure the salt water will not erode the tool). *"I cleanse and purify this tool."*

Pass the tool through the incense smoke: *"I sanctify this tool that it may help me manifest my will."*

Anoint the tool with Oleum (and draw or paint any magickal symbols upon them if you already haven't – you can do that step beforehand if necessary): *I dedicate this tool to my practice of magick.*

In the name of [Daemons Invoked], please bless these things I hold sacred in your honor and let them serve well my will. So be it.

The Tools can now be used.

Creating Effigies

Effigies are a tool for magick in that they are physical representations of a person, place or thing on which the magick is to be worked. The most popular effigies you may know of are the infamous voodoo doll or the poppet. Effigies can be made of wax, cloth, straw, wood, or just about any substance you can think of. They are often charged with a pillar rite. When the effigy represents a human being, a piece of hair or other personal item of the person it is representative of is used in the effigy's creation to bond the effigy to the person. We often hear of effigies used in execration magicks (cursing), but effigies can be used for love, health, and other types of magick you might be working for someone else.

Once again, effigies are charged like any magickal item. Usually using a standard pillar ritual. They are often anointed with an oleum of the purpose for the magick. They can be sent to the victim as in a curse, or they can be kept in a comfortable location as with a healing spell and later given to the person they represent as a gift.

The Types of Magick and Magickal Methods

By S. Connolly and Kelly Schneider

Magick can be arranged by Type, Purpose, and Method.

There are technically two main types of magick. There is spell work, also known as kitchen witchery, and there is ritual magick (i.e. ceremonial magick). Both forms of magick have workings that range from the simple to the complex.

Magical purposes can range from the low simple and mundane and even primal as in execration magicks and love/lust magick (Thaumaturgy) to the highest spiritual enlightenment magick (Theurgy). This is how we determine high magick from low magick. Low magick deals with mundane matters in the physical realm, whereas high magick is more apt to deal with

81

spiritual transformation. For example, your Wiccans and Hedge Witches and whatnot tend to work a lot of low magick, only occasionally treading into high magick. Your ceremonial magicians work more high magick.

There are a plethora of magickal methods. Methods are the way in which we employ the magick. Some magickal methods rely on candles, others rely on meditation exercises, other rituals are performed astrally. There is color magick, stone magick, divinatory magick (it's both a purpose and a method depending on how it's used), blood magick, sex magick, herbal magick, and sigil magick. The list goes on. Magical method takes on many forms, each relying heavily on knowing correspondences, symbolism, the purpose of certain actions, etc... It would be a virtual impossibility to cover every aspect of magick in one book. However, we can give you a general overview of some of the more common methodologies and help you develop a core foundational knowledge, which you can build upon for your personal magick practices.

Contrary to some belief, all methodologies can be used for all purposes and can be employed in both high and low magick. This means that you can use color and candle magick, for example, in tandem with high magick. For far too long, books about magick, and various schools of occult thought have been separating magick by method and type.

The reality is that **magick is magick**. It's not really high or low, or black or white. It is what it is without any extra labels attached. It is the authors' beliefs that magick, whether used to transform the self or your current work situation, works much the same way no matter how it is applied or which model you draw inspiration from. The purpose for doing it may be either mundane or spiritual, but the end resulting goal is still CHANGE IN CONFORMITY WITH ONE'S WILL. Period.

The Astral & Magick

Nick Schneider & S. Connolly

Astral magick requires the magician to know how to effectively perform astral travel. That is, to leave the body and ascend to the astral plane. In the astral world, time has no meaning. The physical no longer matters because there, the universe is mental. This is why so many people will erroneously mistake magick done in the astral temple for imagining or daydreaming about the work. While imagination is a wonderful ingredient, you do have to ascend the soul and mind. Hand in hand with Astral work is Dream Work, wherein you learn to leave your body and travel to the astral during sleep. You can even meet up with other magicians in this manner. Learning to ascend to the astral plane, let alone dream walking (which takes a great deal more skill) requires meditation skills and the ability to concentrate. Sadly, these are not skills the magician can learn from reading a book. You need to perform meditation exercises to learn how to ascend to the astral plane. Once there, you can create your own temple and perform any magickal work necessary. However, I highly advise against making the astral plane your sole means of magickal work. As was said earlier in this book, the mental without the physical makes for an imbalanced and half-assed magician.

The Imagination as a Tool for Effective Magick

By S. Connolly

Learning to use your imagination during magick is essential for both focus and astral work. This includes methods of communication with the Daemonic including Ascension. It is vital the magician can close his/her eyes and actually see the object of their desire or the desired outcome of the magick. Being able to focus and imagine will strengthen intent, thus you'll find you are able to manifest your true will more often. You will also find that the sharper your imagination, the higher your success rate at astral temple work. Remember, astral travel is the practice of actually leaving your body behind and ascending to another plane of existence. It's not just imagining -- but the imagination does help considerably.

To exercise your imagination, I suggest practicing guided meditations. Meditation is such a vital skill for any magician because it teaches us so many useful skills like being present, observing emotion, being still, how to breathe, connecting ourselves to all that is, focus, and how to imagine. Any guided meditation CD will do. Check Amazon or your local bookstore. There should be many available. Or - get together with a friend and guide each other through meditations you create yourselves. This can be a rewarding and relaxing exercise and great for magickal study groups.

Astrology & Magick
Valerie Corban, S. Connolly

Using astrology to guide magick is as old as magick itself. Planetary influences are believed to infuse magick with additional energy and specific properties. For example, curses are ruled by Mars, the warrior planet. So you might choose to do a curse when Mars is most prominent to activate its full influence. Moon phases are important to numerous magicians. New moons are considered good times to perform magicks that cultivate new beginnings, relationships, jobs, or whatever one might want a fresh start with. Waning or dark moons are a good time to perform magicks dealing with closure.

The following are some standard Planetary Rulerships and information used by magicians of every ilk. Note that the Daemonic Correspondences can be adjusted to your particular hierarchy or whichever Daemonic entities you affiliate with the Sephiroth, planet, plant, color, or tarot card.

Planet	Day and Number	Colors	Tarot Card	Daemon
Sun	Sunday 6	Yellow, Gold	The Sun, the sixes	Flereous or Flaros
Moon	Monday 9	Purple, silver, blue, pearl white	High Priestess, the nines	Unsere, Hecate, or Lilith
Mercury	Wednesday 8	Orange, violet, multi colored	The Magus, the eights	Ronove or Delepitore
Venus	Friday 7	Green	The Empress, the sevens	Rosier or Ashtaroth
Mars	Tuesday 5	Red	The Tower, the fives	Satanchia or Agaliarept
Jupiter	Thursday 4	Blue, purple	Wheel of Fortune, the fours	Belial or Bael
Saturn	Saturday 3	Black	The Universe, the threes	Satan, Atem, or Lucifer

Planet	Godforms	Sephira	Perfumes
Sun	Horus, Ra, Bast, Sekhmet, Atem, Satan, Flaros	Tiphareth Beauty	Frankincense, cinnamon, Egyptian kyphi
Moon	Isis, Hecate, Unsere, Tezrian	Yesod the Foundation	Jasmine, ginseng, aloes, camphor, lotus
Mercury	Mercury, Hermes, Thoth, Anubis, Maat, Delepitorae	Hod the Glory	Storax, mastic, white sandalwood

Venus	Astarte, Hathor, Rosier	Netzach Victory	Rose, benzoin, sandalwood
Mars	Horus, Mars, Agaliarept, Lucifuge	Geburah Severity	Tobacco, pepper, dragons blood
Jupiter	Jupiter, Amoun, Ammon, Mammon	Chesed Mercy	Cedar, saffron
Saturn	Saturn, Isis, Hecate	Binah	Myrrh, sivet, storax

Planet	Metal	Precious Stones	Animals	Rules
Sun	Gold	Yellow diamond, jacinth, topaz	Phoenix, lion	Leo
Moon	Silver	Moonstone, quartz, pearl	Elephant, dog	Cancer
Mercury	Quicksilver (mercury), alloys	Opal, agate	Jackal, swallow, ibis, apes and baboons	Gemini and Virgo
Venus	Copper	Emerald, turquoise	Lynx, leopard, dove, sparrow, swan, cats	Taurus and Libra
Mars	Iron and steel	Ruby, bloodstone, garnet, red topaz	Basilisk, horse, bear, wolf	Aries and Scorpio
Jupiter	Tin	Turquoise, amethyst, sapphire, lapis lazuli	Eagle	Sagittarius and Pisces
Saturn	Lead	Onyx, pearl,	Crocodile,	Capricorn

		star sapphire	goat	and Aquarius

Planet	Rituals involving	Plants	Vegetable drugs
Sun	Money, honor, promotion, success, the support of those in power, friendship, healing	Acacia, almond, angelica, ash tree, bay tree, chamomile, heliotrope, lovage, marigold, mistletoe, peony, rice, rue, rosemary, saffron, st. johns wort, sunflower, walnut	Datura, alcohol, digitalis, coffee
Moon	Travel, visions, divination, dreams, magic and love	Acanthus, almond, cabbage, cucumber, dogs tooth violet, iris, lettuce, white lilies, mugwort, poppy, privet, pumpkin, white roses, turnips, watercress, willow tree, wintergreen	Orchis root
Mercury	Intellect, memory, science, creativity, business, magical conjurations, divination, prediction, eloquence, the gift of tongues	Anise, azaleas, bittersweet, camphor, caraway carrots chicory, cinnamon, cloves, dill, fennel, fern, frankincense, hazelnut, honeysuckle, lavender, licorice, lily of the valley, marjoram, mulberry tree, mushrooms, myrtle, oats, orris root, parsley, parsnip, pomegranate, sandalwood, savory, scabious, valerian	Peyote, herb mercury, and all cerebral excitants
Venus	Love, marriage, friendship, pleasure, beauty,	Artichoke, bean, birch, blackberry, catnip, cherry tree, columbine, daffodil, daisy, dittany of crete, feverfew, foxglove, geranium,	Damiana and all aphrodisiacs

		artistic creativity, imagination, fertility	gooseberry, ladies mantle, ladies slipper, mints, mugwort, peach, pear, pennyroyal, periwinkle, plantain, primrose, raspberry, rose, strawberry, tansy, thyme, vervain, violet, yarrow	
	Mars	Energy, courage, battle, conflict, death, curses	Aloes, anemone, asafoetida, barberry, basil, box tree, broom, chives, coriander, dragons blood, galangal, garlic, ginger, hawthorn, honeysuckle, hops, mustard, nettles, onions, parsley, peppers, pine, radish, rhubarb, rocket, sarsaparilla, shepherds rod, tarragon, tobacco, woodruff, wormwood	Nettle, nux vomica, absinthe, all irritants and caustics
	Jupiter	Honor, riches, friendships, health, the hearts desires, luck	Asparagus, balm, borage, briar rose, cedar, chervil, chestnut, carnation, costmary, dandelion, fig tree, fir tree, hyssop, jasmine, linden, lungwort, maple tree, myrrh, oak, pinks, roses, sage, sumac, verbena	Opium, cocaine, all analgesics
	Saturn	Knowledge, familiars, death, reincarnation, buildings, bindings, overcoming curses, protection	Aconite, barley, beech tree, beet, bitter aloe, comfrey, cypress, elm tree, gladiolus, hellebore, hemlock, hemp, holly, ivy, juniper, medlar tree, mullein, nightshade, patchouli, poplar tree, quince, rushes, safflower, sloe, sorrel, tamarisk tree, yew	Belladonna and all sedatives

The planetary symbols:

Moon	Mercury	Venus	Sun
Mars	Pallas	Juno	Vesta
Ceres	Jupiter	Chiron	Saturn
Uranus	Pluto	Neptune	Earth

Moon Phases & Magick

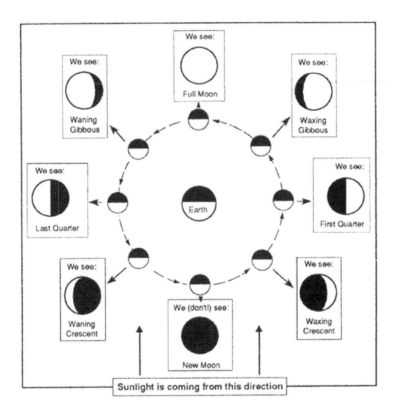

New Moon: New Moon magick can be performed from the day of the new moon to three-and-a-half days afterward. Utilize the new moon for starting new ventures or for making new beginnings. Also, it is a good time to perform love and romance magick, or magicks for health or job hunting.

Waxing Moon: From seven to fourteen days after the new moon you can perform constructive magick, such as love, wealth, success, courage, friendship, luck or health.

Full Moon: From fourteen to seventeen-and-a-half days after the new moon would be best to perform rituals for divination, protection, and prophecy. Any working that needs extra power, such as help finding a new job or healing for serious conditions, can be performed now. Also, love, knowledge, legal undertakings, money and dreams are good purposes for magick now.

Waning Moon: The waning moon runs from three-and-a-half to ten-and-a-half days after the full moon. The waning moon can be used for banishing magick, or for ridding oneself of addictions, illness or negativity.

Dark Moon: From ten-and-a-half to fourteen days after the full moon runs the dark moon. The dark moon is an ideal time to perform work to rid oneself of bad habits, to perform binding spells, for exploring our darkest recesses and for developing an understanding of our angers and passions. Also, this is a good time to bring justice to bear. Plainly put, Dark Moons are perfect for cursing.

Astrology & The Magician

Some Magicians are made while others are natural magicians. A natural magician is one with innate strong gifts or magickal skills. Oftentimes, it can be determined which natural gifts, if any, a magician has by looking at the magician's tropical natal chart. (S. Connolly believes this should all hold true with the Sidereal Natal Charts as well.)

It will often take an astrologer well versed in reading these signs to find the markers in a chart.

The following are some of the markers that will suggest someone is a natural magician. Depending on how many of the markers there are, or how pronounced, in conjunction with other chart characteristics, will determine how strong the ability is.

- Mars and Mercury Conjunct
- Mars and Mercury Conjunct in the upper left sextile at thirty degrees(or close to – indicates VERY strong ability for magick and an ability to deflect magickal attacks or negative energies from external sources). In the right upper sextile it indicates a chart of Set – or the Chaos Chart (people whose magickal ability may be out of balance in this world, but more pronounced interdimensionally or on other planes of existence).
- Water Signs (Pisces, Cancer, Scorpio) in all the occult houses (4, 8, 12). The straighter on – the more pronounced the ability of the magician. If it's just a sliver, then the ability diminishes.
- Pluto in an occult house or water sign (suggests mediumship ability).
- Fire and water in the occult houses indicates a magician with high energy.

95

On that note, by viewing the chart of a natural magician, the astrologer can tell which areas or types of magick are prominent. A magician with activity in the house of healing, for example, may be good at healing magick. A magician with Venus in the 12th house may be good at love magick, or parting lovers.

It would be impossible to go through every possible marker or combination in this book, however, if you find your have one or more of the markers indicated, chances are you are a natural magician to some degree.

Now mind you in suggesting there are natural magicians I am in no way saying that those without the markers have no magical ability or no ability to learn magick. Natural magicians simply don't have to try as hard to learn and cultivate certain skills that other magicians will try for years to cultivate. Sometimes successfully, sometimes not. The reading of a natal chart is merely suggestive of the potential for innate abilities.

Elemental Magic
By S. Connolly

EARTH rules all things mundane, financial, stability oriented, and physical. Ritual work should ideally be preformed when the moon is in one of the astrological signs governed by that element: Taurus, Virgo, Capricorn. Some of the better known Earth Daemons are Ba'al, Belial, and Belphegore. Goetia elemental correspondences may be different.

AIR rules all things educational, enlightening, and thought related. Ritual work should ideally be performed when the moon is in one of the astrological signs governed by that element: Gemini, Libra, Aquarius. Air Daemons may include Lucifer, Lucifuge Rofocale, and Ronove (Ronwe). Goetia elemental correspondences may be different.

FIRE rules over passion, lust, creativity, and action. Ritual work should ideally be performed when the moon is in one of the astrological signs governed by that element: Aries, Leo, Sagittarius. Daemons of fire include Flaros (Flereous), Satan, and Amducius. Goetia elemental correspondences may be different.

WATER rules intuition (divination), emotions, and wisdom. Ritual work should ideally be performed when the moon is in one of the astrological signs governed by that element: Cancer, Scorpio, Pisces. Water Daemons may include Leviathan, Verrine, Astarte, or Wadjet. Goetia elemental correspondences may be different.

Elemental Balancing
(From The Complete Book of Demonolatry by S. Connolly)

Being balanced elementally is important for the magician for several reasons:

1. Having too much or too little of one element within yourself can cause your magick to fizzle, backfire, or cause intensity issues.

2. Certain rituals will imbalance you and cause physical or mental health issues. So knowing how to regain that balance is important and knowing how to balance yourself depends on knowing what you naturally lack or have in excess.

3. Certain magickal skills can be harder to develop if you have too little of one thing or too much of something else.

Figuring Out Your Elemental Makeup and Identifying Imbalance:

You start out by taking your natal chart (You can get a free one at www.alabe.com) and looking at which planets you have in which signs. For example - if your Mars is in Cancer, you have one water. If your Pluto is in Sagittarius, one fire. If your N. Node is in Capricorn and your Rising sign is in Virgo - that's two earth. You will end up with 12 of these (all the planetary bodies including the N Node and your rising sign). Then you add them up based on element.

Now mind you that is only an indicator of where elemental imbalances might occur, and you might get imbalances that don't coincide with your chart due to whatever you may be doing.

For example, expending too much energy on the emotional can either deplete water or cause you to build an excess of water. It's different for different people. The key is getting to know your elemental makeup and how different rituals, work, and situations effect that balance or imbalance.

For Reference:

• Aries (FIRE)
• Taurus (EARTH)
• Gemini (AIR)
• Cancer (WATER)
• Leo (FIRE)
• Virgo (EARTH)
• Libra (AIR)
• Scorpio (WATER)
• Sagittarius (FIRE)
• Capricorn (EARTH)
• Aquarius (AIR)
• Pisces (WATER)

Some Imbalance Possibilities:

Air Imbalance – An air imbalance might have symptoms of trouble catching one's breath, thinking too much instead of doing, or not being able to think clearly.

Fire Imbalance – A fire imbalance may be identified by lack of motivation, exhaustion, being quick to anger, irritable, or extremely thirsty.

Water Imbalance – Water imbalances can be identified by extreme thirst, severe emotional mood swings, and the inability to go beyond feelings to find reason.

Earth Imbalance – Characteristics of an earth imbalance could include feeling lethargic, tired, and overly pessimistic.

If your chart is heavy in certain elements and light in others, it might be best to do regular balancing to help with a natural imbalance. For those of us who are naturally more balanced based on more balanced charts, an imbalance will be easier to identify.

To balance yourself, use a self cleansing or grounding or the following Elemental Balancing Ritual. For those new to magick, realize the reason so many Daemonolatry rituals are often done inside elementally balanced ritual circles is to keep the magician balanced. This negates (for the most part) the need for constant banishing and cleansings so prominent in other systems. Certainly there are situations where banishings and cleansings are quite useful. See previous sections for more about this.

Elemental Balancing Ritual

As always, be reminded that Daemonic Magick relies on two things: A. Daemons B. The Natural Elements that make up our universe.

It is important to remember that healing rituals are no different. Water is the element of healing. Leviathan is the lord of water (in some hierarchies anyway). His colors are blue, gray, and sometimes white.

Why we get sick - all sickness is caused by physical and mental strains/stresses and environmental influences. We get sick when our bodies lose their natural balance. Sometimes it's due to Elemental Imbalance. It is, essentially what it says. Your body becomes imbalanced and thus unhealthy.

To negate and correct the effects of the imbalance -- you must do, on a regular basis, what is commonly known as an Elemental Balancing Ritual.

This ritual relies heavily on creative visualization.

Set up your altar as you normally would, invoke your elemental Daemonic circle, and sit comfortably in front of the altar. Some people prefer to do this ritual skyclad (naked) as opposed to robed.

First you must remove all of your elements from you. Do this by imagining you are holding a box. Into this box you put all of your elements, one at a time, and then throw the box from you. You may have to fill the box with each element more than once. Imagine Earth as soil and leaves. Imagine air as smoke. Fire as flame and Water as water.

Once you have removed all your elements - and you will be able to tell because you will be exhausted-- you can begin replenishing that which you have freed yourself of. Imagine refilling the box with "fresh" elements. Only fill the box once with each element. Pull the box into you. When this is done correctly you will feel invigorated and energetic. Then you close the ritual as you normally would.

Interesting Note: This ritual can also be modified for different belief systems or to a personal belief system. I have been told it works just as well regardless of which gods you invoke if any.

Herbs & Magick
By S. Connolly

The use of herbs in magick is as old as magick itself. Included in this chapter is information on preparing herbs and making oleums (oils) for magickal use. It is suggested if you are further interested in this topic that you look into it more. There are numerous encyclopedias available that discuss the magickal usage of plants. We have included a brief plant listing with this chapter that includes common plants that have played a historical role in various types of magick from witchcraft to ceremonial magick. It is by no means complete, hence the suggestion that you own at least one good reference book on magickal herbalism if this is an area that interests you.

Another alternative is to intuitively select plants to put into your incenses and oils. For recipes, please see the formulary chapter.

PLANT REFERENCE:
S. Connolly & B. Morlan

Angelica Root (Venus) – Creativity, Feminine. Associated with the Empress card in Tarot

Balm of Gilead (Jupiter) – Consecration, Necromancy, Divination, Love Magick

Bay Leaves (Sun) – Divination, Dreamwork, Love Magick, Consecration, Protection

Belladonna* (Saturn) – Astral Work, Execration, Protection for Warriors

Black Nightshade* (Saturn) – Execration Magicks, Necromantic Work

Blackthorn (Saturn) - Execration Magicks, Self Work, Protection

Black Mallow Flowers (Venus) - Healing, Dream Work & Love

Calamus Root (Sun) – Water, Ascension, Higher Self

Cardamom (Mars) - Lust, Love, Sex Magick, Protection, Clarity

Cassia (Fire) - Purification, Consecration

Cedarwood (Sun) - Healing, Self Work, Purification, Execration Magick, Psychic Development, Protection, Money

Chamomile (Moon) - Dream Work, Money, Higher Self, Moon & Sun Magick, Love

Cinnamon (Sun) - Healing, Knowledge, Luck, Love, Lust, Creativity, Protection, Psychic Development, Money
Cinquefoil (Mercury) - Travel, Wealth, Money, Healing, Purification, Wisdom, Curse Breaking
Cloves (Sun) (Moon) - Money, Love, Protection
Coriander (Mars) - Execration Magick, Love, Healing
Damiana (Mercury) - Lust, Love, Intuition, Feminine
Dittany Root (Fire) - Protection, Moon Magick, Earth Magick
Dogbane (Jupiter) - Love, Creativity, Aids Spirits to Appear
Elder (Venus) - Protection, Knowledge, All Elemental Magick
Fennel (Mercury) - Execration Magick, Protection, Healing, Purification, Fertility, Focus
Galangal (Mars) - Courage, Strength, Aid in Legal Matters, Adds Power, Execration Magick
Grains of Paradise (Fire) - Passion, Lust, Sex Magick, Protection
Hibiscus (Sun) - Love, Lust, Divination, Intuition, Ascension
Jasmine Flowers (Venus) - Love, Dream Work, Money, Meditation, Healing
Juniper Berries (Jupiter) - Purification, Consecration, Mental Magick, Increases Psychic Ability, Healing
Lavender Buds (Mercury) - Love, Peace, Intuition, Dream Work, Lust, Sex Magick
Licorice Root. (Mercury) - Lust, Passion, Fidelity, Necromancy
Mallow Flowers, Black (Venus) - Love, Water Magick, Healing
Mandrake Root * (Saturn) - Protection, Power, Execration Magick, Divination, Fertility, Money, Love
Marigold Petals (Sun) - Protection, Dream Work, Aid in Legal Matters, Psychic Development

Mistletoe (Sun) - Protection, Love, Fertility, Healing, Necromancy

Monkshood* (Saturn) - Hecate Magick, Necromancy, Astral Work, Execration Magick

Mugwort, (Moon) - Strength, Healing, Astral Work, Dream Work, Psychic Development, Moon Magick, Consecration

Myrtle (Venus) - Love, Money, Fertility, Peace

Nutmeg (Jupiter) - Fidelity, Luck, Money, Healing, Concentration, Skrying, Psychic Development

Oak Moss (Earth) - Money, Potency, Fertility, Luck

Orange Peel (Sun) - Divination, Love, Luck, Money, Focus, Centering

Orris Root (Moon) - Love, Attraction, Binding, Divination, Moon Magick, Protection

Patchouli (Earth) - Fertility, Lust, Money, Divination, Love, Sex Magick

Pennyroyal (Venus) - Strength, Protection, Peace, Initiations, Execration Magick

Peppercorns, Black (Mars) - Execration Magick, Protection, Strength, Lust

Poppy Seed (Moon) - Love, Lust, Fertility, Dream Work, Divination, Money, Luck, Moon Magick, Knowledge

Red Sandalwood (Venus) - Healing, Meditation, Sex Magick, Purification

Rose Buds, Pink (Venus) - Love, Friendship, Beauty, Healing, Luck, Divination, Psychic Development

Round Cardamom (Moon) - Moon Magick, Focus, Dream Work, Psychic Development

Rue (Mars) - Mental Work, Protection, Reversing, Love, Execration Magick

Sage (Earth) - Wisdom, Purification, Consecration, Psychic Development, Banishing

Safflower Petals (Mars) - Healing, Sun Magick

Solomon's Seal Root (Saturn) - Protection, Wisdom, Consecration, Mental Work

Spikenard (Earth) - Luck, Fidelity, Healing, Attraction
Star Anise (Moon) - Luck, Psychic Development
Sulfur (Fire) - Protection, Execration Magick, Necromancy
Valerian Root (Jupiter) - Dream Work, Love, Consecration, Elemental Magick, Purification
Vervain (Venus) - Love, Protection, Purification, Peace, Money, Healing, Sex Magick
Vetivert Root (Earth) - Banishing, Peace, Luck, Love, Protection, Dream Work
White Oak (Jupiter) - Protection, Fertility, Strength
White Sage (Jupiter) - Clarity, Purification, Consecration
White Sandalwood (Mercury) - Protection, Healing, Purification, Consecration, Necromancy
White Willow (Moon) - Divination, Protection, Healing, Moon Magick, Dream Work
Wild Lettuce (Saturn) - Dream Work, Hecate Magick
Witch Hazel (Saturn) - Protection, Knowledge, Dream Work, Divination
Wormwood, Organic *(Mars) - Execration Magick, Psychic Development, Necromancy, Protection, Love, Transformation
Yarrow Flowers (Venus) - Courage, Marriage, Love, Psychic Development, Longevity, Dream Work
Yew (Saturn) - Necromancy, Hecate Magick, Astral Work, Execration Magick, Increases Magickal Potency

*Poisonous

Preparing Herbal Mixtures for Incense:

Using a mortar and pestle, (or even a coffee bean grinder, which we prefer) grind the dried herbs into a powder. Use a self-igniting charcoal to smolder the incense on. That is - you light the self-igniting charcoal and then place dry incense powder on it. Use a separate mortar and pestle to grind resins in because they tend to be sticky and gunk up on the side of your bowl. Use a mortar & pestle if you want more of your personal essence in an incense.

Making Cone or Stick Incense
Written by S. Connolly as explained by Valerie Corban and
Brid Delaney

Making stick and cone incense isn't really as tough as people think. Some people will just buy incense blanks (charcoal based are better than wood base in our opinion) and cover them in essential oils then bake them. Others choose to do the mixing themselves. It gives us an excuse to pull out our alchemical lab equipment.

- Ground Herbal Mixture
- Essential Oil(s) or Oleums (magickal oils) if desired
- Ground Charcoal (not the self-igniting kind)
- Gum tragacanth
- Potassium nitrate
- Warm water
- Thin twigs, broom straw, or wooden splints of some type
- Bowl
- Whisk
- Mortar and pestle or coffee grinder
- Wax paper

First you will want to dissolve the gum tragacanth (which you can find in herb stores, a little goes a long way) in warm water. This will create the glue that will hold it all together. How thin your mixture is depends on which kind of incense you plan to make. Stick incense, which we prefer, will hold together with a thin mixture whereas cones will require a thicker mixture. The best way to do this is to put the gum tragacanth into a bowl and add the warm water, whisking it in. 1 teaspoon to about two cups of water is about right. You need to let the gum tragacanth dissolve. Once it's mixed, set the mixture aside (cover it so nothing gets into it). At any time if the glue seems too thick, just add a little more water and whisk it.

Next you make your incense. Add about 2 parts ground charcoal to 2 parts of ground herbal mixture and up to six drops of your essential oils or oleums. Make sure you blend this well. We use our hands. You can use a spoon. Just make sure your mixture is well mixed and fine in texture. Take the incense and put it onto a scale. Weigh it. Calculate 10% of that. Whatever that number is - add that in potassium nitrate. Be careful here. So let's say you have 2 ounces of incense, you would only add .20 ounces of potassium nitrate. Mix the powder in and be sure it's well blended.

Time to add your tragacanth glue. We add it dropper by dropper until the incense is wet. For sticks wet but thick is desired. For cones, think the consistency of dough.

For cones, shape the cones by hand, place them on a sheet of wax paper (on a baking pan is excellent) and let them sit for about 6 days to dry completely. They are ready for use after that. For sticks, you can do it two ways. First, you can dip the sticks in the mixture, pull them out, let them dry a few seconds then dip them again (repeat until the stick has a goodly amount of incense on it), then let the sticks dry. Or, you can keep your glue in a glass, dip the sticks, then roll the sticks in the herbal and potassium nitrate mixture (on wax paper) and then let them dry. A piece of clay that you can stand the sticks in upright, or a wood or clay drying stand (specifically made for stick incense) makes this process easy.

You can substitute Gum Arabic for Gum Tragacanth -- but you'll need to use twice as much and your drying time will increase by 7 days.

If you're really adventurous, you'll grow your own ingredients, distill your own oils, and so on. One last note - resins are tough to work with. If you must use resins (including Frankincense), you're better off burning them on self-igniting charcoals.

Buying quality herbs and plant matter: A good local herb store is always the best place to buy so you can smell and feel the herbs before you buy them. Good health food markets will often sell herbs in bulk. Buying them in bulk is often cheaper. Alternatively, online herb stores like Penn Herb carry a wide selection of ingredients for reasonable price. Of course quality can be fully controlled by growing your own ingredients. Stay away from buying herbs at metaphysical shops just because you're going to pay more and possibly sacrifice quality. (Unless it's something no one else carries or you need it in a pinch). We've been fortunate because several of the women in our group have gardens so we share our harvest with one another. Indoor hydroponic gardens like the Aerogarden are a good choice for colder climates or those who have a black thumb of death. If you are going to grow your own plant matter, grow things that have a dual purpose. Many culinary herbs are used in

112

magick, as are flowers. Grow as much that is native to where you live as you can. If you have a greenhouse you can grow plants year round.

To Dry Plants: Once you've cut the plants you wish to dry, use string and tie them. Then hang them upside down on a covered porch or indoors. Some people will use food dehydrators to do this. Once you've effectively dried your plants, keep them in clearly labeled airtight containers in a cool, dry place. A pantry or root cellar are both ideal. Clearly marked is a key phrase here. You don't want to accidentally mistake dried and ground Hemlock for parsley. We knew someone that happened to and while it didn't kill them, it did make for a not so fun trip to the hospital and a family stomach pumping.

Plant Safety: Know your plants. Know if the plants you use are poisonous or not. If they're poisonous, use care in handling them. Only burn plants that emit noxious fumes outdoors or in a well-ventilated ritual space. Do not ingest poisonous plants. Keep your plants in **clearly labeled** containers. (Pictured below: Deadly Nightshade, *Solanum Nigrum*)

Making Oleums/Ritual Oils : Ritual oils are made by adding oil to plant matter and boiling it. To do this it is often easiest to simply grind all your plant ingredients into a fine powder, add a light carrier oil like grapeseed oil, and then boil. Strain through cheesecloth, bottle, add tincture of benzoin (1 drop per dram) and cap. Oils should be kept in tinted bottles in a cool, dark place. A basement pantry or rootceller is perfect for this. In some recipes, olive juice or water is used in place of oil. All strained plant matter can be re-dried and incorporated back into incense mixtures or it can be put into your compost pile. Oils can be kept six months to one year before they need to be replaced. Water based oleums work much the same way except you boil them in water. ½ hour boiling time is about the standard. Add a drop of your own blood to each bottle of your oleum to make the oleum personal to you. That means you are attuning the oleum to you and making it your own. Once you've added your own blood, do NOT allow others to use your oleum. Keep oleums blood free for group ritual work.

Be careful putting pure essential oils on skin or taking oils internally. Most must be diluted before personal use or you can risk irritating the skin or self-poisoning. If you do get an essential oil on the skin and you experience irritation, immediately flush with water. If irritation persists consult your physician. If you ingest a poisonous essential oil contact poison control immediately. If you are seeking to make your own essential oils you will need a great deal of plant matter and a distillation set up. This is very involved. We won't go into it here. There are numerous books about the subject.

Making the Tincture of Benzoin: Tincture of Benzoin is simply a preservative agent for your oils and salves. It is basically finely powdered Myrrh mixed with Alcohol. In an 8-ounce jar mix Vodka or Everclear with about 2 tablespoons of ground Myrrh. This will keep forever. There is also an alchemical way to make tinctures. See the Alchemy chapter for more information.

Making Salves: Salves are herbal and oil mixtures suspended in animal fats. Pork fat is my favorite method for salve making. I will boil pork fat (bacon grease is good, but it does smell) with the herbs and oils necessary, strain it through cheesecloth, then place it in a plastic bowl. I keep my salves in the refrigerator because they have a longer shelf life that way. Most salves have a shelf life, refrigerated, for at least six months.

Alchemy
By S. Connolly

Alchemy seems to be one of those topics magicians either really dig into and adore, or it's passed over in favor of something less involved and less dry. It is my hope I will be able to cover this topic adequately and in an interesting manner as to make Alchemy more readily accessible to all Daemonolatry magicians. Even those with short attention spans.

In this chapter we'll discuss the processes of alchemy both in a laboratory sense and in the spiritual metaphoric sense. First it's probably important to know that alchemically speaking, the elements are dry, hot, cold, and wet. Considering alchemical process this isn't surprising.

Now onto why alchemy is important to the Daemonolatry Magician and how one can incorporate it into his/her practice. To be blunt – alchemy is a great way to produce Daemonolatry tinctures and other herbal necessities you can add to your magick arsenal. Spiritually speaking, the alchemical process teaches patience and abstract thinking. Think of the spiritual alchemical process as a metaphor for our understanding of ourselves in relationship to the divine and the process for uncovering our own divine nature.

I've broken this section into two parts. The first part will discuss the practical laboratory application of alchemical processes – for the Daemonic magician. The second part will give you a brief look into Spiritual/Metaphoric Alchemy. A book like this does not allow for in depth analysis of such topics so it is advised that serious magicians definitely research further into topics of magick as interest dictates. There are hundreds of books that delve into topics such as Alchemy with much more depth even though this particular book may be the only one that puts Alchemy into context with Daemonic magick.

Some Alchemical Terms

Ablation: Separating one substance from another by skimming it off the top in some manner.

Albification: Turning a substance (matter) white.

Ablution: Purification by washing with liquid, usually successively.

Assation: Reducing matter to dry ash via burning.

Calcination: Heating or burning a substance until it is broken down.

Ceration: Causing a substance to soften and become wax-like. Usually achieved by adding liquid and heating until the proper consistency is attained.

Cineration: Another word to describe heating something until it turns to ash.

Coagulation: (also Coadunation and Congelation) Turning thin liquids into solids as with curdling milk. Sometimes this involves adding something, heating, or cooling the mixture.

Coction (also Concoction): Cooking a substance at moderate heat for an extended period. Kind of like simmering (for the cooks among us), but not necessarily.

Cohobation: Removing the moisture from a substance by applying heat. In this process you'll usually find liquid re-added and the process repeated.

Colliquation: Melting together two fusible substances.

Coloration: Exactly what it says. Coloring a substance by adding dyes or colored tinctures (also dyes). Sometimes it's only a surface coating, other times it's changing the entire color of a substance depending on application.

Combustion: Burning matter or substance in open air.

Comminution: Reducing the substance to powder using a mortar and pestle or forcing it through a sieve of some sort.

Composition: Mixing two substances together.

Conception: The merging of masculine and feminine aspects of substances. What's interesting is this can be taken metaphorically as indicated by substance correspondences, or literally as in male and female parts of flowers.

Conglutination (also Glutination): Turning a substance into a glue like substance, usually by putrefaction. If you want to test this, leave spinach in butter sauce in a bowl at a window that gets sun for about a week.

Conjunction (also Copulation): Joining two opposite components. This can be utilized for polarity purposes, too. Joining of Lucifer and Lucifuge for example. Or Unsere and Euronymous.

Contrition: Reducing something into powder via fire.

Corrosion: Allowing a substance to be eaten by a corrosive material such as something acidic or alkaline.

Cribation: Turning a substance to powder by shoving through a mesh strainer.

Crystallization: Usually formed by evaporation of liquid.

Dealbation: Changing a black substance, via alchemical process, into something very white.

Decrepitation: Splitting apart substances via heating. To test this, add a grain of salt to flame.

Deliquium: Reducing a solid to a liquid by putting it in a humid place where it can absorb water from the air. A good example of this is those canisters of moisture absorber containing calcium chloride.

Descension: The separation of one substance from another wherein one substance sinks to the bottom of whatever it is mixed with. As opposed to Ascension where one substance rises from another into vapor as happens with distillation.

Desiccation: Drying a substance.

Detonation: Burning a substance with the result being an explosion. Substances mixed with nitrate for example.

Digestion: Gently heating a substance to modification.

Disintegration (also Dissociation): Breaking down a substance into its many parts.

Dispoliaration: Turning dead matter into liquid.

Dissolution: Dissolving a substance in liquid.

Distillation: Separating specific components from a substance by heating, thus separating the wanted component from the substance that it turns to vapor, which is then condensed and collected as a liquid.

Divapouration: Producing dry smoke (vapor) from a substance upon heating.

Edulceration: Removal of salts from a substance by washing.

Elaboration (also Exaltation): Purifying a substance by any variety of processes.

Elixeration: Turning a substance into an elixir.

Evaporation: Removing water from a substance via heat or general air-drying.

Exhalation: Releasing gas or air from a substance

Expression: Extracting liquids using a press.

Extraction: Macerating a substance in alcohol for purification. After extraction, the extract is then separated from the left over residue.

Fermentation: Allowing an organic substance to rot and produce gas bubbles.

Filtration: Passing a substance through a strainer, filter, or cheesecloth to remove the pulp or matter of a substance.

Fumigation: Altering a substance by passing it through smoke. This term is often used to describe clearing a temple by filling it with smoke from incense. Of course alchemically, the smoke should be corrosive in some way.

Fusion: Mixing two powders or converting a substance into a new form via exposure to high heat.

Gradation: Gradually purifying a substance by performing the purification process in stages.

Granulation: Turning a substance to powder or grain by grinding, pounding, heating with rapid cooling etc...

Grinding: Using a mortar and pestle to reduce to powder.

Humectation: Allowing a substance to absorb moisture by placing it in a humid environment.

Imbibition: The process of continually adding gradual substance to another substance.

Impastation: When a substance that has been through putrefaction and becomes black, thick and congealed.

Impregnation: Taking a male substance and a female substance, infusing them via copulation and creating a new substance.

Inceration: Adding water to give a substance the consistency of soft wax.

Incineration: Using fire to turn a substance to ash.
Incorporation: Mixing together different substances until they become one body.

Ingression: Combining two substances in a way that they cannot be separated later.

Inhumation: To bury a substance in earth.

Liquefaction: Melting or dissolving a solid substance into liquid.

Maturation: A degree of the perfection of the work.

Melting: Turning metal or other substance to liquid via heating.

Mortification: Allowing the substance to go through a death (usually via putrification), seemingly destroyed but later revived.

Multiplication: Multiplying the power of a substance.

Projection: Using a tincture or ferment on a substance in order to transform the substance.

Pulverization: Beating a substance into smaller fragments using a hammer or mallet.

Putrefaction: Letting a substance rot through use of a gentle moist heat, casing the substance to become black.

Quinta Essentia: An elevated form of a substance. Making of a quintessence.

Rarefaction: Making a substance thin, airy, and subtle.

Rectification: Purification of a substance by repeated distillation (i.e. Reiteration).

Reiteration: The repeated distillation of a substance.

Resolution: A process similar to coagulation where substances are mixed together and become separated when placed in a solution.

Restinction: Perfecting a substance at white heat by quenching it in an exalted liquid.

Reverberation: Igniting a substance at high temperature as within a furnace. Calcination via high temperatures.

Revivification: Reactivating mortified matter.

Rubification: Making matter go from white to red via alchemical process.

Segregation: Separating a substance into all of its parts. The separation of a composite substance into its parts.

Separation: Taking two opposite components together, and removing one from the other. This process is often alternated with conjunction.

Stratification: A process in which a substance is reduced to layers of its various properties in the flask. The heavier parts of the substance will sink while subsequent lighter materials will float to different layers in the flask.

Sublimation: Heating matter to where it gives off a vapor, which then condenses in the cooler upper part of the vessel without going through a liquid phase.

Subtilation: Separating a subtle part of a substance from the bulk of it. For example, separating essential oil from a plant leaf.

Transudation: Sweating the essence out of a substance in drops during a descending distillation.

Trituration: Reducing a substance to powder by applying heat.

Vitrification: Turning a substance into glass by using high heat and sometimes adding lime.

Practical Laboratory Alchemy

Alchemy was the precursor to modern chemistry and pharmacology. Even today alchemy is used for the purpose of distilling oils, creating medicinal tinctures, and for creating magickal tinctures. This is where the practicality of Alchemy comes in. Those who are into creating their own oleums and incenses will definitely want to delve into a Daemonolatry alchemy experiment or two (provided). It is a longer process than your standard oleum making method, but it's worth it.

The Home Alchemy Lab

You can easily start your beginner alchemist's lab with a scale, a mortar and pestle (you can use a grinder, but sometimes crushing the plant to powder is preferred depending on what you're making), wine alcohol, a glass funnel, a measuring cup, ceramic dishes that withstand high heat (Coors porcelain is good), droppers, and a lab burner or gas burner. You can use your electric stove; it's just that gas heat is easier to control temperature wise. Later on you can add distillation devices (you can get inexpensive kits for under $50), graduated beakers, heat resistant glass flasks, test tubes, filter papers, funnels for powder (these can be plastic), lab bottles/jars, porcelain crucibles and so on. There are actual alchemy stores that sell this stuff. That said, let's discuss some laboratory experiments ala Daemonolatry style to get you on your way to a working knowledge of laboratory alchemy. You will also need an outdoor incineration area for turning matter to ash. It can be as simple as a clay pot or pit or a fire urn of some sort. I use an old clay plant pot.

Alchemical Process- Using Spagyric Alchemy to Create Tinctures:

We'll start by making a simple and basic spagyric *Tincture of Lucifer*. The plant ingredient is Melisa Officinalis, or Lemon Balm. Some alchemists will tell you to begin with the dried plant because it will powder easier. I prefer to start with a fresh plant. It won't powder, but it will become a nice pulp yielding a great deal of plant energy and essential oil. However - you can dry the plant (Desiccation) by tying some freshly cut sprigs together and hanging them inside where the air can get at them from all sides.

Since Lemon Balm is ruled by the planet Jupiter and Jupiter rules Thursday, begin this operation on a Thursday just after sunrise (the hour ruled by Jupiter). Over the newly plucked leaves of the lemon balm (or newly dried - try it both ways), recite the enn of Lucifer and offer prayers that Lucifer reveals his wisdom unto you.

Using a mortar and pestle, begin grinding the herb. Some people will suggest using an electric grinder, but for the purpose of alchemical process, it is preferred that the alchemist do this by hand to infuse the proper intent into the matter. Coffee grinders should only be used if the herb(s) you're working with are hard seeds or something that cannot be easily ground to a powder or pulp by hand.

As you grind, imagine that you are releasing the divine matter from the herb and from within yourself.

When you've reached a fine powder (as with dry herb) or a fine pulp (as with fresh herb), place the herb in a jar. Then slowly pour grain alcohol over it. Fill the jar 1-2 inches over the herbs. The jar should not be more than 1/2 to 2/3rds full, as the maceration process will cause some expansion. The fluid will evaporate from the heat, and then condense when it cannot escape. As a result, you will notice the fluid getting darker with each passing day.

First - the liquid should touch no metal so using a plastic lid is ideal. However, you can use plastic wrap between the jar and lid if necessary. Then, wrap the jar in craft paper or tin foil to keep out light. Place the jar in a warm place where the mixture can heat. I prefer to put mine in the full sun garden in the backyard. Make sure you'll put it in a place where you'll remember to shake it daily. It will need to be shaken one to two times daily. While shaking gently, imagine the separation of the essence from the physical plant matter. Do this for 2 weeks. You'll discover your tincture has taken on a very dark hue.

Now that you have your tincture, using cheesecloth or a mesh strainer, strain the liquid from the plant matter, squeezing off the excess liquid from the plant matter by pressing it.

Take the remaining plant matter outside to your clay burning pot and burn the remaining plant matter until it is ash. Carefully collect the ash in a heat safe dish and place in the oven at 500 degrees until it turns into a gray-white (or even completely white) powder. This is calcination and purification. The finer you grind your plant matter during the initial maceration process, the finer your calcinated powder will be at the completion of the purification process.

Keep the matter (salt) separate from the tincture. This particular tincture is meant to be taken internally as a symbolic purification and openness to the wisdom Lucifer has to impart. It will be used before ritual, meditation, or during a self-purification process. Take one glass of distilled water, mix in two drops of the tincture and drink it. Then anoint the third eye with some of the ash. The ash can also be taken internally in very small amounts, grain by grain. Be careful to only take internally tinctures and salts made from plants that are not poisonous.

You can make numerous tinctures in this manner. Tinctures can be added to oils and salves (and will also preserve it) and can be used to anoint, bless, and clear talismans and other items.

A Practical Application: The Creation of a Vegetable Stone

Creation of the stone itself is symbolic of elemental balancing. Making the vegetable stone is very similar to creating the spagyric tincture except that the salts that may be discarded during the making of a tincture are actually kept for calcinations. If enough salt isn't acquired from the process, sea salt can be used. So while creating the tinctures is often about separating parts of the plant matter into different forms and extracting the pure essences. The "vegetable" stone is basically all about the calcinations of the extractions from the plant matter.

First, we will create the tincture as in the previous method. Then we want to take the white ash produced from the process and further process it by putting it in alcohol and then burning the alcohol off. You must use extreme caution when doing this and we recommend doing it outdoors in your burning area. The use of safety glasses and the use of a wire mesh screen to keep hot ashes from blowing onto you or anywhere else is highly recommended. The wire mesh screen will also keep the finer ash from blowing away.

For processing the ashes (salts) of your tincture, continue by re-soaking the ash in alcohol and again burning it off. Do this five times. You can do this indoors if you are very careful and have a gas stove. Your ash needs to be white or white gray before it can be considered properly processed.

You can calcinate salts (sea salt for addition to your stone) ahead of time. Some people choose to do this on the planetary day and hour of the herb being alchemically processed. (Choose the herb based on what you're seeking to accomplish with the work.) To calcinate your salts you'll want to do this via leaching.

Leaching can be accomplished by placing the sea salt in a moderate amount of distilled water, and allowing it to evaporate naturally, or with the assistance of a heat lamp or toaster oven. Setting it under a table lamp that is turned on should be fine. Once the salt has calcinated, scrape it from the container, grind it up, and repeat. If you spread your salt finely across the bottom of your dish, and use just enough water to cover, you can actually accomplish calcinations in 24 hours. This salt can then be added into your processed ashes for the next process.

Okay – now back to your tincture ash (the actual ash from the body of the plant matter). Once you've processed your plant matter into the fine white ash, you will want to reincorporate the tincture into the heated "salts" until fully absorbed. You will add the tincture back drop-by-drop if need be.

In this alchemical process you are imbibing the lifeless plant matter with life once more. Continue doing this (adding the tincture back into the ash matter – i.e. the Stone) for approximately an hour. Then leave the stone and repeat the process once a week (some believe on a Saturday – ruled by Saturn – at an hour ruled by the plant used if you want to get really technical). Continue until your stone will take no more tincture.

Store the stone near a heat source and watch it over the next few months noting any changes. I wouldn't store it in the heat safe dish you used to perform the heating process just because it is going to get hard and it will likely be difficult to get out. Note that the stone will be small and will only be the size of a tip of your finger. The stone can be ingested in small bits, under the tongue, with water, or a small piece can be cut or scraped from the stone and re-incorporated into water for ingestion if you so choose.

It is for this reason you should be careful which plant matter you are using to create your vegetable stone. Do not ingest poisonous plant matter in any form, just in case.

Spiritual Alchemy

It is said that each physical process of laboratory alchemy also corresponds to a path in our own spiritual journeys. Many have said that understanding alchemical process requires some knowledge of Qabbalah since each process of alchemy can be paired with a path or Sephiroth.

The Metaphoric Alchemical process works much the same way. I believe alchemical process is its own, unique model for how we are to discover and embrace our true nature as divine beings on a physical plane of existence.

This process of spiritual cultivation and self discovery is studied in many Hermetic schools of occult thought in a brief text you probably know of -- The Emerald Tablet of Hermes. My personal observations from a Daemonolatry perspective are in italics.

The Emerald Tablet
From the Latin

1. True, without error, certain and most true
2. That which is below is as that which is above, and that which is above is as that which is below, to perform the miracles of the one thing.

3. And as all things were from the one, by means of the meditation of the one, thus all things of the daughter from the one, by means of adaptation.

4. Its father is the sun (*fire - Flereous*), its mother, the moon (*water/liquid - Leviathan*), the wind (*air/gasses - Lucifer*) carried it in its belly, its nurse is the earth (*earth/matter - Belial or Ba'al*).

5. The father of all the initiates of the whole world is here.

6. Its power is integrating if it be turned into earth.

7. Separate the earth from the fire, the fine from the dense, delicately, by means of/to the great together with capacity.

8. It ascends by means of earth into heaven and again it descends into the earth, and retakes the power of the superiors and of the inferiors.

9. Thus, you have the glory of the whole world.

10. Therefore, may it drive-out by means of you of all the obscurity.

11. This is the whole of the strength of the strong force, because it overcomes all fine things, and penetrates all the complete.

12. Thus the world has been created.

13. Hence they were wonderful adaptations, of which this is the manner.

14. Therefore, I am Hermes the Thrice Great, having the three parts of the philosophy of the whole world.

15. What I have said concerning the operation of the Sun has been completed.

It's food for thought. Enjoy.

Blood & Magick
By Brad Morlan, HP

What is Blood Magick?

Blood Magick is well steeped in the history of all religions worldwide. Since Daemonolatry is a blood based tradition, we utilize blood to form bonds with Daemons, as well as giving of ourselves by sacrificing some of our blood in order to honor ourselves as well as the Daemons in the form of offerings and requests. Using blood in rites allows one to increase their personal power.

Blood Magick is simply using our own Life Force to direct our own will towards a specific goal. As we know, magick is defined as bending and shaping reality for a needed/desired change. We can use our own blood, our Life Force, to affect that change.

Blood Magick is a powerful way to change our lives, since it is a part of us, it is more effective since more energy is being utilized.

We can use blood in rites to share with one another, to form more of a connection, both physically and psychically as well as using the energy within the blood as a catalyst for attaining a higher state of consciousness. This is done by ingesting a small amount of blood. Or as in the ever-popular Blood Brother ritual, people would cut a part of their palm, and grab each other's hands, allowing their bond to become more solid, as "brothers" or "sisters". As a child, my sisters and I would have our own version of our rites, and then later that night, the adults would have a more elaborate ritual. Towards the end of the rite, we would partake in a ceremony of sharing Blood Wine. For the kids, it was very simple, no alcohol. The recipe for that is simple, we would have apple juice, with a drop of blood from each of us in the virgin Blood Wine. As I got older, and was able to attend the more elaborate rites, we could partake in the actual Blood Wine. We simply had a chalice of red wine, enough for a drink from each of the people in the circle, and we would add 3 drops of our own blood to the wine.

As such, we anoint candles, sigils and people with our Life Force, in order to better connect with a particular Daemon, to make sacred our intentions and requests to make a change in our lives. The definition of sacrifice is to make sacred. This simply means, that by giving our Life Force as an offering to the Daemons, we are making our work sacred in the eyes of the Daemonic Divine, or to consecrate whatever work we are doing charging it with our personal energy, later to be also charged and mingled with the Daemon's energy to be carried out into manifestation.

Signing a request in blood or creating a sigil in blood is a very good use of Blood Magick. This act makes more concrete our intentions in the Daemonic realm. This attracts the Daemon we are making the request to, and makes it personal to us, thus making it more potent and more honoring to the Daemons. As we visualize and think about the work we are doing, this automatically charges our blood for us with the intention we are working towards. It also helps us to create a sympathetic link to our own intentions, making it very clear and creating a strong focus on what we are trying to accomplish.

Placing a small amount of blood in your incenses and oleums also makes them very personal to your own use, as well as making your bond with the Daemons more powerful, it is an act of selflessness, in that you are offering your own energy, your trust, to the Daemons being invoked to aid your life, or as general devotion. Devotional practices also make a great way to use Blood Magick. As we pray to our Matron/Patron Daemons, you can add a small amount of blood to your prayer cord or prayer beads. If you do not use these, then a small amount of blood on the prayer candle you may be using will be sufficient enough to accomplish the same goal. This is very pleasing and honoring to the Daemonic Divine.

Focus and intent are very important to all types of magick, however, in Blood Magick, it seems to be that using blood makes focusing your intentions a little bit easier, allowing your body and mind to come together to make for a greater experience and personal growth. After all, our blood is a culmination of all the elements in nature. It contains the element of Earth – the cell as a whole, the element of Air – the white blood cells, the element of Fire – the red blood cells, the element of Water – actual physical water in our blood, and the element of Spirit, the fifth element – our own Life Force, the essence of who we truly are, the integration of the other four elements into one cohesive, all encompassing element. This makes this type of magick more in balance with all types of goals, or changes we need/want to make in our lives.

A note should be added here, about writing implements and inks. There are many tools you may use to write your requests or draw a sigil with. I prefer to use a small paintbrush, but you might find it easier to use a calligraphy pen or fountain pen that you can fill yourself. There is one kind that has a plunger that allows you to draw in the ink, or in this case, blood ink, and use it like a pen. Another popular form of writing implement is a quill. You can create one yourself, or buy one from a stationary store. Find what works best for you.

As for inks, this is actually very simple. Take a small bowl, and extract several drops of your own Life Force, your blood and drop it into the bowl, thinking all the while about the goal you are trying to accomplish. Take a small amount of water, and mix it into the blood. You may have to add several more drops of blood to make a strong enough liquid to stain your parchment, or whatever it is you are writing on. When you get the color the way you like it, take a small amount of Gum Arabic, and slowly start mixing it into the blood mixture. When it is an inky consistency, you are ready to use your new Blood Ink. There are many ways you can add to this basic ink, to make it more meaningful to the type of rite you are doing.

Culling or Drawing/Extracting Our Life Force

In order to use our blood, we must extract or cull it from our body. There are many ways to do this. If a woman is menstruating, she may use that blood to make changes happen in her life or the lives of others.

In the past, drawing blood was often harsh and painful. As a child, when we needed blood for a specific rite, it was taken with a razor sharp knife on our left palm just under the thumb, on the fleshy part, only about a quarter of an inch cut. It is important not to cut too far or too deep here, because of the veins in that area, as well as the tendons. My oldest sister cannot move her thumb now, because she cut too deep and cut a tendon. Blood seems to flow better from the hands, however, I have seen many people take blood successfully from other parts of their body. Often times, drawing blood in this way produced too much blood and a nice scar, as well as a reluctance to cut oneself again in the future for other rites. This in some ways detracts from the goal, because of the impending dread of the first cut.

In today's world, however, we have available to us the diabetic pen, or lancet. This produces a smaller amount of blood and far less pain, giving one the added advantage to stay focused on what they are doing.

Before we get into a basic blood rite, a word of caution – Blood Magick is not for everyone. If you have doubts or concerns about using blood, don't use it. Instead, use urine, saliva, fingernail clippings, or hair. Also if you are not mentally prepared for this type of work, then you shouldn't use it. I have seen people drive themselves mad because they weren't mentally stable enough to handle this amount of energy. In today's world, with the possibility of blood related diseases, such as hepatitis, AIDS and such, be cautious of who you share blood with, or come into contact with open wounds.

That being said, the following is a basic rite outline you can easily adapt for your personal needs.

Basic Blood Rite

Gather together the following items and bring them to your ritual area:

- a black candle inscribed with the Daemon's sigil for your desire
- a razor blade or lancet
- a small bowl
- a small amount of rubbing alcohol
- a writing implement (a fountain pen, calligraphy pen, or a quill works well)
- a piece of parchment
- a sigil of a Daemon to represent your specific goal
- Incense of the Daemon being invoked

Cast an elemental circle, invoking Satan or whatever you consider to be the fifth element from the center of the space.

Kneel at your altar. Take the lancet and prick your finger and squeeze out a few drops of blood and anoint the candle with your blood. (if using a razor blade, make a small cut on the fleshy part of your left palm, just under your thumb, going towards your wrist.)

Light the candle and invoke the Daemon with the appropriate enn, or words of your own choosing, something meaningful to you.

Take the small bowl, and place it in front of the candle. Add a small amount of rubbing alcohol to the bowl, about a cap full should be enough.

Take the lancet or razor blade again, and make another cut or prick your fingers again, letting about 10 – 20 drops of blood fall into the alcohol in the bowl. Just enough to make a red ink.

Take your writing tool, and dip it into the blood mixture and take the parchment and draw the Daemon's sigil on the paper, and then write your request with the blood thinking about your goal.

When you are finished writing, take the parchment and fold it in half, then half again. Hold this between your palms, and visualize your end result and feeling how connected you are to the Daemons, your will and your own Life Force. Allow the focus and energy from your blood and the Daemons to enter into the parchment. See the end result.

When you can concentrate no more, set the parchment in front of the candle, and let the candle burn down almost completely. When the flame is about out, ignite the parchment and let it burn completely.

When it is done, take the ashes and the remaining wax, and mix it with the remaining incense in your burner, along with the rest of the blood ink that is left over. Take them all outside and either throw them into the wind, or bury the remains in the earth.

Return to your altar, and close the rite as normal. Walk away and forget about it. Let the magick work. Keep a journal and record your experiences, and the results.

Note: If you have noticed, I have not included an oleum or oil to use with this rite. This is because the blood that is anointing the candle as well as the parchment, is acting as the oleum.

Blood Magick & Recipes

Blood Magick can be a very rewarding practice. There are many applications of blood in magick; one is only limited by their own imaginations. Some of the uses for Blood Magick include, but are not limited to:

- Skrying
- incenses
- oleums
- divinations
- attuning oneself to the elements and nature as well as the Daemons
- cursing
- meditating
- offerings
- prayer and devotion

Here are a few recipes for your reference.

Virgin Blood Wine (for those who don't like or don't drink alcohol)

1 chalice
1 cup of apple juice
a few drops of blood from each participant

Let the blood fall into the chalice, and then everyone takes turns taking a drink.

Basic Blood Wine

1 chalice
1 cup of Red Wine (or wine of your choice)

a few drops of blood from each participant

Same as above.

Blood Ink #1

a small bowl
several drops of blood
a small cap full of rubbing alcohol

This is a really basic recipe, and very liquid.

Blood Ink #2

a small bowl
several drops of blood
a small amount of water
Gum Arabic

Mix the blood and water, add a small amount of gum arabic until the mixture is an inky consistency, easily able to write with.

Blood Ink #3

- a small bowl
- several drops of blood
- a small amount of oleum of the Daemon you are working with
- sigil of the Daemon you are working with

This ink is more for a specific purpose. Take your bowl, and add several drops of your own blood to it, and take your oleum that you have chosen or made and add a small amount of this to your bowl. Mix them together well, and then write on a small piece of parchment, the sigil of the

Daemon you will be invoking to aid you in your rite. When that is complete, burn the sigil, and take the ashes, and mix that into your ink. You now have a purpose ink!

Explore the possibilities and Happy Bloodletting! I hope you get as much enjoyment and fulfillment as I do when working with Blood Magick.

Candles & Magick
By S. Connolly

Candle magick is one of the simplest forms of magick. For non-Daemonolatry spell work, candle magick can be used alone. Within Daemonolatry magick, however, candle magick is used within a prepared, constructed ritual space wherein the Daemonic has been invoked. Candle magick can be combined with Heptameron circle construction just as well as basic elemental circle construction. You can use it in conjunction with modified ceremonial technique, or herbal magick or stone magick.

Focus candles can often be found on the Daemonolatry altar. See the chapter on Color Magick to choose appropriate colored candles for your operation.

So the steps to candle magick within Daemonolatry are as follows:

1. Use appropriate colored candles for the working – the focus candle being the most important.
2. Construct your ritual workspace and invoke the Daemonic.
3. Carve sigils, names, or keywords into your focus candle using a ritual blade.

4. Dress the candle with appropriate Daemonic Oleum or oil with similar properties.
5. Light the candle.
6. Let the candle burn to nothing.

You do not have to carve into or anoint your general ritual lighting candles. That isn't to say you can't, just that you don't have to. The main candle you'll focus on is the focus candle on the altar. Dressed candles can also be used as offerings to Daemons of fire or magick.

Dressing the Candle:

For those of you familiar with basic candle magick this is pretty straightforward. After you've carved your sigils, symbols, names, and/or keywords into your focus candle, you'll want to "dress" the candle. This means you anoint it with a charged oil/oleum congruent to the purpose of your ritual, the Daemons invoked, and the color of your candle etc....

Dressing the candle doesn't just consist of slathering on a coat of oil and calling it good. There is a method to the madness. Hold the candle horizontally in front of you. Place oil on your thumb and forefinger. From the CENTER of the candle, anoint the candle toward the wick in one direction, From the CENTER of the candle, anoint the candle toward the base in one direction. So basically – you're anointing from the center OUTWARD. This is thought to help balance the stability of the energy of the candle's color. Personally I find it helps to center and focus the mind on the task at hand. Be in the moment while doing this as you'll end up focusing your energy into the candle and adding to the energy of the color and the charged oil/oleum.

Application: Lighting the Candle and Letting It Burn:

Once you light the candle it is symbolic of taking action toward your will. Some believe that as the candle burns down, your will is transformed from thought to energy. If a candle burns fast, it is often believed the magick is strong and more likely to manifest completely. If the candle burns slowly, it is believed that you may have to use follow up magick to manifest your will completely. Many factors can determine whether candles burn quickly or slowly (including air circulation in your home).

Regardless, you may not be able to burn your candle in one shot. You may have to burn it over several nights before it burns down completely. While your initial ritual is done within the Daemonic charged ritual space, completion of the burn of a candle need not be. That means you can perform your ritual, finish it, extinguish the candle, and then come home the next night and continue burning the candle while you're doing other things. Yes, even ::gasp::, outside a constructed ritual space and without invocation if you feel so inclined.

However, I do recommend at least chanting the enn of a corresponding Daemon 3-6-9 times over the candle after lighting. Then walk away and let it burn. Once the candle has burnt down either put its remains with the burnt requests of offerings, sachets, or whatnot – or simply throw the wax crumbs out.

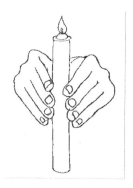

Making Candles:

Hobby stores everywhere sell candle molds, wax, dye specifically made for candles, wicks, and other candle making supplies. Candle making is fairly easy and specialty ritual candles can be made on top of your stove with some wax, dye, heat safe bags (to melt the wax in), powdered herbal ingredients, some essential oils or ritual oils (oleums), a pan of water, and an aluminum candle pouring pot. If you can't afford candle molds, you can make molds out of milk cartons, metal coffee cans (sprayed with a quick release spray specifically made for candle molds) or glass jars.

To start, choose your ingredients including plant matter, oils, color and size of candle beforehand. For those who need exact measurements: use about a tablespoon of dried ground (use a coffee grinder) herbal ingredients for every five ounces of wax and up to 6 drops of oil for every five ounces. You can experiment with this to get your desired result. Get your mold ready by putting the wick in place. Sometimes you'll have to tie your wick to a pencil or wooden dowel and suspend it over the mold to keep the wick centered and straight. Line your aluminum candle pouring pot with a heat safe bag. Put your wax inside. Put a cooking pot with about

4-6 cups of water on the stove -- heat to boiling. Once it's boiling, place your aluminum pouring pot into the cooking pot. This creates a makeshift double boiler. Melt the wax (you can buy thermometers for this). Add coloring, herbs, and any oils at this time. Mix thoroughly. Once it's mixed, pour. Then you let it set. Since wax will settle during a set, you will likely have to do a second pour. So don't put anything away. Once the candle is completely cooled (24 - 36 hours) and ready, remove it from the mold. You can carve sigils into the candles and paint the sigils with an acrylic paint.

A candle burning tip -- burn a candle one hour for every inch it is wide. This ensures an even burn.

Rolled Beeswax Candles:

You'll need:

- Some beeswax sheets (they usually come in about 8" x 16" sheets
- Some primed wick appropriate for a 1" candle
- A paring knife.
- A suitable cutting surface - I like those plastic cutting mats

First, place your beeswax sheet and put your wick along it. Cut the wick about 1 inch longer than the length of your sheet (i.e. the length of your candle). Some people leave some at the bottom, too. Just in case. Lay the wick on the edge of the sheet and start carefully rolling the wax over. This will encase your wick in the center of your candle. You work one end to the other, making sure your rolling is tight and even. Keep rolling, making sure you're rolling the wax straight. Roll until there is no more wax on your sheet (1 sheet = 1 candle) and press the edges firmly, but gently into the candle. Anoint with appropriate ritual oils and light. Beeswax candles aren't often suitable for etching sigils.

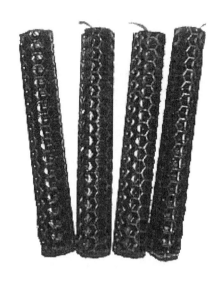

Color & Magick
by S. Connolly

Color has long been used to evoke certain moods and emotions. Along that vein, color plays a large role in magick by evoking a certain mood, atmosphere, or emotional response. This is helpful when you are focusing on your will. Each reminder of your goal or intent is helpful. The following are the traditional and magickal meanings and usage of colors.

WHITE:

White contains all colors. It is often used to promote spiritual enlightenment, to cleanse, purify, and consecrate. It is also used in rituals for healing, blocking, protection and truth seeking. White is the color of lunar energy and is associated with virginity or purity. You can use it to substitute any candle color.

Use the color white for any lunar magicks, divination, spiritual seeking ritual, protection, health, truth finding rite, or during meditation to bring about a sense of peace. White is the color of the element Air, direction East. It is associated with the Moon and Monday and is mutable. The number corresponding to white is 0, and the magickal tools associated with it are divination devices, wands, and burnt offering bowls.

In conjunction with white, you may choose to use scents and herbs associated with the color. For scents/oils, try sandalwood, lemon, myrrh, anise, cedar, lavender, or thyme. For herbs, use mugwort, sage, mint, rosemary, mustard, elder flowers, lilacs, gladiola, ferns, or heather. For woods, birch, elder, almond, ash, cedar, and juniper.

Complimentary stones include opals, moonstone, rose quartz, and amethyst. The associated tarot card is The Fool.

Complimentary Daemonic Forces: Iah (the Feminine All), Diana, Tezrian.

SILVER:

Silver is often used to remove negativity and encourage stability. It can be utilized to dispel negativity and is additionally used to help develop psychic abilities. This color can be used magically for purification, protection, to learn astrology, for divination, for ascension or to uncover your hidden potential.

Silver is associated with the element air, the direction east, the moon and Monday and is mutable. All divination tools are associated with Silver, as are wands.

To choose complimentary scents, woods, and herbs, see the same as White. For metal, silver (obviously). The associating tarot card is The Moon and the keyword for this color is clarity.

Daemonic forces associated with silver include (but are not limited to) Delepitorae, Thoth, Unsere, and Ashtaroth.

GRAY:

Gray is a neutral color and can be employed during meditation to overcome more difficult situations. Magically speaking, this color can dispel negativity through neutralization or cause opposing forces confusion. Gray can be used in water magick, moon magick, ascension or astral work, workings for patience or peace and it can be used for balancing.

Gray is often associated with the element Water whose direction is either North or West (depending on your tradition or preference). It, too, is associated with the moon and Monday. Number correspondences are 1 and 6. The Magickal tool association is the chalice.

For scents try jasmine, chamomile, lotus, vervain, sandalwood, ginseng, wormwood and basil. For herbs consider cumin, cloves, rosemary, birch and feverfew. Perhaps even blackthorn. Its corresponding wood is oak.

For stones, associate onyx, malachite, crystals and moonstones. Tarot correspondences include the Hanged Man and the threes of all suits.

Daemonic correspondences include Leviathan, Marbas, Orias, and Sonnillion.

PINK:

The color pink is often considered the color of romance, love, and friendship. It's magickal purposes range from use in rituals to draw affection and for feminine mystique. It's the color of honor and service. Use pink in magicks for creative pursuits, marriage, attraction, friendship, beauty, compassion, and relationships. Some people may be tempted to use red, but reconsider as pink is the kinder, gentler color.

Clearly it is associated with the element fire and the southern direction. It is often associated with the heart chakra, the planet Venus, the day Friday, and the numbers 0 and 1.

The magical tools associated with this color include wands, thuribles, and offering bowls. For scents, consider rose, apricot, strawberry, lavender, ginger, sandalwood and jasmine. For herbs consider violets, feverfew, pennyroyal, coriander, basil, yarrow, ginseng, and allspice. Woods, sycamore, olive and orange. For stones, use rose quartz, pink garnets, emerald, peridot, or any pink stones. The cards in the tarot associated with pink are the sevens of all suits.

Daemonic Correspondences include Rosier, Ashtaroth, Astarte, Amun Ra, Hathor, Isis, Venus, or Asafoetida.

RED

Use red in sex magick or for energy work, physical strength, victory, or passion. Red is also an aggressive color and can be used effectively in cursing because it is the color of anger, war, aggression, and strength. Some people say you should use red with caution because it is considered a high-energy color. Red can also be used in transformation rituals. Combined with black, you can temper the erratic effects of this color.

Red is clearly associated with the element fire and south. It rules the root chakra and corresponds to the planet mars, Tuesday, and the number 5. The magickal tools associated with this color are candles, thuribles, offering bowls, and swords.

For scents consider dragon's blood, musk, mullein, and cinnamon. For herbs use onion, rose, garlic, hops, peppers, chives, wormwood, tobacco and yew. Woods, use cherry or redwood. Stone correspondences are tigers eye, agate, diamond, ruby, garnet, quartz crystal, and bloodstone. The tarot cards associated with red includes The Magician, the entire suit of cups and fives of all suits.

Daemonic Forces associated with red include Flereous, Amducius, Mars, Thor, Atem, Satan, Kali, Tezrian, Sonnillion, Lilith, or Satanchia.

PURPLE

Purple is the color of power and success. It is also the color of magick and energy and the astral plane. This color can promote manifestations, psychic or otherwise. This is a wonderful color to use for meditation, ascension, astral travel, and divination of all sorts. Keep something purple on your altar at all times to give all your work an extra spark of energy. When seeking Daemonic guides or mentors, purple will promote this. Use purple during workings of ascension, channeling, spirit communications, divination, justice, protection, breaking bad luck, cleansings, removing negativity or curses. You can use purple in place of white.

Believe it or not, purple is often associated with air and the east, however because of it's energy and strong intuitive elements, it is also fire and water. It is associated with the brow chakra, Jupiter, Thursday, and the number 7. Magical tools corresponding to purple are the wand, thurible, and offering bowl (note that in Daemonolatry the offering bowl is often for burnt offerings).

For scents consider sandalwood, jasmine, nutmeg, bay, cedar, and cinnamon. Perhaps even ginger or lotus. For herbs, my favorite - wisteria, mugwort, violets, dandelions, oak, clover, rue, and eyebright. Woods might include lilac and willow. Stone correspondences include all opals, amethyst, sapphires, and beryl. Sometimes clear quartz crystals. Tarot cards associated with purple include Justice and all the fours of all suits.

Daemonic influences could include Mithras, Horus, Delepitorae, Thoth, Kali, Maat, and Hecate.

BROWN

Brown is not one of those colors one generally thinks of with regards to magick. However, brown is a wonderful color for material gain, justice, retribution, clarity, and concentration. Use during rituals to find lost things, and to learn new skills (as brown increases concentration). Anything requiring concentration and a steady mind.

Usually you would reserve brown for workings involving creative pursuits, business, legal issues, or your career. Some people will view brown as fire or air and corresponding directions of east and south. However, I personally prefer to think of brown as very earthy and thus north or west. Brown is associated with the spleen chakra, the number 2, Mercury/Mars (and consequently magick), and the days Tuesday for the physical, Wednesday for the mental, and Sunday for both. The eights in the tarot deck are associated with Brown.

The ritual tools associated with this color are wands and censers. For scents, try jasmine, dill or honeysuckle. For herbs, vervain, valerian, rue, gardenia, flax, buckwheat and ferns. Wood - Lemon, Lime or Orange. Stones might include quartz, carnelian, or moss agate.

Daemonic Correspondences to the color brown can include Satan, Atem, Ronove, Bast, Kali, Lilith, Unserc, Belial, or Belphagore.

BLUE

Blue is considered one of the big spiritual colors and the color for healing, wisdom, inner peace, guidance and truth. Some people believe the shade of blue is of just as much importance. Use royal blues to attract Jupiter energy, promote loyalty, or exert influence. Use light blue for healing and all spiritual pursuits. Use dark blue for healing, creative pursuits, communication, and meditation work.

Light Blue: Healing, Spiritual color; helpful in devotional or inspirational meditations; brings peace and tranquility to the home; radiates Aquarius energy; employ where a situation must be synthesized. Use blue in water magick, balancing, healing, dream work, meditations, inspiration magick, friendship magick, and even magick for peace and harmony.

Blue is often associated with water and North or West. It rules the fifth chakra, the throat. It is ruled by Neptune and Mercury, Saturn, Jupiter, and the Moon. Consequently, it also has many days associated with it including Monday, Wednesday, Thursday, and Saturday. It correlates to the number 3, all the cup cards and The Hierophant. Wands and chalices are ruled by blue.

For scents consider basil, lotus, cedar, camphor, jasmine and clary sage. For herbs try aloe, carnations, daffodils, and calamus. I also like baby's breath. For wood, consider cedar. Stone affiliates include opals, coral, hematite, sapphire, agate, turquoise, coral, and sodalite.

Daemonic forces associated with blue include Leviathan and Buer among others.

GREEN

Green has long been used to promote financial success, good luck, fertility, and rejuvenation. Like blue, different shades of green can be used for various things. Dark greens, for example, can counteract jealousy, greed, or ambitions that seek to cause you harm. Use green in rituals for money, luck, fertility, and earth magick.

Green's element is earth, it's direction north or west, its planets Venus, Jupiter, and mars, and its days Fridays, Wednesdays, and Thursdays respectively. This color rules the heart chakra (fourth), the number four, wands and bowls, sevens in the tarot deck and The Emperor card.

Consider scents of mint, musk, vervain, cinnamon, mugwort, patchouli, sage, vanilla and pine. For herbs you can use thyme, verbena, basil, cloves, mugwort, coltsfoot, pennyroyal or sage. For woods, try oak, pine, elder, and birch. Stone correspondences include green tourmaline, emeralds, peridot, jade, malachite, and coral. The metals gold and silver also apply.

Daemonic rulerships could include Belial, Ba'al, Belphagore and Unsere. Think Earth Daemons clearly.

YELLOW/GOLD

Yellow is one of those off colors that many people don't think of when they think about magick. However, yellow is the color of knowledge, can enhance communications, to help with clairvoyance, and has been used for centuries to repel negativity. It is considered a very mental color. Therefore when working with yellow in magick - use it in workings for creativity, learning, astral projection or clairvoyance, knowledge, understanding, and concentration.

When the yellow is more of a gold, use it in rituals that promote understanding or workings to enhance energy, power, vitality, and to bring success and luck or in rituals needing solar energy.

Yellow is of the element air and the direction east. It rules the solar plexus chakra. It is associated with the Sun and Sunday for the mental, Wednesday for the physical. The numbers 3 and 2 are associated with yellow/Gold as are wands and swords and the tarot cards The Sun, knights, and all sixes.

Scents include lemon, cloves, vanilla, musk, laurel, lavender, and frankincense. For herbs, consider rosemary, sunflowers, daisy, ash,
saffron, and chamomile. For woods, oak. Metal - gold.
Stones, use citrine, tigers eye, quartz, amber, carnelian,
topaz or chrysolite.

Daemonic Correspondences may include Ronove, Anu, Bast, Amun Ra, Lucifer, or Lucifuge Rofocale.

BLACK

Black is the absence of color. It is used to dispel or absorb negativity and to induce deep meditative states. Black is often used in curses meant to remove excess negativity from the magician when the magician has no real intention of targeting a person or situation with their negativity. Others will use Black as a cursing agent for bindings. Black is said to attract Saturn energy. It can also be the color of wisdom, enlightenment, and can help to absorb illnesses and mental conflict as well. For cursing, use with red for more impact! Or to absorb any misdirected energies. Black is often used in necromancy and for magick to keep or reveal secrets or that which is hidden.

Black is a fifth element, contains all the elements. It is often associated with east, Saturn, Saturday and the number 6. Swords and wands are ruled by black and The Death card, all the queens and all the kings are ruled by Black.

For scents, try basil, myrrh, vervain, peppermint, yarrow and yew. For herbs and woods look into oak, flax, cedar, cloves, rue, mullein, mandrake, cayenne and dragon's blood. For stones, onyx, moonstone, pyrite, agate, black quartz, jet, and obsidian.

Daemonic influences that are conjunct with black include Thoth, Hecate, Lilith, Lucifer, Satan, Eurynomous/Euronymous, Baalberith, Babael, Bael, Set, and Anubis

Nine Divinity Color Correspondences:

- **Belial**- Brown, black or green.
- **Lucifer**- Yellow/white.
- **Leviathan**- Blue, grey or white.
- **Flereous**- Red/orange.
- **Satan**-Any.
- **Amducious**- Orange.
- **Verrine**- Blue.
- **Unsere**- Green/white.
- **Eurynomous**- Black/white/gray.

Goetic Color Correspondences (see Appendices):

- **Kings** – Yellow
- **Marquises** – Violet
- **Presidents** – Orange
- **Dukes** – Green
- **Princes & Prelates** – Blue
- **Earls and Counts** – Red
- **Knights**- Black

Divination & Magick

Divination is how one foretells the future or discovers answers to the hidden or mysterious by means of communicating with a spirit or entity or the higher self. There are many methods for divination.

The most common methods among Daemonic Magicians are:

- Ouija Boards (also Spirit Boards)
- Pendulums
- Skrying Mirrors/Crystals/Bowls
- Reading Daemonic Sigils
- Tarot Cards
- Channeling
- Ascension

Admittedly most forms of divination require the person performing the divination to be a medium of some sort. There are four main types of mediumship ability and most mediums will have one to four of these abilities depending on sensitivity.

The first is Clairsentience, *to know*. That is – a medium who just knows things. This ability can actually be broken down into two because some Clairsentient mediums can foretell the future and others cannot. So the first type of medium is the Clairsentient who simply knows things and can translate what they 'know' into words. Intuition is a Clairsentient ability and is actually quite common, it's learning to listen to that inner voice that most people struggle with. The second type of Clairsentient is one that knows what is going to happen (in the future). The third type of medium is the Clairvoyant, *to see*. Clairvoyants pick up things from objects, places, others, and situations as images. So clairvoyance means the medium's mind gives them images that the medium must translate into coherent thoughts. This can be easier said than done. It can take some practice depending on the level of natural ability. The last type of medium is someone who experiences clairaudience, *to hear*. That is – they "hear" whatever it is they're picking up. Not in a psychotic, schizophrenic hearing voices kind of way, but rather they 'hear' whatever they're picking up in their mind. So his or her internal voice may say something like, "Someone died here." Where as a Clairsentient would just know, in their gut, that someone had died, and someone with Clairvoyance might actually get a vision of the deceased. Some mediums might get all three.

Divination can actually be used in magick to, for example, communicate with the Daemonic to learn how to perform certain magicks. Or, to discover if magick has or will manifest. Divination can also be the part of the magickal process of invoking the Daemonic entity. Or, magick can be used to make a divination session more productive (see ritual section toward the end of the book for several divinatory rituals).

Now onto the various methods of divination useful for the magician to, in the very least, know about. If you have tried many of these methods and failed with them or if you are not sure of your mediumship ability, choose the pendulum to work with. Most people have, in the very least, some mild abilities, usually in the form of Clairsentience (intuition).

Ouija/Spirit Boards
S. Connolly

With Ouija/Spirit Boards there is a very specific method of preparation that must be followed if you are going to get Daemonic entities ONLY to come through the board. Otherwise you open the board to anything that wishes to communicate with you and that can turn out really bad. I realize that most people reading this will be surprised to learn that even Daemon Worshipers have a deep respect for the proper use of the ouija/spirit board and that we'd warn the practitioner at all about them. I assure you this warning comes from personal experience. Boards (made by Parker Brothers or not) are NOT TOYS. As a matter of fact, I wish they'd quit selling the damn things at Toys R Us. All it takes is one board and a real medium – and the boards can become very dangerous. Sure – thousands of people use the boards with no ill effects at all. The key component is a medium. Once you put a medium on the board – every "thing" from the other side is going to see that portal open and whoever or whatever gets there first can attach itself to the board. Sometimes that "whatever" is very bad.

Let me share a story just to drive this point home. When I was a teenager I got my first ouija board and contacted my first otherworld entity who called itself Samuel. Samuel started out being very helpful but soon showed his true colors when a friend, we'll call her R, decided to talk back to the board. "Samuel, you're an idiot," she said. Next thing we knew, a set of invisible hands (that were clearly leaving marks even though nothing was there) were choking R and lifting her off of the ground. She began to turn blue. I yelled at the thing to stop and flipped the board upside down. R was released.

I put the board away and didn't touch it for several months. The next time we pulled it out I took it to my friend S's. When we pulled it out, same thing. We got Samuel. This time, he lied to us and was clearly being a problem. I left the board with S. Several days later she called me to tell me something was in her basement (it was a finished basement so it's not like it was a scary to begin with). It was turning on and off lights late at night and opening and closing doors. It would also travel through the basement causing cold spots and call out her name when she was the only one home.

Whatever Samuel was he had attached himself to the board and was using it as a portal (that I myself had inadvertently opened, being the medium I am) to gain entry into this world, manifesting a full out haunting.

After much research through books (we didn't have Internet back then) we discovered the best way to remove an unwanted "thing" attached to a Ouija board was to burn the board and planchette, collect the ashes, separate the ashes into two or three separate containers, and distribute those ashes into separate bodies of running water. So in one night, we did this, walking miles to the next river and then another mile to a creek (the only running water around).

This effectively removed Samuel from my friend's house and things went back to normal. No more cold spots, no more doors opening and shutting, no more disembodied voices, and no more lights turning on and off.

This is why it is of the utmost importance that for Daemonic Divination work you use a new board that has never been used and **prepare it first**.

Board Preparation

This method of prepping a board will exclude everything but Daemons. You might just want to keep two separate boards.

(Doesn't matter if your board is Parker Brothers or not) You have to prep the planchette.

- Delepitore or Azlyn Oleum OR sage oil
- 1 candle, color of your choice.
- 1 small stone your choice (think - fits on head of pin)

Generally this is done inside an elemental circle by witness of Satan (or your All), Delepitore (or equivalent), and/or Azlyn (or equivalent).

First you anoint the board and the planchette with the oil. Then, you drip candle wax on the planchette to cover it (NOT the indicator window). The sigil of a Daemon of your choice is carved into the wax or drawn on the planchette with oleum. The planchette is anointed again. The stone is affixed, with a tiny dab of glue, at the center of the indicator window (this is why it must be small). You can burn temple incense if you want.

If you do it right - nothing but Daemons will come through the board.

Mind you this will not necessarily make a board work for you. You either have mediumship ability with a board or you don't. This just ensures that nothing but Daemons come through a particular board.

Using The Board

One of the primary ingredients necessary to use a board correctly is you need someone who is a medium. That means – someone who is sensitive to otherworldly entities and with whom the entities can effectively communicate. Some people – by their mere presence – stilt the flow of energies making communication impossible. The medium(s) and the medium(s) ONLY should place up to three fingers on the planchette. Yes, this means that ONE person can work a board by his/her-self. If the medium senses that anyone in the room is blocking him/her, she should ask that person to leave. A block feels like someone holding you back when you're trying to walk forward. You know that feeling? If you feel that – stop, find the block and remove it.

Ask for the Daemonic entity you would like to speak with and the planchette should start moving. I get figure eights, others get circles. Then you begin asking questions. Keep a pad of paper and pen ready (someone else to record the session is ideal). When you have made contact you will feel a feathery, electricity sensation through the top of your hands and through your fingers and you'll also feel a strange energy "pressure" even though your fingers are still resting lightly on the planchette. You may feel that electricity feeling up through your wrists (it almost tickles). It's not an unpleasant sensation, just strange at first.

The Daemonic force or entity responds to each question by moving the planchette from letter to letter to spell out words. More sensitive mediums may also find they get images and/ or actually "hear" in their mind's eye the words before they're finished being spelt out. And when they think the words, the planchette will jump to yes. If you are this type of medium your sessions will be much more productive. Expect that your medium (or you if you're the medium) will be tired after long durations of board work.

Pendulums (Dowsing)
by Mike Delaney & S. Connolly

Using a pendulum is often called "Dowsing". Pendulums really don't require preparation for use. You can anoint them with a Daemonic oleum and if you want to make sure you are communicating with a Daemonic entity, use the pendulum in a constructed elemental space. That usually will keep unwanted visitors out. Pendulums can also be used, like all divination devices, to communicate with your subconscious, higher self.

Hold your pendulum like this:

Alternatively, you can slip the bead/ball usually at the end of the pendulum between your forefinger and middle finger, letting the pendulum hang freely and holding your hand horizontally level. I suggest keeping your elbow on a flat surface to help keep your hand steady at first until you get the hang of a steady hand.

To use the device, ask questions and whichever way the pendulum swings, that's your answer. For some people a counterclockwise swing means no, and a clockwise swing means yes. For others, a pendulum that swings left to right is yes and to and fro means no whereas a circular swing means nothing. You can either decide which works best for you, or ask the Daemonic energies (or what or whomever you are communicating with) to show you yes or no (repeat for clarity).

For whatever reason, pendulums are just more accessible to more people, mediums or not. This method of divination can be easily learned. The only difficulty is that for the most part, you can only ask yes or no questions. Some people will dowse using a pendulum over an ouija/spirit board so the pendulum can swing over letters to spell out words. Others will simply write answers or charts on a piece of paper and the pendulum will swing to the answer. This really depends on what you're doing.

Skrying Mirrors/Crystals and Bowls
by S. Connolly

Skrying is a form of divination in which you peer into a reflective surface and visually see images. This method of divination will work best for people who have some clairvoyant abilities. The three most common forms of Skrying are Mirror Skrying, Crystal Skrying, and Bowl Skrying.

To prepare your Skrying equipment you can anoint the devices directly with oleums of Daemons for divination or you can add appropriate sigils to the devices themselves. For Skrying mirrors, you can put the sigils on the frame. For crystals, you should probably leave them intact and untouched. For Bowls, you can paint sigils directly onto the outside of the bowls. As with most divination sessions you probably ought to consider working within a balanced, Daemonically charged circle for both balance and to keep unwanted influences (entities or energies) out of the way while you work.

Creating the Mirror:

You can buy a Skrying mirror. They're basically mirrors with a black backing. Or, if you have some time and ambition, you can create your own mirror.

The first step is to buy a picture frame with glass intact (or a piece of glass that will fit into a frame). Do not buy plastic! Make sure it's real glass and the thicker the glass, the better because it gives more depth. Choose a frame that has some aesthetic appeal for you (i.e. something you really like). You can get frames at dollar stores and thrift stores inexpensively.

Remove the glass from the frame and clean it completely (same process for a mirror). With some glossy black oil based enamel paint, paint one side of the glass (or the back silver side of the mirror). You will need to apply as many coats as necessary to make sure no light passes through. Allow the paint to dry completely between coats.

Paint any sigils or symbols you wish on your frame. Finally, put the glass (or mirror) back into the frame, the paint side of the glass on the inside. Make sure you have some cardboard or felt board against the painted side to keep the glass from getting scuffed. Use a collector plate stand to prop your Skrying mirror up (or if you're using a frame that came with a stand, that can work too) and you're done. You can get collector plate stands at hobby and craft stores and usually large discount stores like Wal-Mart or Target.

Finally – you can use a regular mirror. However, many people won't get results with a regular mirror unless they're very sensitive. You can try it and if it works for you, great. But if it doesn't work, try a black mirror.

Crystals:

There are numerous crystals you can use for gazing. Some are cut in the shape of pyramids or other geometrics. The most popular are crystal gazing balls. Glass can be used in place of crystal, but some believe that crystal itself allegedly lends better to gazing/Skrying. Regardless, the ball should be kept clean and free of fingerprints and dust.

Skrying Bowls:

Your average Skrying bowl is dark in color (either black or some other dark color) and you put water, ink, oil or blood into the bowl for Skrying to create the reflective surface. Skrying fluids used in the bowl should be of even color. So mix liquids beforehand, for example if you're diluting blood in water, or ink in water, or using blood or ink in oil. Some liquids separate. In some methods of Skrying this is desirable. In others, it's not. Depending on whether you're reading the shapes in the water (as with tea leaf reading) then you might use oil in a water-based fluid, or vice versa. If you're not doing that kind of "reading" or Skrying – a fluid, solid color with no separation is best. Inks, blood, and waters often work well together. Oil is one of those substances you should use alone for standard Skrying.

How to Skry

Within a prepared ritual space, flank your Skrying device with candles, then gaze into your Skrying device and clear your mind. Completely let go and allow the images to come. Usually the reflective surface will fade to black (or seem hazy or smoky) and then the images will come forth. Sometimes they're clear, sometimes not. Try your best not to give a voice to the images, let them come and go. Just remember them. When you pause, write down what you've seen or say aloud what you see (having a recorder there, human or electronic is handy), giving your mind time to process the images. If we try too soon to process and define the images, we can end up stilting the flow of the images and holding ourselves back from stronger images. For some people, skrying is not easy because the images are far too disturbing or unsettling for them to handle. Others won't get images at all because they have no gifts for clairvoyance. Some people with clairsentience or clairaudience claim they can hear or know from a skrying device and the mirror simply helps them hear or know better. Some people will actually use a mirror to channel. The only way to know if Skrying works for you is to try it. If it doesn't, there are plenty of other divination devices and methods to try and learn. If the images are weak – you can continue to practice and hone your skill as eventually they'll become stronger.

Reading Daemonic Sigils
by Brid Delaney & S. Connolly

Contrary to popular belief, the idea of Reading Daemonic Sigils drawn on cards, carved into or painted onto stones or clay is not anything new. Reading Daemonic Sigils is a fairly old practice. Probably as old as the practice of working with Rune Stones and Tarot Cards. The concept is pretty much the same.

Each card, stone or clay stone has painted or engraved on it a sigil of a Daemonic name. Traditionally, a person makes his or her own cards, clay tablets or stones using sigils of Daemons (s)he is familiar with. These are kept in a bag or jar and when a situation arises that the person needs guidance on, one of the cards, stones or clay pieces is pulled. Brid's mother-in-law used to do this.

Whichever Daemonic sigil you pull is the answer to the inquiry (or the wisdom you seek in the situation). So, for example, if you are angry with a co-worker and you need to know which action to take and you pull Unsere, this would mean you should try to be understanding and work through your differences with the co-worker because things could get better. If you pull Amducius, a confrontation might be prudent or imminent. If you pull Belphagore, it could mean it's time to update your resume` and you should seek employment elsewhere.

You can also use standard Tarot Card layouts in much the same way by pulling a sigil for each position and then reading the sigil (by understanding what each Daemon represents) based on the position in which it falls. See the Tarot Card section to learn more about positioning and performing readings in a prescribed sequence.

Tarot Cards
by S. Connolly

Tarot Cards are one of the most common forms of divination. Now while you're usually not contacting the Daemonic through the cards (or you could be), you can still use cards within a balanced ritual space in order to connect with your own internal Daemonic wisdom or insight. Usually – reading cards is about connecting with your higher self and your intuition in order to find the answers. By reading the cards the intuitive can get a sense of what has happened, what the present situation is, and what will happen if the current path is followed. This means that the outcome presented by the cards is not fixed.

To read the cards, the person doing the reading may have the person the reading is for shuffle the cards then cut the cards three times toward him/herself (if the question is about them personally) or cut them three times away from themselves if the question is about another person. If the person the reading is for is not present, the reader can concentrate on that person and perform the reading that way. Very sensitive readers can give very functional and accurate readings from long distances. To begin the reading, the reader will lay the cards out and read the cards starting from the past, moving to the present, and finally to the final outcome.

Some readers will read the inverse meaning of cards, others will not. From my experience the *good* readers will not merely memorize the little booklet that came with their set of tarot cards and give everyone a stock reading of what the cards allegedly mean. Instead, true empaths, intuitives, and mediums will have studied the cards a great deal, will read from the symbolism of the card and what the cards mean to them and will use the cards as a tool to sort out their empathic or intuitive feelings about a situation.

A very common tarot layout is called the Celtic Cross.

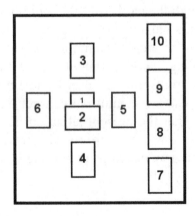

1. Present Position
2. What crosses your present position.
3. What is influencing the present position (what's in the asker's head).
4. Distant past foundation.
5. What lies ahead.
6. Recent past foundation.
7. The path to the final outcome.
8. The path to the final outcome. Influences.
9. The path to the final outcome. More Influences.
10. The final outcome.

Additional cards can be laid out on each of these areas to gain more insight into a specific influence or situation.

Or, a more simple layout is the past, present, future layout where only three cards are pulled. There are numerous methods by which to read. Even Daemonic Sigils (and even Rune Stones) can be pulled out and read using much the same layouts.

To learn to read the cards you will need to practice for many years before you get good at it. Each card is part of a sentence. If you pull more than one card for each position (I do) you will read each card in context with the one next to it. For different people and different readings – the same card could mean something different depending on where it is in the sentence. The Chariot and the Sun next to the Ace of Coins might suggest a financial windfall prosperous to the person the reading is for. The Chariot and The Sun next to the Ace of Cups could mean a wedding or the beginnings of a beautiful friendship. The Devil next to The Tower next to the Three of Coins could mean financial troubles that are enough to cause a change in how someone lives his/her life. The Devil next to the Three of Coins next to the Knight of Swords could mean financial problems due to a friend or sibling who is irresponsible. So while the basic meanings may be ever-present, none of your "sentences" will be the same.

It's okay to start learning to read by using the books that give you a general idea of what each card means. The person serious about learning to read cards, however, must eventually graduate past the pull the card, regurgitate memorized information, repeat - stage. This involves taking time to meditate on each card and write down everything that card means to you. A valuable exercise is to get one of those color-your-own tarot decks and basically to meditate on each card and color your own, adding your own symbolism.

Once you've attached a meaning to a card they will become easier to read. Cards can also be a valuable meditation device to use during ritual and magickal workings as representations of what you want to accomplish with the working. Anyone who cannot graduate past the "use the book" or who thinks they have to memorize the cards in order to read them is one who likely doesn't have a gift for accessing the internal intuition required to read cards. If you find you cannot, after years of practice, read the cards without use of a book, or if you have had to memorize the book and cannot go beyond it, consider this may not be a good divination device for you.

Channeling
by S. Connolly

Channeling is basically a process wherein you allow a Daemonic presence to take over your body so that it can perform physical action, or more often, can use your mouth to speak directly to others in the room.

Oftentimes, I don't recommend channeling unless you are working with several people. Not so much because it's dangerous (if you do it within a prepared and balanced ritual space!) or anything like that, but rather there's not often as much use for channeling unless you're with other people. Sometimes, the person channeling can get lost in the feeling of having their mind disconnected from their body, and won't remember what was said. Other times, the person channeling could panic (if it's their first time) and it's useful to have someone else there to help bring them back from the experience.

In this section I'll explain some merging techniques and controlled channeling techniques that will help you channel. If during the exercises you do go into channeling, don't panic. The Daemon will recognize when you're ready to return and will leave your body. I've only heard of two people who have actually passed out from the experience. This is why you'll want to perform this operation on the ground (with a blanket nearby just in case) or where you won't have any danger of falling and hurting yourself (i.e. like sitting in a chair).

If you are a part of a group or have an open-minded friend, you can do your experiments with these people. The method is that once you invoke and merge with the Daemon, the group asks questions and the Daemon answers.

Why Channel?

Channeling can be useful during group divination. I have a friend who used to do weekly group channeling lessons wherein the Daemon they were working with, Belial, put the group through guided meditations and offered practical advice on self work. Unfortunately I was unable to attend their meetings so did not witness this first hand. But from those in the group I talked to, they were getting a lot from it.

I've personally used channeling (with a Daemonic entity) in paranormal investigations as a way to identify what is happening in a house or location.

How does one channel?

There are three basic steps to channeling. Invocation, merging, and allowing the Daemon to take over the body. The last part is the hardest for most people because it's instinctive for us to want to maintain control of our bodies. For others, this is going to come quite naturally.

A Note of Warning: When I say channeling is not dangerous, I mean, it's not dangerous for mentally stable individuals who are working within a well prepared and balanced ritual space. This means you have invoked Daemonic entities into the space so that nothing else can get to you or disturb the work or slip into your body while you're open to it. Not all spirits or entities are Daemonic and not all are friendly. I suggest working with the Daemons Ashtaroth and Azlyn during divination using a pentagram ritual configuration at which each point an elemental is invoked (don't forget your fifth element) using the appropriate Enns. Ashtaroth and Azlyn would be invoked from the center.

A Channeling Meditation:

Meditate on the Daemon of your choice. Use an Enn to invoke the Daemon if you wish. Allow their energy to surround you. Surrender to it. Merge with it. Remember your breath. Relax. Allow all emotions, feelings, and thoughts to flow freely. Their thoughts become your thoughts and vice versa. You are intertwined with this Daemon.

[Note - the point of this exercise is not to BECOME the Daemon. That is impossible. However, you can merge with a Daemon by intertwining energies empathically.]

To Channel, you simply let go and allow the Daemon to take over when you feel that you and the Daemon's energies are merged sufficiently.

What to Expect:

Many people describe the feeling of hearing someone talking with their voice, but it not being them. They often report feeling disconnected from their own mind and body and surrounded in blackness. I have had this same experience. The second you feel panicked or like you want to return into your mind to regain control, the Daemon will usually step aside and allow you back in. I say usually because I have heard of rare instances where a Daemon stayed for several hours past its welcome because it had a very important message to impart. I've never heard of an instance of this continuing for more than several hours though.

More importantly you should know the people involved could get really freaked out by a Daemon or spirit being channeled. It's important you discuss with the participants what they should expect so that no one is caught off guard or panics during a session. The others present should expect the medium's voice and personality to completely change. (S)he might use words or phrases (s)he would never use, her face may contort and take on a different appearance, her voice may sound gruff or even plural, and in some instances those present may experience paranormal phenomena during the session including actually seeing physically manifested entities separate or merge with the host medium, stray lights and shadows, sounds, and even objects moving. I have experienced all of these phenomena at least once during a channeling session, so expect it just in case.

To leave the state of Channeling at will, simply tell the Daemon (obviously in your mind) that you would like to return to your body now. You should find yourself back in your body and in full control of your faculties. You may also feel like you're waking up from a nap. Channeling can be a very strong and unbalancing experience. If you find yourself imbalanced by channeling (as being connected to a Daemon like that is like being plugged into a power plant), be sure to balance yourself before and after each session.

Ascension
by S. Connolly

Ascension is a method by which we can commune with the Daemonic Divine on an alternate plane of consciousness. Think of it as connecting with the universal consciousness. It's the best of both Insight Meditation and Channeling, but it all happens in the ascended meditative state. Most people receive images during ascension, making it a very effective meditative state for learning more about the Daemons and their plane of existence.

Many Daemonolaters use ascension for divination, to learn how to perform certain rites, to see physical manifestations of the Daemons, and to learn more about the nature of the Daemonic. Ascension is also an effective tool for self work, meaning the Daemons will often impart wisdom through the practitioner's ascended states.

To begin, most people will use what I call a "Ready Ascension Formula", meaning a ritual to ascend to that particular plane of consciousness wherein we meet the Daemonic Divine head on. As you gain more experience and confidence, you'll discover you have developed your own method to ascend to this particular state. The following exercises will teach beginning ascension practitioners helpful methods to learn to ascend, and will help seasoned practitioners hone their skills and analyze their own methods of ascension.

Ready Ascension Formulas:

Many Daemonolaters believe that ascension is best achieved when we face our fears because it brings our awareness into ourselves and makes us more sensitive to the ascended state. That's often why those who don't practice "fear facing" will report their ascension attempts always result in cloudy, faded, or dark images that won't clear up.

PLEASE NOTE: *You can substitute Tiger Balm (you can buy this from any drug store in the section where they sell sports creams) for anointing oil and replace incense recipes with an incense of your choice. You also don't necessarily need incenses or oils. Those with allergies may choose not to use incense at all. The primary purpose in these formulas is to stimulate the senses to invoke atmosphere and a heightened state of awareness. Their secondary purpose is to invoke the proper conditions for effective ascension. But you can reach an ascended state without them.*

To Ascend to the Daemonic Plane
Richard Dukanté

1 part rose
2 parts chamomile
1 part camphor

Mix into oil and anoint temples. Place a parchment on which are drawn 12 Daemonic sigils of your discretion. Place this beneath your mattress or beneath your sleeping place. Light a white candle. Place an image of yourself outside yourself and project your consciousness into it. Go through black caverns and face your fears one by one. Only then shall you emerge onto the plane. If you do not, your fears have not been faced.

Invocation To Speak With a Daemon
(from Dukanté grimoire)

The Daemon Conjuration Of Richard Dukanté (circa 1963 - the Grimoire of Richard Dukante Book 1 Page 50) Being a working wherein the Daemon of the practitioner's choice may be called upon willfully.

Upon the altar must stand three tapers. One of Black, One of White, One of the castor's element. Within the Castor's taper the Daemon's name must be inscribed upon it along with the name of Satan. [meaning actual - SATAN]

Present also must be the dagger and chalice of water taken from a flowing river or from the falling rain.

The invocation incense shall be burned within the thurible during the entire rite: 2 Parts Sandalwood, 5 Parts Graveyard Dust [mullein], and 3 Parts Devil's Claw.

You Shall begin by lighting the tapers upon the altar after having writ the aforementioned inscriptions on the center taper. Set the incense alight within the thurible. Cast the circle by invoking each element in the language of Daemons -

- Earth - Belial - Lirach Tasa Vefa Wehlic Belial
- Air - Lucifer - Renich Tasa Uberaca Biasa Icar Lucifer
- Fire - Flereous - Ganic Tasa Fubin Flereous
- Water - Leviathan- Jedan Tasa Hoet Naca Leviathan

Begin the Invocation: I, [your name], do invite thee, [Daemon's name]. In the name of Satan [or insert the name of your highest deity], I request you come forth.

Hence you shall draw your own blood from your palm and let three drops fall into the chalice. Mingle it with the water and invite all present to drink from it. Do not drink from your own blood lest you invite the Daemon into you.

You shall draw a circle upon the ground the width of the taper at least. Within this circle, inscribe the sigil of the Daemon you doth conjure. If this sigil is unavailable, use an inverse pentagram or DZ. You shall pour the remainder of the chalice contents within the circle - for it is your energy the Daemon will use to rise. " 'Tis this energy that is blood."

Over the circle you must say:

Reayha bacana lyan remé quim [name of Daemon].

Place the castor's candle within the circle. From this circle - the Daemon shall emerge from the flame and you may speak with him freely until the candle is extinguished.

Finding Your Personal Key

A "key" is basically your own method of entering the Daemonic plane. For some, it's an actual key used to unlock a specific door to the Daemonic plane. For others, the key is a sigil, place, or thing they visualize that will help them get onto the Daemonic Plane. For me, the sigil of Delepitore, merely thinking of it, will often pull me directly into an ascended state. I've trained my mind to do this through repeating the visualization each time I practice a session of ascension. This alleviates the long process of ascending (through visualizing halls and doors in your astral temple).

Perform the following meditation to find your key. If you find the right key, the image will naturally be the first thing you want to see whenever you enter the temple to perform ascension. Sometimes it will take a few tries before you find the key that works best. You'll know if the key isn't quite right if you find your mind shoving it aside in favor of something better.

Ascending to the Daemonic Plane

The final step in learning ascension is to learn to carry a question or desired outcome into the ascended state with you. This way, you can come out of the ascended state with answers and direction. So, for example, if you enter an ascended state with the desire to learn a personalized incense recipe to work with Asmodeus, you can come out of the ascension with that recipe. You can also discover sigils, Enns, and other important information. Or answers to problems or self-work you are currently performing.

So your first step for this ascension session is to choose something important to you. Something you wish to discover about a Daemon, a rite, or yourself.

Use your key to ascend to the Daemonic Plane. Give the Daemons control of your state and simply follow, watch, and listen to what they're telling you.

Now sometimes you'll find that what you think is important - the Daemons don't agree and they'll tell you something else. It's also perfectly okay to go into ascension with no expectations. The latter allows the Daemons to impart wisdom with you as they see fit and necessary, and they WILL inevitably give you something to chew on. That's just how they are. So going into ascension with no preconceived notions is a wonderful exercise for adepts who are seeking their next area of study or personal growth, but have been unable to find it on their own.

It is often suggested that you do not attempt to practice ascension night after night for months at a time because it can make you feel drained or compromise your health. Sometimes the revelations are so profound you'll need several months break in between sessions to work on the issue or to mull over the experience. Sometimes revelations from ascension aren't clear until several days afterward.

Ascension can be a cumbersome method of divination because of this. If you want instant gratification or an answer right now, you may or may not get it during an ascension session.

Gematria & Magick
by S. Connolly

Gematria is the method of assigning a numeric value to letters and calculating the numeric values of words to find their hidden (numeric) meaning. Gematria is the fundamental method by which magick squares (including Enochian Tablets) are produced. The following article also appears in *The Complete Book of Demonolatry* and is repeated here as a complete lesson in Gematria and the creation of magickal tablets/squares. It is important the magician understand that Gematria is a fundamental part of both Enochian Magick and Qabbalah, two of the three great pillars.

Magickal Tablets for Daemonolatry: A Complete Course

This lesson is meant to teach you the basics of how a tablet works. Tablets are an effective magickal tool because they are elementally, numerically, and alchemically balanced.

Let's just say that in most magickal traditions of the ceremonial variety, the complete knowledge for creating personalized tablets is something that's saved for the adepts of the upper echelon and inner circle. Most beginners start working with the basic Enochian tablets (watchtowers of the elementals).

I can say from personal knowledge that many traditions make it deliberately confusing. In some traditions they even say that only males can create and use tablets. Obviously this myth came about from a time when women were denied certain knowledge and practices.

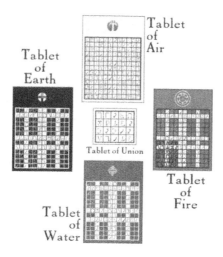

In the traditional Enochian Tablet you start with a square 13 down by 12 across (symbolic of the zodiac, alchemical properties, and aethyrs of the tree of life). The squares are broken down. The sixth and seventh squares in from the left side and 13 squares down and the seventh square down and 12 across represent the great cross (equal armed). Then you have the four quadrants, which are elemental as well as alchemical. The quadrants are 6 down and 5 across. Each quadrant is further broken down into kerubic squares, lesser squares, and the sephirothic cross (Christian oriented obviously since the whole system of Enochian magick was originally Egyptian and converted to a Christian bend with angels et al)

But all of this will just confuse you because there are many ways to create magickal tablets that are elementally, alchemically, and numerically balanced and attuned to a certain deity (Daemonic or other).

I do think it's important that all students of Daemonolatry learn as much as they possibly can about other schools of occult thought including magickal tablets because it's all interconnected with Hermetics (i.e. Khemetics), which is the foundation for Daemonolatry anyhow.

The following method is how my teacher taught me. Once you start with the basics you can work your way forward and the more complex systems of Gematria (like the actual Hebraic version) will make more sense. We started simple with basic Gematria and the English language as used for the Enochian system of Magick. First, on a piece of paper write out the Daemon's name you want to create the tablet for.

On the next pages you will find the values for letters (there are many other considerations depending on how complex you want your tablets to be) .

Note *just FYI - you should know that for most tablets, each letter in English also corresponds to a zodiac sign and element as well as tarot card.*

Here are the Gematraic values for each letter in English (for letters with two values, the first is the primary value and the second is the secondary or alternate value):

A=6
B=5
C=300
D=4
E=10
F=3
G=8
H=1
I=60
J=60
K=300
L=8
M=90
N=50
O=30
P=9
Q=40
R=100
S=7
T=9, 3
U= 70
V= 70
W=70
X=400
Y=60
Z=9,3

First, let's start out by figuring out the gematria value of your name. Experiment with this using your name and the names of others to discover the hidden meaning in the numbers of a name.

You can get meanings from the Sepher Sephiroth. Most people have a copy of *Crowley's 777 and Other Writings*. If you don't, I suggest getting one. It has the Sepher Sephiroth in it. Though you might want to stay away from the Hebraic Gematria at first because it can be confusing.

Let's do a tablet for Lucifer. It's a short name. First you want to figure out the value of Lucifer.

$L = 8$
$U = 70$
$C = 300$
$I = 60$
$F = 3$
$E = 10$
$R = 100$

Add all these numbers together. You get a grand total of 551.

You can further break down 551

$5 + 5 + 1 = 11$

Break 11 down further as $1 + 1 = 2$.

That is the lowest property you can reduce it to. 551 has no value, but 11 is a number that has the meaning, *"the special fire or light of the sacred magick of light/life"*. The number 2 is the Sephira of Wisdom. This obviously describes Lucifer very well.

Now you can kind of decide on the size of square you want and how you are going to choose to arrange it. Mind you this is simply a method of creating effective magickal tablets that will teach you about Gematria and all the alchemical and elemental properties of the mathematical construction of a tablet. These tablets, I've found, are just as effective as any.

Personally - I'd choose to create a 9x9 square only because I'd want the representation of the nine divinities and the ninth sephiroth represents the foundation or basis. The nine divinities are the foundation or basis of Daemonolatry so this works.

This means you'll have a total of 81 squares to work with. Draw this up on a sheet of graph paper and use a highlighter to color the fifth row across and the fifth row down. Now you have an equal armed cross and four quadrants.

For now - let's stick with English. On the highlighted row down, skip the very first square. Now spell LUCIFER - one letter per square - going down. Do the same across. The 'I' will be in the same place so they will intersect at the exact same point.

Right now let's say your top left quadrant is AIR (because you want to start with the element of Lucifer). For whatever reason, let's assume your top right quadrant is WATER. The bottom left quadrant is EARTH, the bottom right quadrant is FIRE (for this example's purpose). There are four alchemical properties associated with certain combinations so you can place the elemental quadrants where you want them just in case you didn't want air at the top left.

Elemental Alchemical Properties:

- Air + Water = Humidity
- Earth + Fire = Dryness
- Earth + Water = Cold
- Fire + Air = Heat.

You could also break this down into zodiac decans but we won't go that far.

Now technically you could spell Lucifer diagonally through the quadrants as well, but let's not. Instead, Let's condense the elementals to four letters each. Lucifer is LCFR, Leviathan will become LVTN, Belial will become BELL, and Flereous will become FLRS.

With another highlighter or colored pencil of a different color (you can use colors of the elements if you wish) in each quadrant color the four center squares of each quadrant. From right to left, top to bottom, spell out the four letters of each Daemon name.

EXERCISE - what is the numeric (gematraic) value of each of the elementals spelt as they are? What is the lowest value you can take that number down to? How many empty squares do you have left over? The answers are on the next page.

	L	C		L		L	V	
	F	R		U		T	N	
				C				
	L	U	C	I	F	E	R	
				F				
	B	E		E		F	L	
	L	L		R		R	S	

30 Squares Used
81 Squares Total
51 Squares Left Over

LCFR = 411 to 6
LVTN = 92 to 11 to 2
BELL = 31 to 4
FLRS = 118 to 10 or to 1

READING TWO

So now you know the basic construction of a tablet we are going to work on building a tablet more complex.

How about adding a sigil to a tablet? Aside from a pictorial representation (actual sigil) added to a tablet somewhere at its midpoint, why not build one right into it?

Get a piece of graph paper.

Let's start with another 9x9 tablet because it's small and easy to work with. Plus, 9 + 9 = 18 and 1 + 8 = 9. You may choose a larger tablet with a different numeric meaning.

For the purpose of this example - we will work with the following sigil (Verrine):

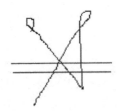

Since I want the value of the sigil to be 1 because it represents the Sephiroth Kether in the tree of life. (You can choose any value for the sigil you want) Were I using Crowley's Hebraic Gematria – 1 would be representative of the letter A. In the modernized Enochian Gematria number system we're using for the purpose of this course of study (see reading one) the letter H is the only letter with the value of 1. Therefore we will use the letter H.

H								H
	H						H	
		H				H	H	
			H		H		H	
H	H	H	H	H	H	H	H	H
H	H	H	H	H	H	H	H	H
			H				H	H
		H					H	
H								

Can you see the likeness of the sigil within the tablet? You can color the tablet any way you wish. I chose blue for this particular tablet because blue represents healing to me. It also represents relaxation and renewal. Choose colors that represent the sigil and tablet purpose most closely.

How many squares does this sigil use? How many squares are left over?

Squares used – 34
Squares left over – 47

An alternative to creating a Verrine based tablet would be:

	V	E	R	R		I	N	E	
V									E
E									N
R									I
R									R
I									R
N									E
E									V
	E	N	I	R		R	E	V	

In this instance, the actual sigil of Verrine sits at the center of the tablet and his name encircles the tablet on all four sides. There is still enough room for elemental quadrants here, and numerous other properties based on the purpose of the tablet.

How many squares does this sigil use? How many are left over?

- Squares used - 29
- Squares left over – 52

You might wonder why I keep asking you how many squares are used and how many are left over. The reason for this is that you will need to know what is left over to eventually complete the tablet.

You can also create the tablet first, then embellish it with the sigils wanted surrounding it.

Remember, the tablets in these examples are not completed. That is a surprise for the next lesson. In the meantime, let's discuss, more in depth, more aspects of the magickal tablet. Not only can individual quadrants or words within the tablet be added up for numeric significance, but they can be added across and down and as a whole for their numeric value.

A simple example to illustrate this would be:

H	H	H	H	H	H	H	H	H	= 9
H	H	H	H	H	H	H	H	H	= 9
H	H	H	H	H	H	H	H	H	= 9
H	H	H	H	H	H	H	H	H	= 9
H	H	H	H	H	H	H	H	H	= 9
H	H	H	H	H	H	H	H	H	= 9
H	H	H	H	H	H	H	H	H	= 9
H	H	H	H	H	H	H	H	H	= 9
H	H	H	H	H	H	H	H	H	= 9
= 9	= 9	= 9	= 9	= 9	= 9	= 9	= 9	= 9	= 81

The value of the columns and rows of this generic tablet = 81

$8 + 1 = 9$

Or $81 + 81 = 162$

$1 + 6 + 2 = 9$

Now let's try a more complex example (you might want to copy this page to calculate it):

L	S	A	T	A	N	A	S	N	=
E	L	B	A	L	A	B	L	A	=
V	H	U	L	U	L	U	H	H	=
I	H	P	C	C	C	P	H	T	=
A	L	U	C	I	F	E	R	A	=
T	H	P	F	F	F	P	H	I	=
H	H	E	L	E	L	E	H	V	=
A	R	B	A	R	A	B	R	E	=
N	S	A	N	A	T	A	S	L	=
=	=	=	=	=	=	=	=	=	

I've left space in the table for you to total all of the values of each row and column. Once you get the values down and across – add the value of the column and row together and then take it down to its lowest calculation.

Reading Three

Tablet Properties

Colors:

Here are some basic color correspondences you can work with. If any of these aspects doesn't seem to fit for you – you are more than welcome to add colors that you associate to the purpose of your tablet more readily.

- **Red and Orange** – Fire, action, love, lust relationships, creative work, anger, passion.
- **Blue and Gray** – Water, emotions, empathy, intuition, creative process, healing, divination, fertility.
- **Yellow and White** – Air, enlightenment, education, life lessons, planning.
- **Brown, Black, Green** – Earth, stability, financial matters, mundane matters, physical aspects of fertility, knowledge, trust, grounding/balancing.

Numbers special to you:
Consider numbers that might be special to you like birthdates, anniversaries, etc...

Alchemical and Elemental:

- **Elemental** = a part of the natural universe essential to life. Earth, air, fire, water.
- **Alchemical** = parts of the natural universe combined to create something different. Humidity, dryness, cold, and heat are some examples.

Daemonic Properties:

See the various Daemon listings in *The Complete Book of Demonolatry* or other resource to find Daemons that correspond to your tablet's purpose.

Planetary Properties:

Ruling Planets

Sun

This is the center of existence. In astrology it symbolizes everything we are trying to become, the center around which all our activity in life revolve. This Planet (also known as a luminary and a star) represents the self, one's personality and ego, the spirit and what it is that makes the individual unique. It rules the zodiacal sign Leo, a fire sign. Everything in the horoscope ultimately revolves around this singular body. It is the Sun, which gives strength to the other Planets, which is why this Planet occupies a key role in Astrology. It is the symbol of strength, vigor, wisdom, dignity, ardor and generosity, and the ability for a person to function as a mature individual.

Moon

Since the Moon is closest to Earth it influences us more deeply than any other Planet. The effect is very personal, very intimate. Whereas the Sun gives us our spirit, it's the Moon, which gives us our soul. The Moon is goddess-like in that it symbolizes mother and the relationship between woman and child. The moon (also known as a luminary) speaks to the women in one's life and their role as nurturer. This planet rules zodiacal sign Cancer one among the watery signs.

Mercury

This Planet implores us to express ourselves clearly. Mercury represents your capacity to understand the desires of your own will and to translate those desires into action. In other words it is the planet of mind and the power of communication. Through mercury we develop an ability to think, write, speak and observe- to be aware of world around us. When Mercury goes retrograde (the appearance of traveling backward) our communications will be challenged. Mercury rules the zodiacal sign Gemini and Virgo.

Venus

It symbolizes the harmony and radiance of a rare and elusive quality, the beauty itself. Venus is all about pleasure, especially pleasure shared with someone else. This Planet concerns itself with love, romance and harmony in our emotional attachments, marriages, friendships and other unions (like business partnerships). Venus also deals with the pleasure we derive from our possessions. Luxuries (jewelry, paintings, expensive cars), a beautiful home and a sense of refinement all belong to Venus's interests. This Planet ruling the zodiacal signs Taurus and Libra appreciates the exquisite nature of things.

Mars

Mars is the action Planet of the Zodiac. Your Mars Sign defines what you desire and how you express that desire. This Planet commands you to stand up, be noticed and get things done etc. Ambition and competition are also within Mars's realm. Mars also rule the power and confident expression of the individual. Mars is the ruling planet of zodiacal signs Scorpio and Aries.

Jupiter

Jupiter influence thinking capacity of a person. In astrology it rules good luck and good cheer, health, wealth, optimism, happiness, success and joy. It is a symbol of opportunity and always opens way for new opportunities in life. Jupiter is the minimization of limitation and the emphasis on spirituality and potential. While our success, accomplishments and prosperity are all within Jupiter's realm, its negative influence can deteriorate into laziness and sloth. It rules the zodiacal signs Sagittarius and Pisces belonging to fire and watery elements respectively.

Saturn

Saturn plays the role of a taskmaster in the Zodiac. Saturn commands us to get to work and to work hard. Saturn rules time, old age and sobriety. It can bring depression, gloom, jealousy and greed, or serious acceptance of responsibilities out of which success will develop. Learning life's lessons is key to this Planet, in keeping with its role as teacher. It rules the earth sign Capricorn and the air sign Aquarius.

Uranus

Uranus brings with it a new way of looking at things, and its approach is best met with an expanded consciousness. Uranus rules unexpected change, upheaval, and revolution. It is the symbol of total independence and asserts the freedom of an individual from all restriction and restraint. It is a breakthrough planet and indicates talent, originality and genius in a horoscope. This planet rules Aquarius an air sign.

Neptune ruling the watery sign Pisces, awakens a sense of higher responsibility often causing guilt, worry, anxieties or delusions. In short, Neptune is

Neptune creating an illusion -- of what is enchanting on the outside and captivating within. Sleep and dreams are also lorded over by this Planet.

Pluto This Planet influence transformation, regeneration and rebirth. This Planet is about all that is secret and undercover, that which is hidden from view. Pluto starts its influence with a minor event or insignificant incident that might even go unnoticed. Pluto rules the fire sign Aries and water sign Scorpio.

Letters and The Zodiac and Alphabet (from Modern Enochian Magick correspondence examples):

A = Taurus
B = Aries
C, K = Fire
D = Spirit
E = Virgo
F = Cauda
G = Cancer
H = Air
I, J, Y = Sagittarius
L = Cancer
M = Aquarius
N = Scorpio
O = Libra
P = Leo
Q = Water
R = Pisces
S = Gemini
T = Leo
U,V,W = Capricorn
X = Earth

Z = Leo

Reading Four

Completing the Tablets

In reading one we started with the following tablet.

	L	C		L		L	V	
	F	R		U		T	N	
				C				
L	U	C	I	F	E	R		
				F				
	B	E		E		F	L	
	L	L		R		R	S	

Now I am going to complete this tablet. This is an Air Tablet. It already has all of the Elementals present except for Satan (or the All). I am going to include Lucifuge Rofocale, too. Since Lucifuge Rofocale fits balanced around the outer edge (and represents my Da'ath) that is where I will place him. Satan will wrap around each element in an L shape. In this instance I used both gray and yellow for air, blue for water, bluish green for earth, and red for fire. I used a deeper gold for Lucifuge Rofocale to show his fire side. I chose a deep gray for Satan to represent the whole and the balance within.

215

L	E	L	A	C	O	F	O	R
U	L	C	S	L	S	L	V	E
C	F	R	A	U	A	T	N	G
I	N	A	T	C	T	A	N	U
F	L	U	C	I	F	E	R	F
U	S	A	T	F	T	A	S	I
G	B	E	A	E	A	F	L	C
E	L	L	N	R	N	R	S	U
R	O	F	O	C	A	L	E	L

This table contains the following Numeric Properties (you get to figure it out):

Vertical Value:
Horizontal Value:
Total Value:

This tablet's sole purpose is a representation of the air elemental. Does the calculation prove true to its purpose?

When I translate the tablet to Enochian, it looks like this:

Your assignment for this reading is to complete one of the following tablets based on YOUR personal preference. If you choose the Tablet of Lucifer from Lesson 1, modify it differently from the one above. (See end of lesson to learn how to do this in word)

EXERCISE: Choose one of the following tablets and complete it.

	L	C		L		L	V	
	F	R		U		T	N	
				C				
	L	U	C	I	F	E	R	
				F				
	B	E		E		F	L	
	L	L		R		R	S	

H								H
	H						H	
		H				H	H	
			H		H		H	
H	H	H	H	H	H	H	H	H
H	H	H	H	H	H	H	H	H
		H				H	H	
	H						H	
H								

	V	E	R	R	I	N	E	
V								E
E								N
R								I
R								R
I								R
N								E
E								V
	E	N	I	R	R	E	V	

Tablets Questions and Answers

This section is included, with answers, to see if you have fully understood the tablet readings. Work through them slowly. If you don't get the same answer, try to figure out why.

PART 1

1. What is the value of your name and its meaning according to the Sepher Sephiroth?

2. Calculate the value of LEVIATHAN. What do you get? What is the lowest number value you can get from it? What are the meanings of Leviathan based on these numbers and the Sepher Sephiroth? Based on the Sepher Sephiroth (Crowley's 777) and LVTN.

LVTN= 486. =(18)=(9). (18) Hatred, the antique serpent. (9)= Fire of Sorcery, Beloved, enchanter, and Chesed. (486)= foundations (as in LVTN's place around sephira)

or – based on Gematraic numeric system presented (using primary number): **2**

Leviathan= 220 2+2+0=4

220: The elect, heroina, augusta, domina, ye shall cleave, cean, elegant, giants

4: father, hollow, a vein, proud.

Using the secondary value: 214 = 7 – the lord of armies, the Sephira of firmness and victory.

3. The numbers 7, 6, 9/3, 6, 50 spells what name in English? What is the value of this name and it's meanings according to the Sepher Sephiroth?

Satan. Primary: (78)=(15)=(6). Steam/Vapor, Pride, # Geburah , Monogram for the eternal, He who impels. Secondary: 72 = 9

4. Why do some letters have more than one number associated with them? (A basic answer is fine, but feel free to write more if you've done in depth research into this.)

The primary and secondary have to do with placement value. For example the primary would be used in cases of capitals indicative of proper nouns denoting the specific vs. the common. The primary and the secondary. The first number is primary, and the second number is secondary. Use the secondary number if the letter is in the middle of a name.

5. Why was a 9 x 9 square chosen for the tablet of Lucifer created in the reading example?

Because the 9th Sephiroth, Yesod, represents the foundation, and the foundation of Daemonolatry are the nine divinities.

PART 2

Assignment Tablet

1. What is the total calculation of the assignment tablet in reading two (using the gematria letter number values from reading one)? Did you use a primary or secondary value for T? Notice anything about the vertical and horizontal calculation using the primary vs. secondary values? Either way - the total value of the tablet still comes out the same when condensed to the lowest number. What is its lowest calculation?

Total calculation Primary = 5520 = 12 = 3
                 Non Primary = 5484 = 21 = 3
3 = The Sephira of understanding.
Down and Across the non-primary values are both
2742 = 15 = 6

   2. Explain why I might have chosen the colors I chose. Would you have chosen differently - and why?

- Blue – Leviathan – Water (element)
- Red – Satanas – (Fire) the whole.
- Yellow – Lucifer – Air (element)
- Green – BAL = 19 = 10 = 1 – The whole. Green was chosen to balance the tablet, which was lacking in earth and stability.
- Gray – H – has value of 1 – the whole – the Sephira of Satan – Gray seemed an appropriate color due to the subtle shades of gray in everything.
- Light Blue – P – has the value of 9 – the whole. Light blue, for me, is a calming/balancing color and 9 is the foundation or balance.

3. Why, do you think, I used 8 H's and 4 P's. Look at numeric values and colors to figure it out.

H = 1 and there are 8 polarities in the nine divinities.
P = 9 and 9 x 4 = 36 = 9

4. What is BAL? Why, do you suppose I chose it?

BAL = 19 and represents manifestation and contains a balance of light and darkness. Further broken down it is 10, which is the Sephira of Kingdom, exalted. Further broken down to 1 – it is the whole. BAL (a shortened version of Baal – the primary Earth) connects the physical to all that is, and is representative of the missing earth in this tablet to achieve balance.

5. What does all of this information suggest about the purpose of this tablet?

This is a tablet for balance, to achieve a connection with all that is. It would be used in ascension, for divination, and/or for Ordainment of members of the Priesthood. It represents an understanding of the whole and the connection between the mundane and the spiritual.

SIGIL TABLETS READING

1. Can you figure out why I spelt Verrine forward and backward around the outer edges of the second reading tablet?

For balance in the tablet top and bottom.
- V's in opposite corners for balance = 140 = 5
- E's in opposite corners for balance = 20 = 2

2. What would be the numeric meaning of a tablet 48 x 48?

2304 = 9 -- the same as a 9x9 tablet.

3. How can someone choose colors for certain aspects of a tablet?

Based on elemental, purposeful, alchemical, and/or planetary correspondences that have meaning to the Daemonolater him or herself.

READING THREE

1.Calculate the Value of the Tablet in Reading 3:
   Vertical value: 3870
   Horizontal value: 4113
   Total value: 7983 7+9+8+3= 27 2+7=9

What is the tablet that I created in the final reading for?

The foundation of Air

More About Magickal Squares (Tablets) & Magick Words

While the previously discussed tablets are lettered with numeric value assigned to each letter, when it comes to numeric tablets exclusively they are often referred to as Kamea (translates to magick square). They are also used in Qabbalah. Perhaps some of the most popular Kamea magick squares you'll find are the planetary ones like this Kamea of Saturn below. There are numerous books out there with a great deal of detail on the various magick squares. Start with Agrippa and work your way to Abramelin (not the Mather's translation). Add up all the columns of the Kamea below and see what you get.

4	9	2
3	5	7
8	1	6

Here is the Kamea of Jupiter. Add this one up:

4	14	15	1
9	7	6	12
5	11	10	8
16	2	3	13

The **Sator Square** is an example of a word square - - another form of the magickal tablet. Back in Medieval Rome one could find this square inscribed on everything from eating utensils and drinking vessels to being inscribed above doorways. It was, essentially, a ward to keep evil spirits at bay.

The Sator square is a kind of crossword puzzle, rather than a mathematical magic square. Sator Arepo Tenet Opera Rotas. And while each of these words is simply a word – putting them into a coherent sentence from the Latin is difficult. It doesn't translate well. It is widely accepted that there are two possible translations of the phrase including 'The sower Arepo holds the wheels with effort' and 'The sower Arepo leads with his hand (work) the plough (wheels).' Arepo, it is assumed, is a direct name rather than a word that can be translated. Many have taken it to mean "deity" in some form, but the word Arepo itself has confounded even the most astute of Latin scholars.

S	A	T	O	R
A	R	E	P	O
T	E	N	E	T
O	P	E	R	A
R	O	T	A	S

Another example of a magical word square:

M	U	S	E	S
U	N	E	V	E
S	E	Y	E	S
E	V	E	N	U
S	E	S	U	M

Finally, we have magical words, which are also used as amulets. The most popular being **Abracadabra** (which was used as a talisman against illness and for healing illness):

ABRACADABRA   ABRACADABRA
ABRACADABR   BRACADABR
ABRACADAB   RACADAB
ABRACADA   ACADA
ABRACAD   CAD
ABRACA   A
ABRAC
ABRA
ABR
AB
A

Another being Akrakanarba, which is a dissolving spell:

AKRAKANARBA
KANARBA
ANARBA
NARBA
ARBA
RBA
BA
A

They are used much like Akrammachamari (a Coptic conclusion of invocation), where the magi would dip a wand into a magickal mixture, or a fountain pen into a magical ink and the word would be written on the ground or on parchment as the magi spoke it. Thus activating the power of the word. This makes the amulet or spell and if on paper it can be carried by the person using it. Such magical words can also be sewn into cloth or stamped into leather.

Consider all of these options when working with magick squares, numerology, and letters/words in your talismans and magickal work. They do have a place in

Daemonic Magick. And yes – you can create your own
Kamea, word squares, and magical word "reductions".

Sex & Magick
by M. Delaney & S. Connolly

Sex magick can be one of those uncomfortable topics, even among magicians. Some people think it's completely perverse or they expect it somehow revolves around having sex with Daemons. On the contrary, it is neither.

Sex magick is about harnessing the energy of orgasm and directing that energy toward the work being performed. This type of magick can be done alone or with a partner (or multiple partners if you choose). Sex magick can be one of the most rewarding forms of magick for the couple that practices together.

First some ground rules:
- o Always practice safe sex.
- o Do not practice sex magick with people you don't know well (I know, duh, but it needs to be said).
- o If your ritual involves pageantry of any kind, costumes, or "props" make sure all those participating agree to this.

- o If your ritual involves B&D or S&M, make sure all participants agree to this, know their place, and know the safe-word beforehand.
- o Make sure every participant knows his/her role during the rite and that everyone is focusing on the same thing. It's a shame to waste a perfectly good rite (and orgasms) when one of the participants is only there for the sex but not the magick or vice versa.
- o Do not practice sex magick with persons who are not aware that this is what you're doing. For what it's worth – masturbation is far more effective than the ritual done with a participant who is unaware of the intention or goal behind the sex act. This means you don't invite someone who is not a magician into your ritual chamber for sex, or use your unaware significant other, or the person you picked up at the bar, for sex magick. An unaware person can scatter the energy or even worse, panic during sex once they realize they're a part of a Daemonic magickal working.

Why practice sex magick?

- Sex magick produces a great deal of energy at orgasm. More energy than most standard magickal workings.
- To give birth to servitors or thought forms because such a large concentration of energy is initially needed. An orgasm is a very balanced way to get this amount of energy in one shot (no pun intended).
- To infuse amulets or magical tools with your essence (many times replaces blood or is

used in conjunction with blood for a more powerful working), especially if you can masturbate with the tool or upon it.

Things One Can do with Sexual Fluids:

Once you collect sexual fluids you can use them to anoint objects, put the fluid in inks or oils, or use them in a personal perfume. Semen and lubricant sexual fluids can also be placed into food or drink, but use caution with this due to the possibility of spreading disease.

Working With Daemons During Sex Magick:

Choosing Daemonic forces to work with during sex magick is no different than choosing which Daemons to work with in any other method of magick. Choose the Daemons that most suit your purposes and who carry the attributes most closely associated with what you hope to accomplish with the working. Asmoday/Asmodeus presides over a great deal of Sex Magick and if invoked during a sex magick ritual, is said to increase the energy of your sex magick ten fold. You still construct the ritual space as you would with any other ritual. Within the ritual chamber – be sure to place sigils in places where the participants can see them. This helps with focus during orgasm. If, at the moment of orgasm each participant can focus on a sigil, it will help bring together all that energy.

Working With Sigils During Sex Magick:

Some rituals call for you to carve sigils onto waxed paper for use during sex magick. This is so you can masturbate on it or have intercourse on top of the sigil without ruining it or worrying about ink running into your carpets or onto someone's ass. You may alternatively place sigils strategically around the room so that at the moment of orgasm all participants can shift their focus to the sigil, and the intent of the ritual to begin with. Sigils can also be painted, in oleum or ink, on the chests and backs of the participants.

Do you focus on the sex or the magick?

Be present and in the moment during the sexual act. It's at the point of orgasm that you need to have the ability to focus on the magickal purpose of the ritual to send the energy in the right direction rather than allowing it to dissipate into the ether. However, please note that some magicians believe that being in the present moment through orgasm is fine, too. That there is no need to focus the energy toward the intended goal. Experiment both ways and see what works for you.

The Feminine Blessing of Magickal Items:

Invoke Unsere or Lilith. Start slowly and gently caress the labia and inner thighs. Let the labia and clitoris swell. Insert two fingers into the vagina to be sure she has lubricated. Use a drop of Daemonic oleum (make sure all ingredients are safe for contact with skin, especially delicate membranes, I could tell you a story about peppers, but I'm sure you can guess) with lubricant on the item. Gently insert it into the vagina. Have the female participant tighten her muscles to hold the object inside her, or use one hand to do it for her. Massage the clitoris to orgasm while chanting the Enn of Lilith. For smooth objects, the object to be blessed can be gently used as a dildo or used to gently massage the clitoris to orgasm as in the case of stones or even wands. For daggers, only insert the handle side and be very careful of sharp edges or ridges. For additional energy, bind her hands and tie her legs and knees open. Blindfolds heighten the experience.

The Masculine Blessing for Magickal Items:

Invoke Satan or Asmodeus. Binding the male participant and using blindfolds will increase sensation and

233

make the orgasm more powerful. Place the object to be blessed between his legs. You may use the item to caress his erect penis. Stimulate the inner thighs, penis, and the prostate (insert a well lubricated finger (you can use gloves or a condom for this) or an anal stimulation device). The prostate is located just a few inches in, it should be easy to find as it is a walnut-shaped and sized button that should be firm and swollen. Masturbate him to orgasm and use the resulting semen to anoint the item.

To Create Servitors/Thought Forms

Servitors or thought forms (i.e. entities you create to serve you and your will) can be used to do the magician's bidding. They need a great deal of energy for their initial creation and they will need regular feeding. Treat your servitors or thought forms as familiars. They will do what you ask of them provided they are well cared for.

So to initially create the Servitor you will need a strong energy source. From my own experience, the orgasm is the best method to acquire this much energy in one instance. The more participants, the stronger the Servitor. In this I am not necessarily suggesting orgies. Clearly you should only participate in sex magick with people you know, trust, and with whom have the same magickal goals as you. Sometimes it's better to just work alone to create a servitor or with one partner so that you are the sole master of the servitor you're creating.

Ideally, to create your servitor you will want to clearly outline what you expect your servitor to do for you, give it a name, and give it a symbol or sigil of your design. Give it a form if you wish. Then, within a ritual space conducive to the work (usually overseen by Ba'al or your highest Daemonic god form), you will want to masturbate or have intercourse to orgasm. At the point of orgasm, channel all of your energy to the name and sigil and imagined form of your servitor. Repeat this ritual for 7 days. Around day three or four, you will really start to feel the presence of this being you have manifested. Feed your Servitor once a week for the first month, and once every two weeks after that. If your servitor is used often, you will need to feed it more often.

Keeping more than one servitor is a great deal of work and requires the magician to expend a great deal of energy. So consider this before choosing to create more than one. My wife keeps a servitor as a ward against negativity or anything or one who wishes to harm our family. This Servitor has literally thrown people out of our house. See the warding ritual later in this book to learn more about warding and home protection. A good Daemon to work with for creating servitors (I've found) is Marbas, though any Daemonic force for the purpose of your servitor will be just fine.

Sigils, Symbols, & Magick
By S.Connolly

Sigils and Symbols are important tools in magick because they offer the magician something to focus on. It's important to remember that the symbols or sigil is not a thing of power itself until the magician gives it power. The magician must first put intent and meaning into all symbols before use. This includes those pre-made symbols and sigils found in various magick texts such as this one.

Using Sigils & Symbols

You can use symbols and sigils in a variety of ways. First – they can be worn as amulets. They can be inscribed upon objects (including candles for candle magick). They can be used as talismans. They can be left on an altar, hung over a doorway or on a wall, they can be written on paper and burnt! Most people's magickal education will give them pause to do this.

For those of you who haven't read The Complete Book of Demonolatry, in Daemonolatry, sigils can be burnt and buried. Don't worry. Burning the sigil is not considered disrespectful. It's not a way to "control" the Daemonic. By burning sigils or personal symbols on a "request", we are merely transforming the symbol into a different form. It's almost considered an alchemical transformation that sends the intent to where it needs to go and purifies and perfects our will. Matter cannot be created or destroyed, it can only change form. So all the intent that went into the sigil or symbol is merely transformed and sent to the Daemonic Divine.

Creating Sigils & Symbols

This can mean one of two things. Either you create sigils and symbols of your own making, or it can mean the method by which you construct the sigil or symbol itself.

Let's first discuss creating personal sigils and symbols. In the act of creating a new symbol or sigil, many magicians believe one should be in an ascended state. Begin with a meditation or your key or whatever it takes to put you into that state where you are open to Daemonic suggestion and inspiration. See the Invoke Creativity ritual under Magickal Operations if you need help. First you must define what your intent is. Then – give that intent a physical shape in the form of a drawing. That is basically what sigils and symbols are. They're pictorial representations of a Daemonic Force, Emotion, or Idea. Once you've recorded the symbol, it can be created more completely (as in its physical construction), consecrated, charged, and used as you see fit.

As with any tool, sigils and symbols can be constructed of various materials. Some people are knowledgeable enough to use metals. Others have used cloth, thread, yarn, beads, paint, pencils or markers, clay, paper and even wood. It really depends how you wish to use the symbol or sigil and whether or not you wish it to be permanent or not. The only limit on this is your imagination. I had a student who used yarn sewn into paper. I knew another Daemonolater who stamped her sigils into leather. Be creative.

Circling Sigils vs. Uncircled Sigils

Circling a sigil in Daemonolatry magick puts the Daemonic force in perspective as a part of the whole. Whereas leaving the sigil uncircled is focusing on the Daemonic force itself. Circle or uncircle based on what you're focusing on.

Combining Sigils

Existing sigils can be combined to create an entirely new sigil by incorporating all the lines of both sigil into one. This is a perfectly acceptable and common practice in Daemonolatry magick. It's good when you wish to have more than one Daemonic sigil inscribed on an amulet but there just isn't room.

For more information on Daemonolatry specific Sigil Magick see M. Delaney's book **Sanctus Quattordecim** *where he explains combining and trining sigils to incorporate all the attributes.*

Talismans/Amulets & Magick
By S. Connolly

Talismans and Amulets are magickal items a magician will carry with him/her to keep his/her mind focused on a desired outcome. Talismans and Amulets are often charged with certain properties so that when held or kept in a certain place – they will influence situations according to their purpose. Amulet is often the word we use when we mean a talisman that is worn around the neck of the person who seeks the influence of the magickal properties infused into the talisman. So really – they're both the same thing. And really – they're no different that magickal sachets or gris-gris/mojo bags either except in design.

Using Talismans & Amulets

Talismans and amulests are very versatile magickal items in the Magician's arsenal. They can be used in everything from cursing to healing and everything in between. Choosing which incarnation your talisman should take will depend a great deal on what you are going to use it for. A protection talisman for a female child's room, for example, could take the form of a pretty white sachet with white ribbon suspended above the door. The sachet may contain proper stones, herbs, bones and sigils.

Creating Talismans & Amulets

A sigil itself could be a talisman or amulet. See the previous section for ideas on how to use sigils. One of my favorite methods of making of talismans: Buy those glass stones you can get at the hobby store. You can buy a big bag of them for relatively cheap and get all different colors. You can paint sigils onto them (or carve them with a dremel if you're careful), and you can anoint them with oil. They keep a charge really well and are highly portable. See the Rite of Making (Charging Amulets & Talismans – and just about anything else) in the Energy Work section in this book for more.

I made a green money Talisman with the sigil of Belphegore on it and keep it in the cash box at work. I also keep one in my purse and a clear one (with the sigil of Satanchia) for safety in my car glove box. I will add them to sachets as well.

My second favorite method of making talismans and amulets is using Sculpy clay (it's a brand of clay that can be baked in your home oven). The clay comes in all sorts of colors. You just make a circle (or any shape you want) carve your sigils and symbols into it, put a hole in the top for the metal ring if you're going to turn it into an amulet, and bake. Afterwards, you can add a coat of glaze (depending if it's something you're keeping). The clay amulets/talismans are great for burying, wearing, adding to sachets, and giving as gifts.

Cleaning/Clearing Talismans & Amulets

For some people, Talismans and Amulets can begin absorbing what I call "astral sludge" or "residual negativity". To clear or cleanse your Talisman or Amulet, first consider what it's made of. You may not want to use water or oil on clay or substances that can rot or dissolve. Instead, you can leave them in salt for a few days or sprinkle them with a clearing tincture. The alcohol in the tincture could damage certain substances so consider that. You can also re-anoint the item with oleum. Or – wave the amulet or talisman through incense smoke. Regardless how you do it, keeping your amulets and talismans clean and charged with the proper energy is an essential everyday task for some magicians as some magicians have a stronger energy and will attract a great deal of residual energy to themselves.

Cleansing Options:
- Clean the item with water, let air dry, wave through incense smoke, put it through fire, then re-anoint or re-charge.
- Let the item sit in salt for several days.
- Sprinkle the item with a clearing tincture.
- Wave the item through incense smoke from incense made of sage, sweetgrass, or frankincense.

If you find you attract a great deal of residual energy:
- Do not wear any amulet for more than a day at a time.
- Do be sure to cleanse your amulets and talismans daily.

Stone Magick
by Kelly & Nick Schneider & S. Connolly

The use of stones in magick goes back to very primitive cultures. Each type of stone is said to have its own energy and power. People would carry or wear stones to aid in everything from protection, to strength, to healing. Stones can be used to purify and cleanse or even banish negativity. You can use a dremel tool to carve sigils into hard stones.

To consecrate a stone or stone amulet, anoint it with the Daemonic Oleum of choice and chant the appropriate enns and/or prayers over it.

To charge a stone with a particular purpose you would construct your Daemonic ritual space, place the stone upon your altar or cup it in your hands, and infuse it with the energy for its purpose by meditating on it, reciting incantations over it, and directing all your energy into the stone. Some rituals require you to paint a Daemonic sigil upon a stone and to carry the stone with you (however you choose).

To cleanse a stone ridding it of any residual energy, leave it three days in salt if the material can handle it, three days in water provided it won't dissolve, and three days on your altar to dry and re-stabilize it. If you're using a softer stone, do not immerse in water for long durations and only leave it in salt if the stone and salt are both dry because soft stone may erode. Waving stones through incense smoke may be enough to clear most unwanted energy.

To use the stone you would place into in a clay amulet with appropriate sigils carved alongside them or on the underside, keep it in your pocket or purse (with sigil painted onto it or not – depending if you wanted to reuse the stone for different purposes or not), or use it during ritual likewise. You may also create necklaces with stones by gluing them into a setting.

To construct a clay amulet with stones: Create a disk. Make a hole at the top for the metal ring that will run through it to place the amulet on a chain or strap of leather for wearing. Draw any sigils on the back or face of the amulet using clay tools or a paperclip. Push the stone(s) into the clay to make a place for it/them. Then, once the amulet is baked (we prefer baking the clay amulets with the stone in them) and cooled, gently remove the stone, put down a layer of hot glue or super glue, then replace the stone. That should help hold it. Otherwise you risk the stone falling out as we've discovered simply baking the stones into an amulet doesn't always work to hold it there. Use paint or marker to highlight any sigils or markings if desired, then brush a layer of lacquer over the amulet to protect it. Consecrate the stone, charge it, then use. Cleanse as needed, however do not set clay amulets in water as they'll crumble. Instead, simply dip them in water once and pat dry with a towel, then re-consecrate. Note that you will probably have to continually replace clay amulets and soft stones due to normal wear and erosion.

Some basic properties of stones:

Note: There are no definitive stones corresponding to individual Daemons. To learn additional virtues of stones and ways of working with stones, the practitioner should seek the wisdom of the Daemon(s) Bathin, Marax, Foras, Bifrons, or a Daemon of magick such as Delepitorae or Thoth. To match a stone's properties to the Daemonic force being invoked – simply pair up properties. For example, if you're doing a working to increase Mental Acuity and are invoking Lucifer choose Citrine. When working with Fire/War Daemons, pair them with Black Agate. This is a very simple thought process that any magician worth his salt should be able to handle without being hand-held or handed a definitive list.

Basic Properties including Elements

Alum: Earth, Protection
Amazonite: Earth, Balancing, Success,
Amber: Fire, All purpose
Amethyst: Water, Protection, Balancing, Healing, psychic
Ametrine: Air/Fire, Compatibility, Subtle Body blockages
Apache Tear: Fire, Protection, luck.
Aquamarine; Water, Purification, soothes emotions.

Aventurine: Air: Balancing, Motivation, Intuition, Peace, healing, luck

Argonite: Fifth Element, Centering, meditation

Azurite: Water, Dreams, divination, healing

Banded Agate: Fire, De-stressor, protection

Beryl: Water, Love, psychic healing, anti-gossip

Black Agate: Fire, Protection, courage

Blackwhite Agate: Earth, Protect physical harm

Bloodstone: Earth, Healing, removing blocks

Blue Lace Agate: Water, Peace, happiness

Brown Agate: Fire, Success

Brown Jasper: Earth, Grounding

Calcite: Water, Centering, healing, soothing

Cats Eye: Earth, Wealth, beauty, healing

Carnelian: Fire, Peace, passion, protection from external energies,

Chrysoprase: Earth, Happiness, calming, friendship

Citrine: Air, increase mental power, wealth, balance, transmutes negative energies

Coral: Water, Fifth Element, elemental power

Crystal Quartz: Water, Purifying, Astral Projection

Diamond: Fire, Spirituality

Emerald: Earth, Exorcism

Fluorite: Wisdom, spiritual growth, meditation, healing.

Fossils: Fifth Element, Elemental Power

Garnet: Fire, Energizing, manifestation, expanding awareness

Geode: Earth, Free Spirit, courage, astral travel, communication, ascension,

Green Agate: Earth, Fertility

Hematite: Earth, Strength, mental enhancement (learning, memory), focus, original thinking

Herkimer Diamond: Fire, Beauty

Howlite: Air, calms communication, facilitates emotional expressions, dispels negativity

Jade: Earth, Prosper, lucid dreaming, bridge between

physical and astral
Jet: Fifth Element, Divination
Lapis Lazuli: Water, Increases spiritual awareness
Lava: Fire, Protection
Lodestone: Fire, Attraction
Malachite: Earth, Fertility, insight into health issues, release negativity,
Marble: Water, Protection
Moonstone: Fifth Element, Divination, balancing, new beginnings, confidence, connects physical to emotional.
Moss Agate: Earth, growing things (like plants)
Obsidian: Earth, protection for gentle souls
Onyx: Earth, past life recall or meditations
Pearl: Water, Love, money, protection
Pink Fluorite: Water, Analytical about relationships
Quartz: Fifth Element, Purification
Pumice: Air, Eases childbirth or pain of any sort
Pyrite: Fire, Success, energy, new business or creative ventures
Red Agate: Fire, Peace, calm
Red Jasper: Fire, Blood of Isis
Rhodochrosite: Fire, Energy, love. Peace
Rose Quartz: Water, Love, friendship, self love
Ruby: Fire, Wealth, power, courage, focus energy
Salt: Earth, Banishing, cleansing
Sapphire: Water, Love, meditation
Sardonyx: Fire, Marital happiness, relationship harmony
Selenite: Water, Energy, reconciliation
Smokey Quartz: Earth, Grounding
Sodalite: Water, Meditation, Calms, alleviates fear (great for ascension practice), clarity, truth
Sugilite: Water Fire, Activates the third eye, magick,
Sunstone: Fire, Energizer
Tigers Eye: Earth, Luck, honesty, beauty, focus energy, strengthen energy.

Tourmaline: Fifth Element, aids in sleep, aligns subtle bodies

Turquoise: Water, Protection, wealth, healing, inner strength.

Planetary Stone Correspondences

Moon - Moonstone, Gypsum, Pearl, & Quartz
Mercury - Opal, Agate Serpentine, Tigers Eye, Citrine
Venus - Emerald, Turquoise, Malachite, Beryl, Aventurine, Sapphires
Sun - Chrysolite, Topaz, Zircon, Crystal
Mars - Garnets, Rubies, Bloodstones, Jasper
Jupiter - Amethyst, Lapis Lazuli, Sapphire, Topaz
Saturn -Onyx, Jet, Lapis Lazuli
Pluto – Garnet, Ruby
Uranus – Turquoise
Neptune - Aquamarine

Zodiac Stone Correspondences

Aries - Red Jasper or Bloodstone
Taurus - Red Coral or Sapphires
Gemini – Alexandrite or Agate
Cancer – Amber or Emerald (Moonstones also)
Leo - Cats Eye or Onyx
Virgo – Peridot or Carnelian
Libra – Malachite or Peridot
Scorpio – Bloodstone or Beryl
Sagittarius – Moonstone or Topaz
Capricorn - Lapis Lazuli or Ruby
Aquarius – Amethyst or Garnet
Pisces – Pearl or Amethyst

The Three Great Pillars of Magick

S. Connolly

The Three Great Pillars of Magick, all interconnected and inter-related (those who have studied them for years know what I mean) are Hermetics, Qabbalah, and Enochian. You may be asking yourself – what do these have to do with Daemonolatry? Well, first, the foundation of the religion of Daemonolatry is Hermetic (well, actually Khemetic and Canaanite, but Hermeticism is the Greek version of Khemeticism anyway). Qabbalah, if you read between the lines, is also very Hermetic, and so is Enochian (read the Hermetic Theorems and then compare with John Dee's Hieroglyphic Monad and if you need more proof, come talk to me.). The following pages simply contain some of my notes and applications of these systems to Daemonolatry Magick. If you are interested in learning more about the Three Great Pillars, there are numerous books out there that explore all three of these topics adequately.

On that note, I would like to make mention that it is perfectly acceptable for a Daemonolater to modify the rituals of Golden Dawn and/or Thelema or Khemetic traditions for use in Daemonic Magick. This is simply done by substituting God-Forms and names you don't identify with, with ones you do (and who carry the same attributes obviously). It also requires modification of offensive symbolism, sigils, methods, etc... For those of you who fear modification and consider it sacrilege, definitely don't look into a forthcoming book by High Priest B. Morlan and myself with modified rituals for Daemonolatry from other magickal and occult traditions. It will likely only offend you.

Enochian & Daemonic Magick

Enochian is a magickal system put forth by Dr. John Dee and Edward Kelley in the late middle ages. Allegedly it was gotten from a form of ascension (channeling) with "angels". Angels, from where I'm sitting, are just different aspects of the Daemonic Divine. Disagree if you will.

As a magician I can tell you that I frequently incorporate Enochian invocations (created by myself) into my magickal operations. I have even used straight up Enochian rituals when it suits the work. I have also successfully used modified Enochian gate/pillar opening rites for raising energy. Enochian as a language (a barbarous tongue as they say) is wonderful vibrated and has an energy all its own. It is, in a way, very similar to the Daemonic Enns in that quality.

So, as a magician, it's entirely up to you whether or not you wish to experiment with Enochian. The Enochian spirits are another story altogether. I think you'll find these Daemons (Divine Intelligences) have a very different feel from Dukante Daemons and Goetic Daemons. Some Daemonolaters I know have even refused to work with Enochian spirits due to the unsettling feeling they seem to

251

evoke in the magician. From my own observation it's just their nature to exude the energy they exude and to cause those sorts of feelings of uneasiness in those who work with them.

They dwell in a very dark place. I know this from personal experience. Of course face your fear and work with them more than once and you'll find they're very curious and can be quite helpful and wise. I have yet to meet a Daemonic Force I didn't like and I adore the Enochian spirits.

Then there is the question of the Aethyrs and their correspondences. It is up to you which Daemonic forces you wish to work with when exploring the Aethyrs.

So ultimately I do work with Enochian (including Enochian Spirits) depending on the work I'm doing and the energy I wish to utilize during the work. I encourage the magician to incorporate into his pathwork what works for him.

Hermetics & Daemonic Magick

The best reason I can give for any Daemonolatry magician applying principles of Hermetics into Daemonolatry Magick can be found in a little book called The Kybalion. This book illustrates the base Hermetic Principles and the foundation upon which the universe and all magick may, in theory, work. In a lot of ways these ancient ideas about how the universe works are being analyzed now in theories of Quantum Physics and String Theory. That's really all I have to say about this topic and Magick at this moment. There is plenty of information out there about this topic, therefore there is no need for me to really delve into it. If you understand Khemetic/Canaanite Daemonolatry as a religion, you'll understand how a basic understanding of Hermetic principles can help the magician. As above, so below. It's all interconnected.

Qabbalah & Daemonic Magick

Qabbalah is centered around the Tree of Life. A simple blueprint of man's quest to understand the divine both internally and externally. This model contains 10 sephira (11 if you count Da'ath), four worlds, 22 paths, and three pillars. In this section we will discuss, on a very basic level, how Qabbalah works in conjunction with Daemonolatry and consequently, Daemonic magick. Firstly you should know that there is no definitive model of which Daemons fit into which Sephira of the tree. This can vary from person to person based on personal pantheon. Each man's tree is his own. Ultimately, however, a Daemonic force that, for the practitioner, envelops that idea represents the idea behind each Sephira.

The Demonolatry Tree of Life and the Qlippoth

Reprinted with Permission by S. Connolly

The Nine Demonic Divinities are the cornerstone of traditional Demonolatry practice. This article will delve deeper into the symbolism of the nine, and will give you several different perspectives of the symbolism as much of it can depend on the way the individual thinks and how that individual perception helps the individual along his or her personal path work.

The idea of the nine is nothing new. Nine has always been an important number dating back to the ancient Egyptians who were the first to herald nine as the number of foundation and balance. However, they honored ten different deities in their tree of life. In Demonolatry, technically we honor ten as well. The Nine Divinities and the Self.

But before we get to that, let's first go over who the Nine are, what they symbolize, and their elemental breakdowns according to some Daemonolaters.

255

Once again, the following are the **Nine Demonic Divinities**. They are repeated again and again because they are important. Memorize them.

Satan
Lucifer
Flereous
Leviathan
Belial
Verrine
Amducious
Unsere
Eurynomous

Next, we'll again list their purpose, Enn, Rituals, Seasons, and how some Daemonolaters have seen them and corresponded them. That way you don't have to flip around the book to reference them for this section.

- *Satan* - King : _Tasa reme laris Satan - Ave Satanis_ - Direction: Center/All ; Color: All ; Months: All ; Seasons All ; Rituals- Any.; Satan appears as a sage wise man with silver hair and black eyes. His eyes have been described as seeing nothing and seeing all. However their color or features are non-descript.
- *Lucifer* - Air Elemental : _Renich Tasa Uberaca Biasa Icar Lucifer_ - Direction: East; Colors: White Yellow; Month: March; Season: Spring; Ritual: Enlightenment, spring equinox, initiations. Lucifer appears with long, black hair and blue eyes. His voice is considered average though he seems overly excited most of the time. He wears pendants of eagles. Twin to Lucifuge.
- *Flereous* - Fire Elemental : _Ganic Tasa Fubin Flereous_ - Direction: South; Color: Red, Orange;

256

Month: June; Season: Summer; Ritual: Baptism, action, love, solstice. Flereous appears as a tall man with long, red, course hair and red eyes. His voice is low and hissing. His expression is that of placidity.

- **Leviathan** - Water Elemental : *Jaden Tasa Hoet Naca Leviathan* - Direction: West; Colors: Blue, Gray; Month: September; Season: Autumn; Ritual: emotions, initiation, equinox, healing, fertility. Leviathan appears with long black hair and blue/gray eyes so striking it is as if you are staring into the waters of your own soul. His voice is low, his speech reserved. He is also shorter than Lucifer and Flereous, but stands a hair taller than Belial. He wears an amulet of his own sigil.

- **Belial** - Earth Elemental : *Lirach Tasa Vefa Wehlc Belial* - Direction: North; Colors: Green, Brown, Black; Month: December; Season: Winter; Ritual: initiation, new beginnings, winter solstice. Belial appears with hair colored black and white like salt and pepper (some people report his hair to be blonde). His eyes shift from brown to green. His voice comes off as being quite normal, though he speaks with resolute confidence in everything he says. He often seems perplexed or confused by some great mystery. He is not as tall as some of the other elementals.

- **Verrine** - Demon of Health : *Elan Typan Verrine* - Direction: Northwest; Colors: Blue, white; Month: November; Season: Late Autumn; Ritual: healing.

- **Amducious** - The destroyer : *Denyen valocur avage secore Amducious* - Twin to Asmodeous. Direction: Southeast. Colors: Orange; Month: May; Season: Late Spring; Ritual: war, action, dispel old.

- **Unsere** - (Female) Fertility and Sorcery : *Unsere tasa lirach on ca ayar* - Direction: Northeast; Colors: Green and White; Month: February; Season:

Late Winter; Ritual: Wisdom, patience, motherhood.; Unsere has deep green eyes like the fertile plains of Ireland [Adrianna's note - I saw her with blue eyes]. Her hair is brown with strands of spun silver. Her eyes smile and sparkle. Her energy is gentle and nurturing. She travels often in a cowl-hooded cloak. Most memorable are her thin, delicate, pale hands. She dissolves as a mist. She is said to often appear to women during or after childbirth to breath life into infants. [Delaney Grimoire Reference]

- ***Eurynomous*** - Demon of Death : *Ayar Secore on ca Eurynomous* Direction: Northwest. Colors: Black and White; Month: October; Season: Late Autumn; Ritual: New beginnings, death, rebirth, celebration of death, Halloween. Eurynomous appears as a shadow or wraith. Or as a common man with white or translucent hair and pale or white eyes. His energy is calming and cool. He also holds the book of the dead. He often communicates vi baoith raimi Kairtey - or as invisible hands.

From the Purswell Grimoires- Elemental Breakdown of the Nine
Satan: All
Belial/Eurynomous - Earth
Lucifer/Verrine - Air
Flereous/Amducious - Fire
Leviathan/Unsere - Water

From the Purswell Grimoires - Purpose Breakdown of the Nine
Enlightenment: Lucifer/Belial/Satan
Creative: Leviathan/Unsere/Verrine
Destructive: Flereous/Amducious/Eurynomous

These Nine are, indeed, the foundation or balance and can consequently be put into the tree of life (by my perspective) as such:

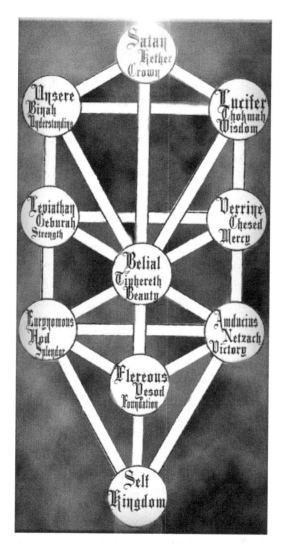

It is important to know that in the Tree of Life, the left pillar is Severity, the middle pillar is Mild (neutral), and the right pillar is that of Mercy.

My thinking behind placing the nine in this manner was thus: Flereous begins as the foundation, that special fire or light that we all come from. He leads to Eurynomous in the splendor of transformation from the actual physical consciousness to the spiritual physical consciousness, which leads to Amducious. Amducious is the physical warrior and the spiritual victory that leads to the perceived mental and emotional beauty that is Belial. Belial is the beauty of the physical and mental. He leads to Leviathan who represents emotional and mental strength and it is in that strength that we find Verrine, who is mercy. Mercy and Verrine in turn lead to Unsere and the feminine understanding. It is in understanding that we discover the masculine wisdom and ultimately a bond with the Divine – Satan.

It is also important to know that instead of considering there are two of each elemental as suggested in one of the listings aforementioned, I took an alchemical look at the Nine Divinities. Four were elemental and four became alchemical.

In my interpretation of the Nine, in regards to the Tree of Life, Flereous, Eurynomous, and Amducious represent the physical consciousness. Belial, Leviathan, and Verrine constitute the mental consciousness. And finally, Unsere, Lucifer, and Satan represent the spiritual consciousness.

10. The Self (Malkuth, Kingdom). We are the physical manifestations of the divine.

9. Flereous (Yesod, Foundation) is the foundation in fire. There would be no life without the sun or the desire for life. It is from fire, which our universe began. Therefore it is the foundation of life and an essential element. Fire also represents the desire. Desire for life, knowledge, and earthly pleasure.

8. Eurynomous (Hod, Splendor) is the splendor, earth transformed air (Dry). There is splendor in transformation and change of consciousness. Change is always severe, hence it's place on the pillar of Severity. Death equals the change from fire as in a mutable rebirth. The Baphometic Fire Baptism is the perfect example of this.

7. Amducious (Netzach, Victory) is air transformed fire (Heat), the victory over the physical emerges transformed victorious. It is the mastery of the physical will and over the limitations of the physical body. While Amducious may seem destructive, force is ruled by will whereas change happens regardless. Therefore just as Amducious can choose to be destructive, there is more power and strength in being able to will oneself toward mercy. Hence the reason Amducious sits on the pillar of Mercy.

6. Belial (Tiphereth, Beauty) is the beauty of Earth. In those things tangible as earth, Belial connects the physical to the mental bringing about an awareness of beauty for all things.

5. Leviathan (Geburah, Strength) is emotional and mental strength through water. In recognition of the physical and mental there is strength. Strength can be seen in the resistance of water. This leads to an emotional maturity necessary to move on to Verrine and mercy.

4. Verrine (Chesed, Mercy) is water-transformed earth (Cold). From emotional stability and maturity comes strength of intuition, which leads to mercy and the recognition of that which needs to be healed. Healing the Self, and others, is merciful to the self and others.

3. Unsere (Binah, Understanding) is fire-transformed water (Vapor/Steam). She leads to an understanding and feminine wisdom of the self and others. She is the connection from the mental to the divine/spiritual. This leads to enlightenment.

2. Lucifer (Chokmah, Wisdom) is air and wisdom. This enlightenment and wisdom is being able to see the whole in conjunction with the sum of its parts in order to reach gnosis.

1. Satan (Kether, Crown) is the source and the divine and consists of all elements and alchemical conjunctions and transmutations. He is the eternal spirit and the Divine.

We all start at 10 and work our way to 1 on our individual paths to spiritual enlightenment. Additionally, I felt this was important:

Physical:
Flereous is neutral and combined of the physical, mental, and spiritual. Eurynomous is feminine spiritual. Amducius is the masculine physical

Mental:
Belial is neutral and combined physical, mental, and spiritual. Leviathan is the feminine physical. Verrine is the masculine spiritual.

Spiritual
Satan is the neutral divine. Unsere is the feminine mental Lucifer is the masculine mental

I tried to further break them down into positive negative, but found that each of these Demons possess both positive and negative aspects.

You may be wondering why I did not include Da'ath. After discussing it over with others, we came to the conclusion that Da'ath had to be Lucifuge Rofocale. See this book's cover to discover Da'ath. He represents the spiritual breath that connects the body to the mind to create the whole of the physical manifestation of the Divine – Our Selves.

- **Lucifage** - High Command (Control) : _Eyen tasa valocur Lucifuge Rofocale_ His twin brother is Lucifer. Lucifuge is often seen as a father figure who gives sound advice and who is firm but often quiet.

But none of this is a new idea. Not by a long shot. People have been working with nine far longer than recorded history.

Many people believe the Tree of Life was a creation from Jewish mysticism. The truth is it goes further back. In the ancient pyramids of Egypt, the following was discovered:

1 - Atem
2 - Shu
3 - Tefnut
4 - Geb
5 - Nut
6 - Osiris
7 - Isis
8 - Set
9 - Nephthys
10 - Horus

Of which we can put into the tree of life as thus:

Notice that Atem is also the source of all, Kether, just as Satan.

It would also be difficult to discuss the Tree of Life without including the Qlippoth. The Qlippoth, also known as the Tree of Death, allegedly shows the opposite the Arch Angels. This is a very Christian viewpoint. Daemonolaters do not believe in black or white or good or evil. Therefore, this particular tree, as seen by many of us, is merely a difference in hierarchy (and aspect) and nothing more.

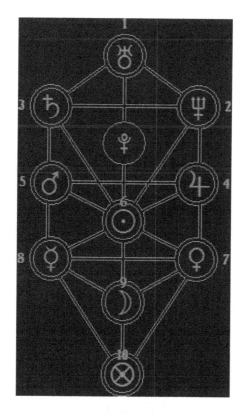

THE SPHERES

1. URANUS

2. NEPTUNE

3. SATURN

4. JUPITER

5. MARS

6. SUN

7. VENUS

8. MERCURY

9. MOON

10. EDEN

DAATH - PLUTO

THE QLIPHOTH
ARCH-DEMONS
1. SATAN (LUCIFER) & MOLOCH
2. BEELZEBUB
3. LUCIFUGE ROFACALE
4. ASTAROTH
5. ASMODEUS
6. BELPHEGOR
7. BAEL
8. ADRAMELECH
9. LILITH
10. NAHEMA
CHARON?

Please Note: This article first appeared in the Summer 2006 issue of Black Serpent and again in *The Complete Book of Demonolatry* and has been included in this book because it was worthy of inclusion as further exploration of the Nine Demonic Divinities and the magician's exploration of Qabbalah.

Qlippoth (Tree of Death):
Because most Khemetic/Canaanite (i.e. Traditional) Daemonolaters don't really put things in neat little black and white boxes, we do not have a Qlippoth model. Instead - we acknowledge that the road to creation is the same as the road to destruction - just different degrees of the same. We acknowledge that the Daemonic forces we place in the Sephira can easily switch sides and become their opposite as Zagam/Zagan teaches us. For some Daemonolaters, they will use a Qlippoth model with different Daemonic names that is separate from their Tree of Life model in order to work with more destructive forces. Some magicians still need that separation in order to focus more clearly. You should feel free to do the same. Each magician's Tree is his own. For Luciferian Qlippoth, check out the work of Michael Ford. He does a good job delving into Qlippoth quite extensively.

Da'ath
The ultimate path of the Knowledge is through Da'ath. This is the great abyss the magician must traverse to know the true self and to manifest his own true will.

Basically – Da'ath is the sephira that connects the mental in ascension to the spiritual. So if you look at the tree of life, your bottom tier is the physical world. Your middle tier is the mental world, and the top is the spiritual world. All the paths connect these three worlds together. Da'ath is on the path where you ascend or connect directly from the mental to the highest Godform or deity (or even universal consciousness) without having to die or pass into the spiritual to get there. It's Da'ath that is often seen as the magician's biggest obstacle because some believe that you have to cross it if you are ever going to be able to connect to Kether directly while still in the physical body. Some magicians call it the VOID, it's also known as The Great Abyss because it requires the magician to somehow overcome and ascend above the trappings and baggage that the physical world inflicts on physical beings (which is ultimately the goal of most magicians). In a nutshell - in Da'ath is everything that holds you (the physical being) back from merging with Kether (the Divine source).

The Four Worlds & Daemonolatry

Azilut is the Divine world - this is where the source energy comes from. All things come from Azilut. Then you have Beriah - which is the beginning of the process of creation (the "idea" -- the universe is mental after all). It's considered the first separation of the divine. So anything that comes from the source, technically is Beriah. Many Daemonic magicians view Daemons as residing here whereas Satan/Atem/Akasha/Ba'al/El resides in Azilut. Yetzirah is the initial formation of the physical. In Qabbalah - this is basically where our souls come in. So the human soul (or physical life energy source) is Yetzirah, it is the energy field that shapes us. And finally - you have the physical world -- the energy transforming from an idea and taking shape as the souls -and finally the physical Asiyyah -- where matter comes together to create the physical world.

So in a magickal model - you start with raw energy (Azilut) - you have an idea of what you want it to be (Beriah) - you gather that energy together via ritual (Yetzirah) - and it creates a physical manifested change according to your will (Asiyyah).

Some food for thought: A top down study of the Tree of Life is about the process of Magick. A study of the tree from the bottom up is a study of the spiritual evolution of man and his connection to the divine.

The 22 Paths and Daemonic Correspondences for Each:

Aleph - Ra or Satan
Beth - Delepitore or Isis or Thoth
Gimel - Rashoon and Astarte
Daleth – Rosier
Heh - Atem or El or Ba'al
Vav - Satanchia or Osiris
Zain - Azlyn or Ashtaroth
Cheth - Lucifuge Rofocale
Teth - Belial
Yod- Isis or Delepitore
Kaph - Ra or Satan
Lamed - Sonnellion or Leviathan
Mem - Leviathan
Nun - Hecate, Eurynomous, Baalberith, Baba'al or Azlyn
Samekh - Kasdeya or Zagam
Ayin - Wadjet or Ra
Peh – Amducius
Tzaddi - Azlyn or Ashtaroth
Qoph - Asaphoetida or Ashtaroth
Resh - Belphegore
Shin - Asmoday
Tau -- Tezrian or Sonnellion.

Working the Tree:

Working the Tree is a phrase I often use to describe how the magician contemplates the tree, his spiritual evolution, and how knowing himself helps him to manifest his own will. This means a few things. First - that the magician worth his salt must eventually evolve past the "I want stuff" phase of magickal practice (low magick) and into the "I want to understand myself and the universe and how to get what I want from that understanding" (high magick).

So in order to work the tree we all start at Malkuth and work our way up. It is when we reach Da'ath that a magician can either be destroyed or redeemed by himself. Some people must deconstruct in Da'ath because the knowledge is too much. It is not for the self-conscious, self-loathing, or the ego driven, or those in denial of truth. Some believe that Da'ath is a force that one must not swim against, but rather allow the current to take us where we need to go. Swimming against the tides of Da'ath only makes one sink faster. The ultimate goal for the magician is a spiritual evolvement to commune with, and come to know, Kether. The Source of all that is. The Alpha & the Omega. The Beginning, The End. The All is One. Of course we must still travel through Binah (understanding) and Chokmah (wisdom) to get there.

Some magicians will tell you that Qabbalah amounts to nothing more than mental masturbation (I've heard this phrase a lot on the Internet these days when Qabbalah comes up). I suppose this depends on whether you actually find a way to practically apply it to your everyday life, or if you simply sit around lamenting about it. So I must respectfully disagree. It's only mental masturbation if you're an armchair theorist and do nothing in attempt to apply what you've learned.

Timing & Magick
By Valerie Corban & S. Connolly

Timing in magick can be important for even further focusing on your desired outcome. The following chapter will teach you how to find the right corresponding times to perform magick. Some magick will be done on days of importance to you so that it holds that much more power. See the moon phases information in the Astrology chapter for more information about planetary and moon phase correspondences.

To use the planetary charts on the next page you need to know what time sunset and sunrise will happen (keep a Farmer's Almanac for this). Divide the hours in between by 12, and you will come up with the times for the daylight hours. You repeat for the nighttime hours and will come up with the planetary hours. Only rarely do these hours equal 60 minutes, because during the summer the days are longer (i.e. the hours of light are longer), and during the winter the days are shorter (meaning the hours of darkness outweigh the hours of light). Use the following tables to determine the planet that rules each hour of the days of the week.

You would essentially time your magick to correspond with a planet whose influence you seek.

Planetary Hours Sunrise

Hour	Sunday	Monday	Tuesday	Wednesday	Thursday	Friday	Saturday
1	Sun	Moon	Mars	Mercury	Jupiter	Venus	Saturn
2	Venus	Saturn	Sun	Moon	Mars	Mercury	Jupiter
3	Mercury	Jupiter	Venus	Saturn	Sun	Moon	Mars
4	Moon	Mars	Mercury	Jupiter	Venus	Saturn	Sun
5	Saturn	Sun	Moon	Mars	Mercury	Jupiter	Venus
6	Jupiter	Venus	Saturn	Sun	Moon	Mars	Mercury
7	Mars	Mercury	Jupiter	Venus	Saturn	Sun	Moon
8	Sun	Moon	Mars	Mercury	Jupiter	Venus	Saturn
9	Venus	Saturn	Sun	Moon	Mars	Mercury	Jupiter
10	Mercury	Jupiter	Venus	Saturn	Sun	Moon	Mars
11	Moon	Mars	Mercury	Jupiter	Venus	Saturn	Sun
12	Saturn	Sun	Moon	Mars	Mercury	Jupiter	Venus

Planetary Hours Sunset

Hour	Sunday	Monday	Tuesday	Wednesday	Thursday	Friday	Saturday
1	Jupiter	Venus	Saturn	Sun	Moon	Mars	Mercury
2	Mars	Mercury	Jupiter	Venus	Saturn	Sun	Moon
3	Sun	Moon	Mars	Mercury	Jupiter	Venus	Saturn
4	Venus	Saturn	Sun	Moon	Mars	Mercury	Jupiter
5	Mercury	Jupiter	Venus	Saturn	Sun	Moon	Mars
6	Moon	Mars	Mercury	Jupiter	Venus	Saturn	Sun
7	Saturn	Sun	Moon	Mars	Mercury	Jupiter	Venus
8	Jupiter	Venus	Saturn	Sun	Moon	Mars	Mercury
9	Mars	Mercury	Jupiter	Venus	Saturn	Sun	Moon
10	Sun	Moon	Mars	Mercury	Jupiter	Venus	Saturn
11	Venus	Saturn	Sun	Moon	Mars	Mercury	Jupiter
12	Mercury	Jupiter	Venus	Saturn	Sun	Moon	Mars

Magickal Meanings of Days:

Monday is ruled by the **Moon**. Its colors are shades of white, silver, and gray. Monday is a good time to perform magickal workings for protection, divination, dream-work, and to discover that which is hidden. Female magick associated with the moon can also be done on Mondays. Asafoetida and Azlyn are Daemons associated with Monday.

Tuesday is ruled by **Mars**. Its colors are shades of red and orange, the colors of fire. Perform execration magicks, magick for courage and strength, and even magick for learning on a Tuesday. You may also consider defensive magicks here. Amducius, Ronove, and Lucifuge Rofocal are associated with Tuesdays.

Wednesday is ruled by **Mercury**. Wednesday is male energy ruled by the planet of communications, Mercury. Wednesday's colors are yellows, grays, violets, and opalescent colors. Wednesday has the energies of mental clarity, communications, writing, strategy, divination, young people, knowledge, business negotiations, teaching, addictions, reason, debt, fear, loss, self-improvement and healings. This day is also good for groups and travel. Lucifer and Ronwe are examples of Daemons that rule Wednesday.

Thursday is ruled by **Jupiter**. Thursday is male energy ruled by Jupiter, the planet of abundance and luck. The colors are royal purple and royal blue. This day has the energies of luck, growth, expansion, generosity, male fertility, older men, masculine side of the female, legal matters, health, honor, wealth, clothing, desires, men's professions and spiritual attainment. Belphegore, Verrine, and Belial are Daemons ruled by Thursday.

Friday is ruled by **Venus**. Friday is female energy ruled by Venus the planet of love. Its colors are pink, aqua, greens and pastels. Friday has the energies of love and pleasure, peace, romance, marriage, attraction, friendships, gentleness, ease, partnerships, art, music, sexual matters, affairs of the heart, physical beauty, scents and perfumes, social activities, women's problems, protection and affairs. Rosier, Astarot, and Asmodeus are ruled by Friday.

Saturday is ruled by **Saturn**. Saturday is female energy ruled by Saturn the energy of discipline and structure. Its colors are blacks, dark purples, dark gray, and indigo. Saturday has the energies of obstacles to overcome a block, spirit communication, meditation, life, freedom, self-discipline, protection, but also limitations to give or break energies, locating lost items and people, the elderly, endings, death, the destroying of disease and pests, constricting and those constricting you, psychic defense, and cursing. Eurynomous, Baalberith, and Tezrian are examples of Daemons ruled by Saturday.

Sunday is ruled by **the Sun**. Sunday is male energy ruled by the Sun, its colors are Oranges, yellows, gold, white and this day has the energies of health, leadership, healing, prosperity, self-knowledge, happiness, ego, hope, joy, strength, individuality, authority figures, fathers, husbands, protection, power and spirituality, promotions, power and fortune. Satan, Delepitorae, Thoth, Leviathan all rule (or are ruled, depending on perspective) Sunday.

Magickal Development & Energy Work

by Selinda Dukante, Darrek Mallory, & S. Connolly

Energy work is not just about building and releasing energy, but also understanding how it feels physically, mentally, and emotionally. Also how it looks. This chapter will discuss building energy, focusing the energy, manipulating the energy and sending it. This discussion will also cover thought forms and servitors – or energy beings of the magician's creation.

One of the first exercises I'd like to discuss is being able to see the body's energy signatures. Certainly there are forms of photography that can capture the body's energy fields, but I think it is prudent most magicians attempt to learn to see this energy that is invisible to the untrained naked eye. The exercise we often give our students is to place their naked arm against black background (wear black as to not distract yourself). Then, look at the arm until you can see your aura. Most of our auras will change color based on our emotion at the time, however they do have a prominent color that the aura will return to during periods of rest and neutral emotion. A magician can perform this exercise as often as (s)he wishes. With practice it becomes easier. If you can get volunteers, see if they'll sit long enough to have you investigate their auras. I realize this sounds very new age or even silly, but the trained eye can see molecules floating in the air, bumping into each other, and ebbing and flowing with the air in a room.

The next exercise is to train you to the vibration of an object. All things, living and not, have a vibration to them. Pick five objects from around your house. One made of plastic, one of wood, one of paper, one of metal, and something of cloth. Feel each item and write down how its energy feels. Feel the energy of living things. A lover, a pet, a child. How do these things differ? Learn how to feel energy, getting a sense of its vibration.

Finally, you need to learn what energy sounds like. Turn off all the electrical in your house. Listen. Chances are you will still be able to hear the whir of the wires running through your house. Next, go to a secluded spot in nature and sit and listen. Chances are you will hear a different energy. Maybe animal or insect noises (which have an energy all their own). Note your observations and the differences you discover.

Knowing the nature of energy is important if we're going to learn how to raise it, focus it, and send it. Continue these experiments until you feel you have a strong grasp of how to see, feel, and hear the energy signature of the plethora of things we share our world with.

Raising Energy

There are many methods to raise energy. You are going to learn several of them in this chapter. The first is to chant or vibrate a sound or an invocation. Let's practice with a simple Enn. *Ganic Tasa Fubin Flereous.*

Repeat this Enn over and over again, feeling the sounds and vibration as the words move through you. Change the tone and pitch of your voice until you find a combination that produces the most energy for you. Continue chanting this Enn, perhaps while imagining a flame rising higher and higher within you. Record your results in your journal. Experiment with vibrating and chanting various Enns and sounds, noting your observations on the energy raised.

In this next exercise, sit in lotus, half-lotus or cross-legged on the ground. Solid ground or actual earth is best, but if the best you have is the living room floor in your second story apartment, so be it. Rub your palms together vigorously. Then, place your palms together imagining a ball of energy forming there. Feel it take form. It gets larger and larger. Now try to press your hands together. If you've done it properly, you will fell resistance and your hands will move away from each other like magnets sometimes will. It will feel just like this. Keep trying until you achieve the end result. Practicing this exercise is an exercise in building energy.

For advanced students, perform this latter exercise outdoors at night in a dark place where you have a piece of metal or a metal fence close by. Once you finish building your energy ball, throw it at the metal fence or object and see if anything happens. Keep trying. If you're getting sparks you're doing it properly. This is very advanced energy work. I only know a few people who have been able to do this successfully, myself (Selinda) included.

For the next exercise, stand with your legs apart and your arms outstretched to your sides. Your right palm should face up, your left palm should face down (you can alternate sides). Imagine energy flowing around your body, in through the right hand from the ground, over your head, through the left hand, and down into the ground and back around again. Concentrate on feeling the energy. You should feel the flow through your palms.

To ground yourself, press your palms into the earth firmly and 'shove out' any excess energy.

All of these exercises are the foundation for learning to build energy. Practice them until you feel you can raise a sufficient amount of energy.

Focusing Energy

Now that you can effectively build energy it's time to learn how to focus it. Use the following exercise to help you learn focus.

Sit in front of a candle flame. Breathe lightly if possible. Place your hands on either side of the flame, far enough to not get burnt obviously. Building energy between your hands, manipulate it just enough to make the candle flame bend to your will. Make the flame taller by using the energy to compress the flame and stretch it out. Make it shorter and flatter by making the energy you're building between your hands squash the flame down. For a more difficult exercise, try changing the color of the candle flame at will. Yes, it can be done, yet I've only seen a select few people accomplish this. Keep trying. Each attempt at focus hones your skill.

For most ritual work it is by this method that you will infuse objects with the energy of your magickal intent. Practice it until you feel comfortable and confident enough in your focusing skills.

Sending Energy

Sending energy is as much a visualization as it is the physical act of sending the energy you've built up to another place. The first thing you ought to know is exactly where you want to send the energy. Remember the exercise where you build the energy ball and you throw it at the metal object? It's not just the act of throwing, but also the feeling of throwing, and the visualization of throwing the energy. It all works together to create the desired effect, which is sending the energy.

I only know of one way to practice this before putting it to actual use. Put an item at the opposite end of the room. Make sure the object has no strong vibrations or 'feelings' attached to it. Sit across the room, build between your palms a strong, vibrant, happy pink energy. Imagine that energy leaving your hands and going to the item across the room (your energy's destination). Do this until you feel you can no longer do it. Now – leave the room for a few hours. Come back, and feel the object. Does it still feel neutral and unremarkable? Or is the energy vibrant, strong, happy and exuding from the object? If it's the latter, you've done well. If not, try again. You'll eventually get it.

Practice this until you feel you can adequately send energy to its source.

By the way, these are wonderful exercises to do with friends interested in metaphysics, other occultists, and groups. Magician's party games as it were. Or at least that's how we've used them. Everyone learns something and hones their skills and we have fun doing it.

Thought Forms and Servitors

Thought forms and servitors require a lot of energy and time. One of the easiest ways to create a thought form is by orgasm (see chapter on Sex Magick for more) because it creates a strong burst of initial raw energy that can be formed into whatever the magician wishes. However, there may be some reason this is not possible. In instances like that, it's perfectly okay to start with a small ball of energy between the palms on the altar. You may choose to keep the thought form bound in a pillar to begin with as this will allow you to give it constant feeding (even if it's just a trickle) at first. Otherwise, you will have to attend to your new thought form every night for the first month to give it a strong start (i.e. before you start sending it out to do your bidding). I've known magicians who say and believe they can create a thought form in a single ritual. While you can provided you raise enough energy, if you want one with staying power and brawn, you need to give them a month to really form. This will also negate the need for constant feedings or constant needs to create new ones.

Unless that's what you want, of course. If you want a weaker thought form/servitor that will dissipate, you don't need to spend a month on it. A simple thought form created with a few days of feeding will be sufficient for spying, sending messages, or carrying energy short distances. For thought form/ servitors that will serve as protectors, familiars, lovers, long distance messengers or spies – one month is the minimum so it doesn't dissipate half way through its mission. Protective servitors need to be fed regularly with acknowledgement and energy transference. Keep this in mind if you are creating thought forms or servitors for these kinds of purposes.

Charging Amulets and Talismans

Charging Amulets and Talismans can be as simple as holding an item between the palms and infusing the appropriate energies into them, or you can create a pillar ritual, which is simpler, but stronger. Pillar rites are rituals (of various construction) wherein you make pillars of energy within which the object to be charged is encased. The easiest method for this is to place 5 candles in a circle on the altar, and place the object inside the circle. The candles are lit and the circle of candles acts as the perimeter of the pillar of energy. Visualizing a pillar of light and fast moving energy that extends from the ground to the sky creates the pillar. Usually pillar rites are done for several days up to a month at a time to properly infuse items with the required energies. Charging amulets can be done in conjunction with any offering or religious rituals as well as during an actual magickal work. You just need to have the space to do both.

Execration Magick - Cursing
by S. Connolly

Those who know me know that I have a fondness for execration magicks. That is - cursing rituals. Erroneously, my love for the dark arts has given some people the impression that I spend all my free time in a blackened ritual chamber sticking pins into poppets, and continually lighting black and red candles with my victims names engraved in them.

Truthfully I am familiar with curses. I have both cursed others and been cursed by magician ex-friends. However -- for as much as I know about the subject, and the fondness I have for execration magicks, you'd probably be surprised to learn that I use curses quite sparingly. In my youth I may not have bided the courtesies and have allowed my emotions spur an unwarranted curse or two. But nowadays I'll simply bind people or send their own negativity back at them. Such methods are much less energy draining, and far less time consuming than performing curses, which take a great deal of anger and energy to perform. I save curses for those persons and situations where my loved ones or myself have truly been screwed-over or injured. In most instances, persons who deserve to be cursed curse themselves by default so I choose not to waste my

283

time if the person in question will curse himself or herself.

Cursing can help a magician heal after a particularly bad relationship/friendship, or after a traumatic event. The psychodrama can help us come closer to letting go of the past. You can use curses to curse the situation or the feelings you have toward the situation or person rather than directing it at a person. So there are many uses for the curse. It's not just a means to hurt another person.

Some of what I am sharing in this book will shock and possibly even anger the non-aggressive peace loving magicians reading this. For those who share my interest in curses, or for those who have an enemy that needs to be taught a lesson -- this section is for you. You will find rituals and techniques in here that are rarely put into print (if at all).

For those of you who are shaking your heads saying "Tsk, tsk..." or "How immature to include curses and methods for destroying others", just know that understanding how the darker aspects of magick work and by inclusion of such methods here also helps the magician learn how to deal with such things when and if they ever run across them.

This means - in studying curses, you also learn how to break them and repel them. There is no black and white, only shades of gray. Sure - including curses may encourage bad behavior on the part of the magician, but it's been my experience that those who want to curse will find the information at any cost and will use the information regardless. Not to mention many young magicians go through a curse happy phase. No magick book would be complete without the discussion of execration magicks.

284

This section will merely help those new to magick get it out of their system faster and will give the curious (and terrified) a good hard look at what can be accomplished with Execration Magicks. You can also take the techniques for execration and use them for more positive works (including healing and protection). So consider that while reading this section.

"Humans are fickle by their very nature and have the habit of turning on one another. The wise magician keeps taglocks from friends and lovers lest they are later betrayed." - G. Purswell

So now let's discuss ethics. Some of you will say that anyone who chooses to curse someone else must have no ethics whatsoever. I use a test to decide if I should curse someone. First I ask -- did the person emotionally or physically hurt another person (enough worthy for a curse?). Second -- is the victim a rapist, murderer, or stalker? Third -- Will the victim curse him/herself? Fourth -- Will the victim continue hurting you and your loved ones if allowed to continue? Consider the answers to these questions to help you decide if this is the correct course of action - then you wait three days (72 hours). See if the anger is still there and if you've changed your mind. If you have not changed your mind and you're still terribly upset - plan the curse and perform it.

Most curses take a great deal of energy and time to perform, so it is doubtful that they will be something you'll use often.

Also consider the courtesies. The one in particular that tells you not to use magick against other magicians. Why? Because then you usually end up in a cursing war that no one wins.

It's a waste of time, energy and resources. So if you're going to curse another magician, take into consideration what you're getting yourself into and make sure it's warranted.

How to Know if You've Been Cursed

Many younger magicians will assume they're being cursed at the slightest run of bad luck or life obstacles. The first question you need to ask yourself is, do you know any other magicians? If yes – have you pissed any of them off lately? If yes, you could have been cursed.

If no, consider you're just having a run of bad luck. It happens to all of us. Not every day or spot in life is going to be effortless and go your way. We're all going to get sick, have loved ones die, have financial problems, lose a job, break up with a boyfriend/girlfriend at some point in our lives etc. But usually a real curse is evident.

Some signs you may have been cursed –

- Someone tells you you've been cursed. The act of telling someone they've been cursed is a curse by itself. Self-fulfilled prophecy.
- You have a dream of the sigils of Focalor and Valefor, or any other destruction, death, cursing Daemon for no reason whatsoever (i.e. you weren't working with those particular Daemons). Or you have a dream of a Daemon chasing you. These are usually warnings from the Daemons. See, the thing is that Daemons don't always pick a side. But they may choose to warn you instead of help the other person curse you. I've received several such warnings when other Daemonolaters chose to attempt to curse me.

- You've had a falling out with a magician friend and you know that friend (ex-friend) is vengeful and has no reservations cursing you.
- You find burnt remains of paper and wax on your property (or coffin nails or jars of piss and burnt offerings) and you know you didn't put it there.
- You find sigils of cursing Daemons (or incantations in foreign languages or magickal languages) hidden on your personal property (including inside, behind, or under furniture, on your car, or on the outside of your house).
- You are at odds with another magician and suddenly your house feels heavy, black, foreboding, not right, and things out of the ordinary start happening (fighting more with spouse even though there aren't money or marital problems etc...)
- You are given an item with strange markings and upon researching those markings you learn the marks are used to curse.

The reality often is that if you hang out with other magicians and there's a fight, personality conflict, jealousy, or secret dislike of one another – there is a distinct possibility that there are going to be curses thrown around. It's human nature. Your best defense is to be aware (not paranoid) and be prepared.

How to Break a Curse

How you break a curse depends a lot on the type of curse it actually is. It's a lot easier to break a curse if you have physical evidence of it. This usually means you've found the remnants of a curse on your property or you've been given a cursed object, or someone has put a cursing sigil under your dining room table when you weren't looking (don't think I'm being paranoid – this happened to someone I know).

Curse Breaker

For physical symbols – the easiest way to break the curse is to use the Oleum of your Patron/Matron (with your blood added) and draw his/her sigil over the curse symbol. This will make the symbol your own and should destroy the curse. So for example, you find the cursed symbol under the dining room table – you use your blood oleum of your Matron/Patron to draw their sigil over it, done.

To Render a Curse Harmless

For remnants of a curse – light a red candle for the curse's sender, let it burn down, write a request to nullify the curse in the name of one of the death or destruction Daemons, seal with your blood, burn it, add it and the wax remnants from the burnt candle to the remnants of the curse you found and bury it all. For curse jars – simply break them and pour blessed (by Belial and Leviathan or other Earth and Water Daemons) water over them. For coffin nails – anoint them with a Daemonic oleum of your patron (with your blood added) – then bend them with a hammer and throw them into a river or lake.

To Un-Curse an Object

For cursed objects you can either destroy them, or make them your own by cleaning them and re-charging them as wards against the person who gave the object to you. The latter is desirable if the object is particularly expensive or pretty and you'd like to keep it. No sense wasting a perfectly good handbag or mantel clock.

For suspected curses (but no evidence) the best method is to perform a dispel negativity ritual to send the negativity back upon whoever sent it.

A good rule of thumb, as a magician who (in her younger years at least) used devious methods to curse others and who has been cursed (I probably deserved it), is when you have a permanent, bridge burning falling out with another magician – take everything (s)he ever gave you and either cleanse it and make it your own, destroy it, or remove it from your home. Or – when it's initially given to you – make it your own immediately just in case it's a bonded object (unless you've taken a vow to keep the bonded object as in initiation to a group). See the section about bonded objects to learn more.

Warding

Wards are protections you, the magician, put in place to keep unwanted visitors (both physical and otherworldly) and influences from penetrating certain boundaries you create. For the natural medium, establishing wards is helpful if you want to avoid spirits from entering your home or ritual space without your consent. For everyone, wards are helpful in protecting a home from unwanted visitors (of the human variety), thieves, and external negativity or harmful astral funk (i.e. curses or astral funk). Establishing wards can be as simple as performing a purification and then inscribing (in any form – whether by paintings, oleum anointed sigils, wood carvings, or other) protective warding sigils (or even Daemonic sigils, usually of a Patron/Matron or Daemon invoked for Banishing or Warding) on each door and window and wall of the house/space.

Another (more time consuming and energy consuming) method is to create a protective Servitor or Thought Form to protect you or your space. See the section about creating thought forms and servitors for more information.

Establishing Wards Within Your Home or Personal Space

I start by cleansing the space. See the cleansing/purification ritual.

Then, I take the oleum of the Daemonic force invoked and anoint each door, window, and wall with a warding sigil. Some people choose to make the warding sigils more permanent by incorporating them into wall hangings in the form of woodcarving or paintings. In this case, re-establishing the wards would include anointing these permanent warding sigils. You might build into permanent wards a spot where you can place the oleum for reinforcement. An example might be – you create a painting of a warding sigil, but leave one spot of the canvas bare where you will touch the oil to. Or the woodcarving will withstand being anointed with the oil. Etc… Think this through when considering permanent wards as you want them to last. As you are anointing, imagine your ward bright, red (or any color of your choosing – I prefer blue or gray), and glowing – grow outward, forming an invisible wall between that space and the outside world (both physical and astral). Do this once a month to keep your wards strong.

Establishing Wards Upon Yourself

I begin with the Self Purification ritual.

Then, I anoint myself with the oleum of the Daemonic force invoked. I may paint a warding sigil upon my own chest or create an amulet I wear (see charging amulets and talismans for more information) and frequently anoint to reinforce the ward. While doing this – imagine a strong invisible barrier around you.

Daemonolatry Warding Symbols

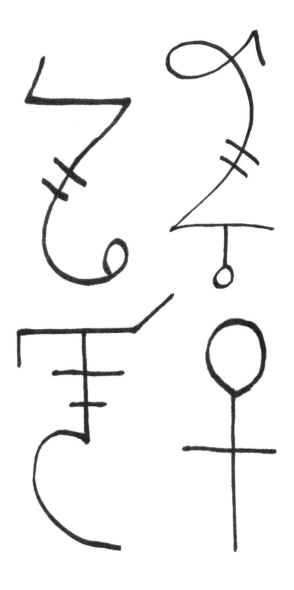

Psychic Self Defense

Aside from creating wards upon yourself or protective servitors, it's always a good exercise for the magician to know how to deflect negative energy or entities at will. A very common meditation for this is to imagine yourself surrounded by mirrors that face outward. Imagine the negative energy or force coming in toward you and bouncing off the mirrors away from you. Once you become adept at this simple visualization, you can add a spin to that and imagine that when the unwanted influence hits the mirror it is catapulted, with sheer force, far away from you at incredible speeds. Once adept at this visualization it can be summoned at any time, with speed, agility, and grace allowing you to deflect anything at a moments notice no matter where you are. **Note:** This is one of those magickal operations where being well versed in astral magick is beneficial.

The following method of psychic self-defense is more practical and can be used against physical persons. It involves using your empathy (ability to feel out a situation emotionally) and understanding people and what motivates them (intellectual). It's prudent to understand that people will often attack others when they feel afraid, threatened, jealous, or their own emotional needs are not being met. Once you realize this, dealing with difficult people can be a bit easier. The boss who yells at you could be terrified of losing his job or may feel inadequate. An overbearing co-worker may be being pushed around at home so over-exerts his/her authority at work to compensate. Someone who feels unappreciated or underappreciated may just need a pat on the back every now and again. By using the powers of observation you can see what the underlying cause of the negativity is and which approach to take with different people with regard to your interaction with them. The general rule here is don't immediately REACT to the negative outburst (thus adding your own negativity to the mix). Instead – observe and feel out the situation first, then make an educated decision on how to react. This, combined with deflecting visualizations, will help you avoid taking psychic and emotional hits from other people. See the section on Psychic Vampirism for more.

If standard deflection techniques including controlling your reactions and visualizations are not working – you may need to do a ritual to dispel negativity.

Rite to Dispel Negativity and Send Negativity Back To Its Source

To perform this ritual you can use simple candle magick (within a ritual construct or not). Invoking the Daemons Amducius, Asmoday, Lucifuge or Satanchia will help you find wisdom in the situation, dispel negativity, and/or deflect other people's negativity back at them. You need a black candle, a personal item or taglock from the other person, some of your own blood, and a ritual knife.

Invoke the Daemons of your choice. Carve the name of your attacker on the black candle. Visualize your wards or deflection. Anoint the candle with the oleum of your chosen Daemon. Light it. Write down exactly what you want on a piece of paper or parchment. Seal it with a drop of your blood. Burn it. Add the taglocks or personal items of your attacker into the offering bowl. Let the candle burn down. Add the remnant wax to the offering bowl. Now you can do one of several things. You can bury the remains of the ritual. You can put it in a sachet and keep it in a clay pot (see offering/request pots for more information) for later disposal. Or you can take these remains and leave them on or near your attacker's personal property. It is said that as the candle burns the negativity will dissipate and be sent directly back to your attacker. I've used this ritual successfully against other magicians, causing their magick to either fizzle or return to them.

Defending Yourself on the Astral Plane or in Dreams

On rare occasion I have had the pleasure of other magicians attempting to attack me astrally or in dreams. Both of these are fabulous methods to terrorize a victim, by the way. However, to protect yourself from these types of attacks you should do several things. First – if you have a public astral temple (one where you might meet others for astral work – even friends) make sure you also have a private sanctuary there that no one else is privy to. This ensures you have a private place to do work. Once you have had a falling out with another magician – it is best to deconstruct and rebuild public astral temples so that it is no longer known to them. Most magicians tend to keep their astral temples private.

If you frequently meet others astrally be careful of creating bonded symbols or keys in the astral that are exclusive to you, but that others know about. Basically - if you use keys – keep them to yourself. If you create a public key (one that others know about) – destroy it when you have a falling out with another magician and create a different one. Basically – the key is something you would visualize to find someone else astrally. It is a link between you if the other person knows it. I have seen people use these against others when a falling out occurs. I have used them against others.

The good thing about Astral attacks is if you're well versed in working astrally – you will be able to summon weapons and defenses to destroy unwanted intrusions into your astral temple without too much trouble.

Dream attacks are a different animal. It requires a magician adept at Dream Walking to attack someone else in a dream. I have never personally attacked someone in a dream and I'm still cultivating necessary skills for successful dream work. However – I have been attacked in a dream. The best method for defending yourself against dream attacks is to learn lucid dreaming. That is – where you become aware you are dreaming and take control of the dream. This means that when you are attacked – you turn on your attacker, summon defenses and attack back. This will usually scare off a dream attacker.

Attacking Others Astrally and In Dreams

It really helps if you know the victim's personal keys. Finding players (people who don't mind talking crap about their friends to other friends who don't necessarily like the other person – be wary of these people, but use them if necessary) they work with astrally and pumping them for information is a possible method by which to gain access, or it could get you in trouble. You can always verify the information you've been given with a Daemonic divination session before using it. Of course the other option is to either seek the person out via their astral self, or seek Daemonic wisdom to help you find them. Once you find the person, become what they fear the most and attack or chase them. It sounds simpler than it is, certainly. However, it's one method by which to put enemies in their place. You may choose to create a sigil specifically for astral traveling to find enemies (Leviathan is good at finding lost things) and placing it beneath your mattress.

However, it is quite probable the person you wish to terrorize isn't someone who travels astrally, but instead is just some person who has wronged you. In this instance, invading their dreams is the alternative. Performing a Dream Ritual of Intent just before bed is going to give you the results you want.

First, you'll want to perform the ritual in your bedroom. Invoke Daemonic forces you wish to employ during the work. For example, you might invoke Azlyn for a stronger dream experience coupled with Amducius to create the calamity you want. Then, focus specifically on what you want to happen in the dream. Put the sigils of your invoked Daemons beneath your pillow or mattress, use a lavender salve on your temples to promote sleep, and use tiger balm on the third eye. Fall asleep focusing on your victim's face and what you intend on doing to them when you catch them. If you're strong enough and if focused on correctly, you will confront these people in your dreams and you can terrorize them to your hearts content. When you wake, you will remember the dream. If you wish to remember it, make notes in a journal about the experience. Then, wait and listen to see if you catch word of how your enemy is sleeping.

Creating Cursed Objects

I've found this works excellent for annoying co-workers, or people I don't particularly like. The object can be anything. I've found metal to not work that well. A porous material works better. Something made out of wood or clay, plastic, or glass works better. Metal attracts too much sludge, and yet nasty energy is easily cleansed from it, too. So choose clocks, mugs, or even key-chains or calendars. A vase of flowers even. Something you can be reasonably certain won't be thrown away or given away is best. Obviously you want the recipient to keep the cursed object or it has no purpose.

(Please note that you can create blessed, healing, or good luck objects the same way. You would just incorporate different Daemons and infuse it with a different purpose.)

Creating a cursed object works much the same way as charging an item with a particular purpose. You can make it more potent by using a pillar rite and charging the object for no less than one month (almost the same process as creating a thought form). Begin charging and finish charging the item during the dark moon.

Clearly you'll want to start by preparing your ritual space and creating your Daemonic circle or ritual construct. I've found a Hexagram construct works well due to the Hexagram altar configuration. You'll want to invoke Tezrian, Amducius, Valefor, Focalor, Eurynomous, and Agaliarept (or six vengeance Daemons of your choice).

First – you need the object. You'll want to make sure that the person you're giving it to will keep it. So choose the item carefully.

You will need a taglock or personal item of the person you want to give it to (if available). A picture of the person will help, too. Nowadays, with everyone's lives so public on the internet, this shouldn't be an issue if you have nefarious intentions. That little statement really makes you consider what you put on the Internet – doesn't it? It should.

Next – you want to create a hexagram with six red candles and white string. Follow the picture below to make sure you tie your string to your candles right. Start by tying the string to the top candle, running it down around the one on the lower right, then over to the one on the lower left, then back up to the top candle (tying off). Then repeat starting at the bottom to create the second triangle.

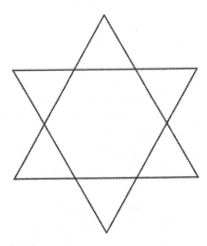

In the center of the hexagram (where there is an open spot), place a piece of parchment with the sigils of all the Daemons invoked on it along with a drop of your blood. On top of that place the taglock or personal item, item, and picture of the person. Imagine the entire set up becoming a pillar of hatred. This must be repeated nightly from dark moon to dark moon in order for the curse to infuse with the item properly. Give the item to the person.

Particularly wicked magicians may create numerous cursed objects (with no intended recipient – just vessels of all their anger and hatred) and send them out into the world just for the kick. Other magicians I've known have infused into objects curses that are kept until needed. They'll sit for years in a temple, bound, gaining in strength and potency – then the magician dies and some unsuspecting purchaser at the estate sale ends up with something particularly nasty that takes strong magick to rectify. So there are cursed objects out there. Of course, as a magician – if you know how to make an object your own, and depending on your ability - you can take a curse off of just about an object.

You may have to employ a similar pillar rite to re-infuse the object with something else.

Creating Bonded Objects

This is a bit of advanced magick I probably ought not include here simply because it's nice to have a few tricks up one's sleeve as needed. However – we're all adults, and most mages will figure this out eventually anyway. This is a particularly useful method of keeping your friends close and your enemies even closer. A bonded object is an item that binds people together – gift giver and recipient. Through a bonded object the giver can send the recipient healing energy and positive energy as needed. On the flip side of that – the giver can also turn this item into a cursed object if the person it was given to betrays the giver.

Some groups, whenever they accept a new person into their group they give them a bonded object (usually in the form of an amulet). The group member vows to take the bonded object knowing that it's bonded. These types of bonded objects are often sealed – meaning if you vow to keep a bonded object – you will not be able to make it your own. So if you ever betray those who gave it to you – expect to be cursed. Sometimes destroying the object will release you from the vowed bond (and the object and the curse), but making it your own likely won't work. Giving it away may or may not work either.

Now here's the scary part (well – for people who receive them anyway). A vow does not need to be made in order to give someone a bonded object. A vow makes the bond between people stronger certainly, and can solidify that portal – but a strong magician can make a pretty good link with bonded object, too. This means that a bonded object can be given to you without your consent or knowledge. Bonded objects are different than cursed objects because bonded objects act as a bond and portal between people and energy of any sort can be sent through them.

A bonded object can be anything. So – you could have a bonded object in your possession right now and not even know it.

Now not all bonded objects are terrible. Parents might give a bonded object to their children when they move away from home for the first time in order to send protection and love at regular intervals. Close friends or siblings may exchange bonded objects for similar reasons. However, false friends or even enemies can give you a bonded object disguised as a well-intentioned gift. As paranoid as I am (for good reason) – I cleanse and 'make my own' every gift I'm ever given by another magician. It would not offend me if I learned my magician friends do the same. I only accept bonded objects knowingly from those I trust completely. I will only take a vow to take a bonded object if I know I can keep that vow (or I know I can destroy and rid myself of the object).

Bonded objects can also be used to send love magick. Just beware of creating a stalker. I've said before and I'll repeat it again (as it's worth repeating), I think love magick is far more dangerous than any curse just because **you may not be able to get rid of what you no longer want**.

Now onto how bonded objects are made.

Clearly you'll want to start by preparing your ritual space and creating your Daemonic circle or ritual construct. I've found a Hexagram construct works well due to the Hexagram altar configuration. You'll want to invoke Unsere, Tezrian, Lucifer, Eurynomous, Amducius and Delepitorae (or six corresponding Daemons to the purposes

300

of protection, vengeance, life, death wisdom, and magick – or whatever infusions you choose).

First – you need the object. It can, literally, be anything from a piece of jewelry to clothing, to a cooking utensil. You'll want to make sure that the person you're giving it to will either know it's bonded and accept it willingly – or that it will be something they will keep and not re-gift or throw out (if they are unaware it's bonded). So choose the item carefully.

You will need a taglock or personal item of the person you want to give it to. A picture of the person will help, too. Nowadays – with everyone's lives so public on the internet, this shouldn't be an issue if you have nefarious intentions. That little statement really makes you consider what you put on the Internet – doesn't it? It should. (Yes – I repeated this from the cursed items section on purpose.)

Next – you want to create a hexagram with six white candles and black string. (Follow the picture below when tying your candles together to make two separate compartment areas on the altar).

In the lower part of the hexagram (where there is an open triangular spot), place a piece of parchment with the sigils of all the Daemons invoked on it. In the upper triangle of the hexagram put the taglocks, and the bonded object. Imagine the entire set up becoming interconnected. It becomes a pillar of energy. Imagine it reaching out from you to the other person (using the photograph of the person to focus on them if necessary). Repeat this for a full month.

Additional Notes on Bonded and Cursed Objects --- the adept magician can advance in magick enough to bond him/herself to an object not in his/her possession by focusing on it and performing a long-distance bonding ritual. In the case of ex-friends/lovers, if you know of an object in their home and you know it well - you can perform a one month bonding ritual to the item - then send cursed energy to it through the portal you've created, thus charging the object as a cursed object. I know, perfectly devious.

Binding Rituals

Binding rituals are the answer when you need something more than a dispel negativity, but you don't want to outright curse someone. You just want them to leave you alone, stop working magick on you, or get them to stop doing what they're doing. Binding is just that – a binding. Bindings come in many forms but my personal favorite is very simple to do and can be very powerful.

You need:
- Red Thread
- 1 High John the Conqueror Root
- 1 Piece of parchment
- High John the Conqueror Oil or Agaliarept Oil

302

- A drop of your own blood
- A black magick marker
- One clay pot with a lid
- One teaspoon of poppy seeds
- One small black bag

Within your prepared ritual space (your circle or ritual space construct is up to you) write your victim's name on the parchment. Prick your finger and place a drop of blood over it. Write your name over your victim's name. Anoint the root with the oil. Wrap the parchment around the root. Wrap the red thread around the root saying:

> I bind [victim] so that she may not speak.
> I bind [victim] so that she may not hear.
> I bind [victim] so that she may not see
> I bind [victim] so that she will leave me be.
> In the name of Agaliarept and the Daemons of Domination, may she be bound.

Chant the Enn of Agaliarept (or other like Daemons) over the root until you feel the root throbbing with binding energy. Put the root in the bag. Add the poppy seeds. Tie the bag closed with more red thread. Throw the bag into the clay pot. Put the clay pot on a shelf and leave it. Forget about it. Eventually the person will go away and stop the offending behavior. If not – a stronger work may be needed.

Do not throw away your bindings. High John the Conqueror Roots tend to soak up binding energy and become stronger with each subsequent use. Eventually you'll have to replace your roots, but re-use them. When you've finished a binding you can untie it, and burn the parchment later on during a cleaning or request ritual (as with request pots, see the ritual section). Although you may find you have to bind more than one person at a time. In cases like this, you can use one root for multiple people, but it does seem to make the magick weaker. Using one root per person is desirable. So keep your stores well stocked.

On that note it is advisable to warn you that bindings can be dangerous. Especially on those who are ill or who may not be in the best of health. I've done bindings that have actually killed people before (unintentionally). I wasn't fond of either woman anyway, but all the same the outcome was quite unexpected. Always remember that sometimes magick works in ways we don't always anticipate or intend. Sometimes we overshoot and a binding becomes a curse. And yet – *we still have to be willing to take responsibility for the magick we work.*

Additional Curses

Cursing a Resistant Foe (Ba'alberith 10 Day)

There are some people who, by their very nature, cannot be cursed or healed or have magick worked on them or for them. For whatever reason, they are resistant (naturally) to external energies. For these people you will have to use an extended curse or get help (meaning you band together with other magicians and work the magick independently, but together). The following is an example of an extended curse that will help you break down the defenses of a resistant enemy.

You will need:

- A red candle (taper)
- A black candle (taper)
- Some gray thread

- 10 pins
- Oleum of Ba'alberith (infused with your blood)
- Any personal items or taglocks from the victim (picture okay)
- 10 pieces of parchment (small squares are fine)
- A magickal ink infused with your blood.
- An additional drop of blood for each of the 10 days
- The Sigil of Ba'alberith
- 1 small jar or square of cloth.

Construct your ritual space in a manner best suited to this working, invoking Ba'alberith from the center of the ritual space by vibrating his Enn *Avage Secore on ca Ba'alberith*. It is best to start this work during a dark moon at the time of Mars. You will perform a series of 10 rituals consecutively. The first night, you will prepare the candles by carving the victims name into both of them. You will anoint the candles with the Ba'alberith Oleum (see the candle magick chapter if you are unsure how to do this). Then, put them in their holders and with the grey thread, bind them together as close to the base as possible.

Underneath the candles place the sigil of Ba'alberith with a drop of your blood on it. Around the candles place the personal items or the victim's picture. Light the candles.

Poke a pin into the candle. Encircle your hands around the candles (as if cupping the sides) and imagine everything you hate about the person, what you want to happen to them, -- imagine that being absorbed by the candles. Imagine that energy ballooning into a sphere and lifting high up into the sky, and coming down on the victim. Imagine the walls around them crumbling. Imagine them writhing in pain on the ground. Imagine them bleeding with open wounds. Now, on the first piece of parchment write the victim's name and your request (for what you want to happen to the victim -naturally). Place a drop of blood on the parchment. Invoke Ba'alberith again with his Enn. Burn the parchment in the offering bowl and leave it there. Extinguish the candles and go about your business.

Day 2: Do the same thing except on tonight's parchment, write your enemy's name, write your name over it, add a drop of blood and burn that.

Day 3: Do the same thing except on tonight's parchment, draw a picture (even stick figures) of your enemy dying. Add a drop of blood and burn that.

Day 4: Do the same thing except on tonight's parchment draw the sigil of Ba'alberith over your enemy's name, add a drop of blood and burn that (being careful to feel respect toward the Daemon and anger toward the foe).

Day 5: Do the same thing except on tonight's parchment, draw your own sigil and/or words of power declaring your power over your enemy. Add a drop of blood and burn that.

Days 6-10 – Repeat days 1-5.

On the tenth night, let the candles finish burning down all the way (if they haven't already). Take the remaining wax, pins, and burnt requests and put them together in a small square of cloth or a small jar. If your enemy is local and you know where they live, either bury or spread the remains of the curse on their property, right outside their car door, or on the doorstep. If the enemy is not local, bury the remains in a remote location. As you bury it say:

> I commit you to the ground.
> You are cursed in the name of Ba'alberith
> Avage Secore on ca Ba'alberith.

306

Some notes on this curse – the pins will fall out of the candles as the candles burn down. Start at the top and work your way down doing about 5 pins per candle. As the pins fall out, put them into the offering bowl and leave them.

**Also note that this ritual can be modified to send someone healing energy. Clearly you'd use different Daemonic, Color, Planetary, and Moon Phase correspondences. You would also leave the pins out and use blue or white as your thread color. Your invocations and written requests will change accordingly as well.

A Disguised Curse/Cursing Paper**

You will need:

- A Red Candle
- 5 Pieces of Paper
- Some water
- Sponge
- Window Screening - enough to attach to the frame.
- Small Wood Frame (old picture frame can be used too)
- Plastic Basin/Tub (Large enough to totally immerse frame)
- Blender/Food Processor
- White Felt or Flannel Fabric
- Staples or Tacks (For tacking screen on frame)
- Liquid starch (optional)
- War Water or other cursing oleum (or oleum of a vengeance Daemon with a drop of your blood).

The first step is to carve the victim's name (or cursing sigil of your own design) in the candle and perform the following while the candle burns.

Write the enemy's name on the first sheet of paper (or a generalized cursing sigil of your own design if you want to make the paper and keep for later use).

Write your curse on the second sheet of paper On the last three pieces of paper draw the sigils of vengeance Daemons and ask for their help in destroying your enemy.

Rip up (into tiny bits) all the sheets of paper and place them in the blender. Fill the blender about half way. Add enough water to run the blender. Add 1/2 dram of oleum. Add water and blend until you get something of a pulp consistency. The thicker the pulp, the heavier the paper you'll be creating. Make sure there are no large flakes of paper remaining.

Next, make your mold. Stretch the screen over the frame and staple it (to attach it). Make sure it's tight.

Next, fill your basic with water about half way. Add the pulp to the water and stir. Add 2 teaspoons of liquid starch (so that you can write on the paper without it bleeding). Stir.

Next, place your mold in the pulp and level it out while submerged, lift out and allow to drain. If the paper is too thick, add more water, if it's too thin, add more pulp. Using your sponge, press out some of the excess water.

Carefully turn the new piece of paper onto your fabric square. The fabric squares help remove moisture. You can hang dry your paper or dry them on newspaper with the fabric sheets still attached. Remove fabric when dry.

Any other papermaking method can be used, too.

Once the paper is dry you can either use it to draw or paint on, frame (and give as a gift), or write a letter to the recipient (pretending to be a secret admirer if need be -- chances are curiosity will cause the letter to be kept).

This paper (if made generally) can be used to make requests for cursing people during other rituals as well.

**Please note that you can also make paper for friendship, love, lust, happiness, creativity, healing, etc... employing this same method, just changing the ritual components to match the new intent.

Psychic Vampirism
By S. Connolly and Anjie Anon

A psychic vampire is someone who feeds off of the psychic energy of another living person. Many of us know of the common types of psychic vampires. These people include users, whiners, victims, needy people, and oftentimes the mentally unstable. These types of psychic vampires are, perhaps, the most dangerous because oftentimes they, nor the people they feed off of, realize that there is psychic vampirism involved or that the relationship is toxic. Oftentimes the people who are being fed on won't even realize it until they have removed the psychic vampire from their life. Suddenly they'll have empathy and energy again and life won't seem as stressful.

Spotting Psychic Vampires

If you have someone in your life who does one of these things – consider that they're feeding on you.

- The person relies on you for their happiness and emotional security.
- The person will manipulate you and blame you for all their problems.
- The person is riding your coat tails in attempt to pave their own way to success.

- The person is a doppelganger and attempts to emulate you.
- Your problems are always smaller than theirs.
- If things are too quiet for too long, they create a calamity or drama in order to get attention from you or to cause you to react emotionally so they can feed.
- They expect your life to revolve around them and if it doesn't they will try to take your attention off of whatever it's on and get it back on them.
- You are constantly dealing with their problems and emotional insecurities.
- They are constantly lamenting about how they're victims to whoever will listen and give them sympathy (i.e. energy).

Now there are several types of feeders. The vampire subculture has their own terminology for this. Here, I'm just going to tell you what I call them. There are the Emo Feeders (ones that feed off others emotions including love, sympathy, sadness, etc..), there are Negative Energy feeders (who feed exclusively off of anger, sadness and more negative emotions or situations), and then there are those feeders that will bleed the creativity and life energy from the successful, motivated people they attach themselves to because they want to be just like those people they feed on.

Some people are a combination of all three. Some people know they're psychic vampires – others do not. Usually those who know they're vampires aren't as reckless as those who don't really understand that they're psychic vampires. The clueless vampires are more dangerous because they're unpredictable. A vampire that knowingly feeds on someone has an end goal in mind and works for their food in a very skilled and meticulous way. Usually they have no intention of killing their prey (destroying the relationship). Vampires who don't know that's what they're doing will feed until their prey is destroyed (the relationship is severed).

There are numerous theories as to why some people feed on one another's psychic energy. The main theory being that they don't have enough energy of their own and must feed in order to keep their energy levels strong. On the other hand, some vampires feed on others so that they don't have to exert themselves by using their own energy.

Becoming a Psychic Vampire

How do you know if you're a psychic vampire? Well, do you fit the description on the aforementioned list? Be honest. If yes, you could be a vampire.

Here's the thing – if you learn you are a psychic vampire there's no need to panic. Not all psychic vampires are bad. Some are quite helpful. Negative energy feeders who don't cause calamities or negative emotions or situations, but rather diffuse them are some of the most beneficial people in our society; and can promote a great deal of happiness and well-being. Other psychic vampires do a wonderful job calming down those who produce too much energy.

The first thing you need to do is figure out WHY you're feeding. Examine who you feed off of and how it makes you feel after you feed. So the key to taking this seemingly detrimental habit and turning it into something positive is to understand it and recognize it for what it is.

For the magician, becoming a psychic vampire is just another method of learning to manipulate energy. A friend of mine learned of her vampiric tendencies after realizing she felt more creative after a fight. Why? Because while those she was fighting with wasted all their time and energy attempting to make her life miserable, she was basking in that "fight" energy and turning it into creative energy – thus leaving her own personal energy reserve alone. She recalled that she would sometimes pick fights just to create this energy and utilize it for a positive purpose. Once it became clear to her what she was actually doing she was able to stop causing problems and concentrate on seeking out and diffusing existing fights. It was better to focus on different, less self-destructive ways to come by a similar energy source that she could use and manipulate to her will.

Being a psychic vampire has everything to do with cultivating and collecting external energy, manipulating it, transforming it if necessary and focusing it toward a desired outcome by aligning it to the magician's will.

Different people have different methods by which they feed. In the case of our example negative energy feeder, she will calm the other people down and take into herself the negativity they had. When she is full with the energy, she may feel like she's had one too many shots of espresso. Something happens within herself where she then takes that energy, transforms it into a more positive creative energy, and then uses it to create art. Regardless how the vampire takes the energy (whether by touch, meditation, or the act of taking in the energy through the other senses), usually that energetic, high, good feeling will last until that energy is used. Depending on the person, a feeding can sustain the vampire for a day up to several months. Then they will have to feed again. Some people don't need to feed – they just choose to feed and may have no set schedule to it.

Feeding can also be used against enemies. The key to being successful relies on the idea that this person has no idea you're feeding off them. Like the case of our example negative energy feeder, she would provoke fights and then cull energy from the resulting emotional response from the enemy. Keep the emotional responses coming, and you're effectively using your psychic vampirism skills to suck the life from your enemies.

Defending Yourself Against Psychic Vampires

Even though some psychic vampires are beneficial, there are those who are not, as illustrated in the beginning of this chapter. So it stands to reason you will want to know how to protect yourself from unwanted feeding. The solution is actually quite simple. A psychic vampire cannot feed if you don't allow it. By this I mean, if you willingly refuse to end a relationship where you're being fed on, you will continue to be fed on. So the first step is to end relationships with the vampire(s) in question. The second step is to take into consideration your own emotions and reactions to situations. Vampires often feed on emotional psychic energy. If you are prone to outbursts (a bad temper, or emotional upset), you might attempt to control your emotions more when around potential vampires. If this is not possible, you should probably stay in – or resign to the fact that someone will likely feed on you (whether they realize they're feeding or not).

Now, there are some instances where you may WANT to be fed on. Yes, I said *want*. Make sure, before ending any relationship with a psychic vampire, that the relationship isn't mutually beneficial. Sometimes high-strung or emotionally unstable people will find themselves feeling calmer and more stable with a vampire around. Trust me – if you are high-strung, emotionally unstable, or extremely energetic you will find yourself drawing vampires to you. It's in the natural order of things. However, if you're just energetic, but you channel that energy into your own success or your life or your hobbies or whatever – and you're relatively stable regardless, hosting a psychic vampire can be destructive and draining.

So consider all of these things when choosing to host a psychic vampire, choosing to get rid of one, or choosing to become one. Merely being aware of psychic vampirism, what attracts it, how to use it, and how to repel it will help you as a magician because it will help you remove toxic relationships and keep beneficial ones just in the mere understanding of how psychic vampirism works.

How the Daemonic Can Be Utilized for Psychic Vampirism

See the ritual in the ritual section about how to become an incubus/succubus for one example of how one can use the art of Glamour/Influence (often coined a Vampire related talent) for seduction. Additionally, working with the Daemon Svengali can help you learn to become a psychic vampire and learn to manipulate and use the energy you have fed for. The typical method of this is to perform a ritual to Svengali seeking his wisdom before you wish to feed, and carry his sigil on you during the hunt. Some vampires have suggested this will heighten the senses, alert you to the presence of an energy source and can help you efficiently utilize the energy you take.

Blood and Vampires
Back in the old days before people got paranoid about blood born diseases, many old school Daemonolaters would practice what is known as the Blood Wine ritual. This is, in a sense, a form of magick. Daemonolaters, by our very traditions, are predispositioned to blood magick so the imbibement (drinking) of blood is certainly no stretch. The ritual is as such, at the end of the ceremony, each participant puts a drop or two of blood into the wine chalice and then everyone takes a drink. It is the mingling of blood, a symbolic gesture of the sect bond between them. Many people will still practice this with select friends, family, or

315

lovers. The alcohol will likely kill any blood born pathogens. For more information about Blood Magick, see the chapter by High Priest Morlan. I believe he's even included a lovely recipe for the Blood Wine. In the meantime, here's another:

Blood Wine
courtesy M. Delaney

- Two cups of orange juice
- 1/3 cup tequila
- 1 shot grenadine
- 5 drops of blood from each participant.

Mix thoroughly. (You can also make a virgin blood wine using juice.)

Creating Your Own Rituals & Spells
By S. Connolly

Self -Creating Ritual

Perhaps it's prudent to take this moment to really define what Daemonolatry Ritual is all about (even magically speaking). Ritual is the act by which you ceremoniously manifest the change and bring about your desired goal (the will). In Daemonolatry it's basically elaborate spell work combined with paying spiritual homage to deity (whether internal or external and by manner of your personal definition) in order to enlist and harness the external energies to give your magickal working more power. The extended length of ritual (as opposed to spell work) is perfect for those who wish to learn to more acutely focus their energy toward a desired goal.

I have included the following because it explains the point of this chapter in a far more eloquent way than I ever could. This excerpt is from Ellen Purswell's book *Goetic Demonolatry* and has been reprinted here with her permission.

I am admittedly not into prepared ceremonial magick as much as I once was. It used to be that I'd spend weeks preparing for a rite. The phase of the moon had to be perfect; the hour spot on, and each ritual component had to be exact. I felt I was cheating if I used substitutions.

In many cases this pageantry of preparation took the meaning out of the rite. Each rite became nothing more than a list of well-rehearsed steps to a final goal that never quite materialized in the way I had hoped. With scrutiny comes wisdom and I realized that the rites had no meaning because I had not created the steps myself, and had not put meaning behind them. Sure carrying a loadstone in your pocket for three weeks prior to the new moon may infuse it with your personal essence, but many ceremonial magick texts don't always give such exact explanations as to why a step is essential thus leaving the practitioner to guess. I also found that stock rituals weren't always effective.

I have become more creative in my rites. Twenty-four years ago I decided to paint my yearly rite of devotion to Purson within the construct of a ritual circle after having invoked the rulers of the elements. The rite had words, certainly, but they were undocumented. There was no step-by-step script for me to follow. Instead, I painted and sang my prayers to Purson. When I was finished, I had an oil painting depicting a face hiding in the smoke, looking over at a strange symbol rising from the sacred flames. Never before had I tapped into such power. The power itself did not lye with an external influence. It hid inside myself as raw creativity.

In her book, Ellen explains the steps to creating ritual. I'd like to elaborate on her steps by adding some of my own in order to walk you through the process of creating effective personal magick rituals.

Let's break down the ritual magickal working into seven parts –

- Define the ritual's purpose and desired outcome.
- Create the invocations or evocations.
- Outline the steps of the ritual:
  - Beginning – invocations (ritual space construct goes here)
  - Middle – the work
  - End - closing
- Assemble the proper sigils, herbal mixtures, and magickal items.
- Prepare the ritual chamber and yourself.
- Perform the ritual.
- Post-ritual follow-up.

Defining the Purpose and Desired Outcome:

The first step to creating any effective magickal working is to define your purpose. Be as specific as you can be. "I need some extra cash" is pretty vague but sometimes a necessary way of putting it. "I want my boss to give me a raise" is more specific. "I want to get a better job" is pretty vague, too. Try adding the field you'd like to work in (be realistic) to that sentence. "I'd like to get a better engineering job" is more specific.

Sometimes being specific is impractical. In cases like that, feel free to define your rituals' purpose and desired goal in broad, sweeping statements. However, being specific has its advantages. First, it helps you focus more clearly on the desired outcome. Second, it gives you a clearer picture of what it is that you really want. Do you really want a raise, or a new job? Don't hint around at what you really want.

Create the Invocations

Next, decide which member(s) of your Daemonic pantheon is/are appropriate to the magickal working and create the invocations necessary (most Daemonolaters use Enns). But since Enns aren't always available – you can write your own and this is okay. For this particular working (to get a raise) I would choose Belphegore. An example (continuing along the lines of wanting a raise) of a created invocation might go something like this:

"Belphegore, of earth, please attend this rite. I call upon you with an offering. Hear me; be present at this rite to bring good fortune."

You can then add another invocation during the body of the ritual (where the work is performed) that better defines the purpose and goal of your working to the external sources you are calling upon. That might go something like this:

"Belphegore, of earth, I ask that you grant me the strength to find stability at my job, and the earthly skills to excel there, so that I might get a raise in pay."

While these examples may not be as eloquent as you might choose to write your own invocations, they illustrate how specific the invocations should be. The more specific the invocation, the more you understand what you really want, and the Daemonic Divine is better able to help you. Asking the Daemons to simply *get you a raise* probably isn't going to be as effective. Keep in mind any colors, symbols, or correspondences you will need to follow to make your Daemonic *guests* comfortable.

Outline the Steps of the Ritual

Next you will want to outline the steps of the ritual. This can be as simple as writing down your invocations for the beginning and middle, and writing down your *"thank you, please depart and drive safely"* for the closing. This means that anything during the body of the ritual (the middle) is fair game. If you would like to perform spells or symbolic action during the work, create talismans or kamea squares, pray, sing, dance, paint, cook, eat – or whatever it is you do during the body of your rituals – you can note it if you are worried about forgetting a specific part.

Otherwise, during the middle of the ritual there are numerous actions you can perform, only limited by your own imagination. For Rites where the middle isn't clearly defined, make sure you have everything you could possibly want within your ritual space or circle including parchment, candles, ink, oils, incenses, paints, canvas, music, cooking utensils etc...

I know it may sound strange to have some of these items within a ritual space or circle, but you must always remember that whatever you are doing during the body of the rite, the more personal the meaning, the more meaning it holds to you. These actions will connect you to the Daemonic Divine, and every action you perform must be done with the purpose and the desired outcome of the ritual in mind.

If you feel like writing a script, do it. If prepared scripts seem to hamper the flow of the ritual, don't use them. As you are planning the working part of your ritual, be sure to note any colors, sigils, or correspondence you want to use during the ritual. You might also want to plan a time for the ritual based on moon phase, hour, etc...

Keep in mind that sigils and talismans can be made during the body of the ritual if you prefer to construct them within a ritual circle. There is power in the making. (See Rites of Making for more information.)

The closing of the ritual can be elaborate or as simple as you wish. In the case of Belphegore I might say something like,

"Belphegore, of earth, thank you for attending this rite. Go in peace."

Basically you are telling your assembled guests (the Daemons) that you appreciate them coming over to help, and you are seeing them to the door like you might a houseguest.

Assemble the proper sigils, herbal mixtures, and magickal items.

Nothing is more frustrating than to have constructed a ritual circle or space only to find you've forgotten something. Make yourself a list of all the things you want and take them to the ritual chamber or space beforehand. That way nothing is left behind.

Prepare the Ritual Chamber and Yourself

Think of this as set up. Some people, during the planning stage, like to draw diagrams of the ritual's layout. Use this technique if it helps you. Having the ritual space set up ahead of time will free you up to prepare yourself.

Some people may wish to bathe in ritual salts or oils. (See the Self Purification Ritual) Others may choose to fast before the ritual. Others still may choose to take their time putting on their robes and mentally preparing themselves for a ritual. Perhaps you want to do all three. Those choices are entirely up to you.

Perform the Ritual

I don't think I need to go further into this. But make sure you've set enough time aside to perform the ritual. Especially if you are on borrowed private time and your roommate/spouse/kids will be home in an hour.

Post Ritual Follow-Up

After doing a ritual working of magick, you can't just sit idly by and wait for a raise or new job to fall in your lap. Nor should you go to work and cuss your boss, or sit at home expecting the phone to ring with a better job offer. Instead, you have to actively participate in magick. That participation means getting to work on time and showing your boss you are competent and deserving of a raise. It means you have to go out and fill out applications.

Then Why Do Magick At All?

This is usually the question people ask me when I tell them to follow through with their magick. Magick, in itself, is a tool to help you focus your energy and to help you draw needed strength from a spiritual, internal, or outside source. It is a tool that you use to influence yourself (the way you are thinking and acting) which consequently changes the world around you. It is by this influence that changes and desires manifest. Think about it. All magick is spurred by the desire for change. The external situation can only change if you *will it* to change.

Creating Spells

Creating spells works in much the same way. The difference is that Spell Work does not necessarily have to be a communion between the self and deity. In Daemonolatry Magick, all magickal work incorporates the Daemonic so in that – spells are often accompanied with Sigil work and Daemonic Invocations. **There may be an absence of a prepared ritual space or circle**. You can use kitchen witchery and still get the same powerful results of ritual. Spells often rely more on symbols and action rather than petitions to the Daemonic in order to help the practitioner manifest his/her will. At the same time, the Daemonic Divine can play a large part in a spell's symbolism.

The handy thing about spells is their ease of use. With simple candle magick you can focus your will for fifteen minutes to get positive results. With spells, I've always felt the power you draw from is primarily internal. This means that you use more of your own energy rather than plugging into the external power source like ritual often intends to do. You will use symbolism (colors, correspondences, words of power, sigils, and herbal mixtures) and you may create (candle magick, herbal mixtures, sachets, and sigils) during the construction of a spell. These actions and symbols draw from your belief in them (or in your knowing that magick does work), thus pulling their strength directly from the self.

If you believe that writing someone's name on a piece of paper, wrapping it around a piece of High John the Conqueror root, and binding it with a red thread will remove the strife you have with the person whose name you've written – it will happen. By performing this simple symbolic action you have already changed the way you think about that other person.

Let's break down the spell into five parts –

- Define the spell's purpose and desired outcome.
- Create the words of power to charge the spell (being specific in your purpose and desired outcome).
- Assemble the proper sigils, herbal mixtures, and magickal items.
- Perform the spell.
- Post-spell follow-up.

As with ritual, spells must be followed up on. Carrying around a sachet for good health isn't going to *make you* eat better and take better care of yourself. But it can *remind you* to choose a salad over a burger – *it can remind you of its purpose and your desired outcome.* If you believe in the spell you can draw personal strength from it.

Does this mean magick will only work if you follow through or that it won't manifest changes without your help? Not necessarily. I've done magick for financial windfalls and had opportunities literally fall into my lap. I've performed curses and watched enemies die unexpectedly. I've done love magick and created stalkers. Take it as you will.

Magickal Recipes - Formulary

See the Incenses and Oleums section to learn how to make Incenses and Oleums. If you are looking for a recipe that isn't here, use the herb guide and match the herbs to the Daemonic attributes (or magickal attributes) you wish to utilize.

Abigor – Poppy, Radish, Goldenseal, Mugwort, Hemlock

Agaliarept – Mullein, Cinnamon, Sage, Cinquefoil, Rue

Altar Oil – I cup olive oil, 1 tsp. Myrrh, 1 tsp. Cinnamon. Steep 30 days

Amducius – Black Mustard Seed, Bayberry, Sandalwood

(Asafoetida/Rosier)
Love Potpourri – Cardamom, Cinnamon, Cloves, Dill, Thyme, Dragon's Blood, Ginger, Lavender, Roses

(Asmodeus)
Herbal Aphrodisiac – Vervain, Fennel

Asmodeus – Cinnamon, Lavender, Agrimony

Astral to Daemonic Plane – 1 part Rose, 2 parts Chamomile, 1 part Camphor

Astral Travel #2 – Lovage, Hops, Valerian, Sage

Aurom Potable – Basil, Honeysuckle, Marigold, Heather, Honey

(Azlyn)
For Astral Travel – Anoint 3rd eye with Camphor

(Azlyn)
Prophetic Dream Oil – ½ cup olive oil, pinch Cinnamon, Pinch Nutmeg, 1 tsp. Anise Seed

Ba'al Oleums – Pig fat, Frankincense, Blood

Ba'al Peor – Salt, Sulfur

Ba'al Marduk – Ground Shellfish

Ba'al Berith – Cocoa, Mullein

Ba'al Zebual – Almonds, Lavender

Ba'al At – Banana Leaf, Salt

Baalberith – Coltsfoot, Saffron, Pau de Arco, Devils Claw, Frankincense, Solomon's Seal

(Belial)
Earth – Mugwort, Skullcap, Cinnamon, Sandalwood, Benzoin, Frankincense, Black Poppy, Hemlock, Patchouli

(Belial/Belphegore/Ba'al)
Money Powder – 1 pinch of each – Allspice, Almond, Basil, Calamus, Chamomile, Cinnamon, Clove, Dill, Cedar, Ginger, Nutmeg, Patchouli, Sage, Peppermint, Vervain, Rose, Poppy, Heather

(Belphegore)
Money Incense – 5 parts Cinnamon, 9 parts Sage, 2 parts Rosemary, 4 parts Thyme, 3 parts Horehound, 4 parts Vervain, 5 parts Hibiscus
Belphegore – Crushed Gum Arabic, Frankincense

Blood wine – 2 cups Orange Juice, 1/3 cup Tequila, 1 shot Grenadine, 5 drops of blood from each participant

Circle Construction Herbal Powder – Rue, Pennyroyal, Vervain, Calamus, Yew

Conjuring Incense – Mugwort, Wormwood, Lavender, 1 grain crushed Frankincense

Contact a Familiar Incense – Hibiscus, Sandalwood, Lovage, Willow, Vetivert, Agrimony

Controlling Oil – Calamus

Cramps (for) – Brew Chamomile and lemon in tea. Add a pinch of Black Cohosh and Valerian.

Curse #1 – Graveyard Dust, Blood, Ashes of curse request

Curse #2 – Thyme, Rue, Orris Root, Devils Claw, Calamus, Vervain, Graveyard Dust

Curse Breaker Incense – Bay, Dragon's Blood, Frankincense

Dagon – Fennel, Calamus, Rose hips, Myrrh

Dispel Negativity Sachet – 1 pinch of each – Juniper, Cloves, Rose petals, Dill, Saffron, Sandalwood, Frankincense, Myrrh, Cumin

Equinox/Solstice Incense – Sandalwood, Orris Root, Thyme, Poppy seed, Rose petals, Benzoin, Myrrh, Frankincense

Eurynomous – Cumin, Poppy, Juniper, Mandrake, Hibiscus

Exorcism/Purification – Garlic and Frankincense

Fast Hair Growth – 2 eggs, ½ can beer, ¼ cup hibiscus, 2 tbsp. Flax Seed, 2 tbsp. Sage, 3 tbsp. Lavender. Let steep 2 hours – Shampoo in and leave for 10 minutes

Favorite Herbal Tea – 1 tsp. Spearmint, 3 tsp. Chamomile, 1 tsp. Rose hips, 2 tsp. Hibiscus

Feminine Mystique – Patchouli, Roses, Narcissus or Mandrake

Fertility – Sandalwood, Patchouli

Fifth Element (Satan) – Elder Berries, Poppy, Nettles, Wormwood, Witchhazel Bark, Alum

(Flereous)
Fire – Arnica, Saffron, Roses, Red Sandalwood, Passion Flower, Cinnamon

Hecate Incense - 2 parts Copal, 2 parts Sandalwood, 1 ½ parts Orris root, 1 part Rose Petals or Rose Essential Oil, 1

part Cubeb Berries, ½ part Spikenard , ¼ part Nutmeg (optional) *Courtesy B. Morlan*

Hex Oil – Myrrh, Mandrake, Creolin, Ginger, Dragon's Blood, Graveyard Dust, Water, Olive Oil

Hex Powder – Myrrh, Mandrake, Ginger, Dragon's Blood, Graveyard Dust

House Protection – Frankincense, Garlic, Myrrh, Sandalwood, Wormwood

Impotency (to cause) – Hemlock, Wormwood, Thyme, Urine, Blood

Incense of Sorcery (Delepitore) – 6 Rose Petals, 1 tsp. Dragon's Blood, 1 tsp. Devils Claw, 1 tsp. Cinnamon, 1 pinch Blood Root, 6 drops Blue Dye dry

Incubus Powder – 1 part Calamus, 4 parts Sandalwood, 4 parts Sage, 3 parts Sarsaparilla

Initiation Oil – Catnip, Oil

Initiation Incense – Sandalwood, Frankincense, Myrrh

Interview Oil – Rose, Lavender

(Leviathan/Dagon)
Snow – Wormwood, Patchouli, Vervain, Hibiscus, Dandelion, Fennel

Lilith – Roses, Sage, Black Cohosh

Love Incense – 5 parts Jasmine, 5 parts Roses, 2 parts Lavender, 1 part Tansy, 1 part Mugwort, 2 parts Fennel, 5 parts Rosemary

(Lucifer)
Air – Goldenrod, Lemon Balm, Lemon, High John Root

Lucifuge Incense – Alum, Garlic, Blue Vervain, Nettles, Pennyroyal Pau de Arco

Lucifuge Oil – 1 cup olive juice, 1 tsp. olive oil, 3 Types of Perfume, ½ cup alcohol

Lucifuge Oleum – Orris, Pennyroyal, Thyme, Sarsaparilla, Grapeseed Oil, Red Devils Claw, hot water to steep

Magickal Ink#1 – Beet Juice, Gum Arabic

Magickal Ink#2 – Dragons Blood Oil, Sandalwood (red), Alum, 1 pinch Gum Arabic

New Beginning – 3 parts Catnip, 2 parts Orris Root, 7 parts Chamomile, 4-5 parts Damiana, 1 part Sandalwood, 4 parts Hops

Oleum of Daemonic Sorcery – 2 Drams Devil Claw, Bloodroot, Ashes of Sigil, 1 cup Blood Oil

Oleum #4 – Wormwood, Cinquefoil, Wild Celery, Polar Leaves

Part lovers – Urine, Mandrake, Mullein, Hemlock, Wormwood, Rose Thorns

Protection #2 – Sandalwood, Hibiscus, Wormwood, Frankincense, Rue

Purification – 1 pinch salt, 5 parts Frankincense, 5 parts Myrrh, 6 parts blessed Thistle, 4 parts Powdered Garlic, 3 parts Benzoin Gun, 3 parts Rosemary, 2 parts Solomon's Seal, 2 parts Gum Arabic, ½ parts charcoal or salt peter

Rashoon – Passion Flower, Eyebright, Cinnamon, Dragon's Blood

Relaxation Incense – Chamomile, Rue, Narcissus, Sage

(Ronove/Lucifer)
Revealing – Sandalwood, Cinnamon, Rose hips

Ronove/Ronwe – Mint, Sandalwood, Nettles, Pinch Devils Claw

Rosier – Berry, Ginger

Sabbat Oil #1 – Hemlock, Wormwood, Corn silk

Sabbat Oil #2 – Betel Nut, Belladonna, Cinquefoil, Wormwood

Sabbat Oil #3 – Wild Celery, Poplar Leaves, Sweet Birch

Sabbat Oil #4 – Parsley, Celery Root, Cinquefoil, Mandrake, Poppy, Vervain, Patchouli

Satan Incense – ¼ cup Ground Sage, ¼ cup Mullein, ¼ Mandrake (ground), 1 tsp. Lucifuge Oil

Sitri Incense – Roses, Rose hips, Cinnamon, Allspice, Yarrow, Mint, Lavender

Sleep Oil – Rose petals, Mace

Sonnillion – Pine, Poppy

Spirit Guide Incense – Mullein, Rue, Sage, Bay

Stop Gossip Incense – Rue, Garlic, Hensbane

Taroon – Mint, Horehound, Coltsfoot

(Temple/Isis/Wadjet)
Altar Incense – Frankincense, Lavender, Myrrh

(Tezrian)
Protection Incense – Myrrh, Frankincense, Clove

Trouble –(To get a fellow co-worker into)– Tansy, Moss, Garlic, Mullein, Rue

(Unsere)
Lemon Grass, Calamus, Mugwort

(Verrine or Buer)
Water Healing – Calamus, Myrrh, Rose, Sandalwood, Thyme, 1tsp Camphor, 2 tsp. Pure Water, 1-cup oil

Verrine – Bayberry, Mulberry, Dragon's Blood, Camphor

Water Incense (Leviathan) – Calamus, Orris, Thyme, Alum, Coltsfoot, Sea salt, Clary Sage

PLEASE NOTE: Most (not all) of these recipes were taken from S. Connolly's private journals. The other contributors to this book donated recipes, too. If any of these recipes resemble those of a former DB Publishing author it is because that person asked Ms. Connolly for permission to print some of her recipes and bases. This is merely mentioned here so that there is no confusion and no one thinks anyone is lifting anyone else's recipes or infringing on copyrights.

Elemental Base Plant Matter

Earth: North, Belial -Patchouli
Air: East, Lucifer - Wormwood
Fire: South, Flereous - Sandalwood
Water: West, Leviathan - Calamus

Selinda's Favorite Base: Olive oil, Parsley, Celery root, Cinquefoil, Mandrake, Poppy, Vervain, Patchouli, tincture of benzoin. *Add elemental herbs to base if desired.*

The Goetic Daemonic Hierarchy Bases:

Elemental/Directional:
- **Amaymon**: Air, East
- **Goap**: Fire, South
- **Ziminiar or Zimimay**: Water, North
- **Corson**: Earth, West

Use a base of any light carrier oil or pure water:

- **Earth Base**, add Sage and Vetivert.
- **Fire Base**, add Ditany and Galangal.
- **Air Base**, add Fennel and Lavender.
- **Water Base**, add Calamus and Chomomile .

*See **The Complete Book of Demonolatry** for more incense recipes.*

Kings – Frankincense

Bael (Fire)
Vine (Water)
Paymon/Paimon (Water)
Balam (Earth)
Belial (Fire)
Zagan (Earth)
Asmoday (Air)
Purson (Earth)
Beleth (Earth)

Dukes – Sandalwood

Agares (Earth)
Barbatos (Fire)
Gusoin (Water)
Zepar (Earth)
Aim (Fire)
Bune (Earth)
Astaroth (Earth)
Berith (Fire)
Focalor (Water)
Vapula (Air)
Amducious (Air)
Vepar (Water)
Uvall (Water)
Crocell (Water)
Alloces (Fire)
Murmur (Fire)
Gremory (Water)
Haures (Fire)
Dantalion (Water)
Bathin (Earth)
Sallos (Earth)
Elgios (Water)
Valfar/Valfor (Earth)

Marquis – Jasmine

Decarabia (Air)
Cimejes (Earth)
Andrealphus (Air)
Andras (Fire)
Amon (Water)
Naberius (Fire)
Ronove (Air)
Forneus (Water)
Marchosias (Fire)
Phenex (Fire)
Sabnock (Fire)
Shax (Air)
Leraje (Fire)
Oriax (Air)

Princes – Cedar

Vassago (Water)
Sitri (Earth)
Ipos (Water)
Stolas (Air)
Orobas (Water)
Seere (Fire)

Presidents – Storax

Gamigin (Water)
Marbas (Air)
Buer (Fire)
Botis (Water)
Marax (Earth)
Glasya-Labolas (Fire)
Foras (Earth)
Gaap (Air)
Haagenti (Earth)
Caim (Air)
Ose (Air)
Amy (Fire)
Volac (Earth)
Malphas (Air)

Earls – Dragon's Blood

Furfur (Fire)
Halphas (Air)
Raum (Air)
Bifrons (Earth)
Andromalius (Fire)

Knights – Myrrh

Furcus (Air)

Magickal Operations

Note that most rituals in this section will tell you to simply construct your ritual space quite inspecifically. This is because it is assumed the magician will take advantage of the various ritual constructs and build their ritual space in a way that best suits what they are doing magically. If you are not this advanced, a standard elemental ritual construction (see chapter on that) will suffice. In other instances you will be given very specific instructions on constructing the ritual space. Nothing is written in stone. You can change a construct or work the ritual in the way that it's written. It's up to you. If we have any warnings or suggestions about how you construct your space -- like say triangles work better than circles or octagons or what have you -- we have noted it. You can choose to take the advice or ignore it and experiment on your own. Read through the ritual before performing them as not all rituals are put in a format with a list of specific needs. Also note that these rituals and operations are most importantly *examples* or advice and can be modified according to your needs. Treat them as **ideas**, not gospel. All rituals are by S. Connolly unless specified.

339

Addiction Breaker

Addiction is a very serious business. It would be silly to suggest that a simple ritual itself can destroy an addiction, however, the ritual as a supplement to professional medical and psychological help can be a powerful activator of your personal willpower, bringing you a step closer to destroying your addiction. This ritual is a curse – a curse to destroy your addiction and is a great example of how one can use a curse against a situation, behavior or feeling rather than a person. This means this ritual can be modified to, for example, destroy our own anger against a person or situation, or remove an obstacle from our lives. Once the negative influence is cursed, it will wither and die.

Need:
- 1 Black Candle
- 1 Red Candle
- 1 Drop of Blood
- Amducius Oleum
- 1 Tiger's Eye (the stone)
- 1 Living Plant (not an expensive one)

First, invoke Amducius from all the points of your ritual space using his Enn and the DZ sigil. On the right of the altar place the Red Candle with the object of your addiction (i.e. the word alcohol, cigarettes, coffee, drugs, food or whatever) carved into the candle. Anoint it with Amducius oil. Next to it, set the living plant. On the left side of the altar place the black candle and the tiger eye stone. **Note** – T*iger's eye is an energy conduit. For those who are sensitive to tiger's eye (who end up with colds or symptoms after prolonged exposure), take care to clear* *your stone daily and leave it on your altar at least 6 hours of every day to minimize your symptoms.*

Next, light both candles. Place a drop of your blood in the soil of the living plant and say, "You are my living addiction and you will wither and die as this living plant dies." Focus all your anger and hatred toward your addiction onto the living plant. Recall all the pain your addiction causes you. All the friends or joys you've lost because of it. Hate it. Project all of this onto the plant. Once you've expended all of your hatred, disown the addiction with a clear statement of intent. For example, "I will stop smoking because it harms me and I love myself. I cannot harm myself anymore."

At this time you may make a request and burn it in the offering bowl. Meanwhile, on the other side of the altar, the black candle will absorb the negativity. Now, take the tiger's eye and hold it in your hands. Fill it with images of your success. See yourself addiction free and happy. See yourself with resolve and strength. The Tiger's Eye represents hope and your own strength to break the addiction. Close the ritual and allow the candles to burn. Leave the plant and let it die. Put the plant in an area you can see it. When you see it say to yourself, "That is my dead addiction."

Carry the Tiger's Eye with you during your treatment or during the period where you are weaning yourself from the addictive substance. When you feel weakness, like you need the substance of your addiction, hold the stone, rub it, and repeat the visualization of being addiction free.

Acquire A Job

This is a ritual I've performed for family and friends when they're experiencing a bout of unemployment. Please note it will only work IF you are actively seeking employment by filling out applications and sending out resumes. It always gives good results by producing interviews within a week of the ritual's performance. While I make no guarantees I do dare the job seeker to try this ritual and see if you get the same results. When a dear friend was unemployed seven months, I did this ritual and he got three interviews the next day, one resulting in a job.

Invoke Ba'alphegore/Belphagore thrice around the altar table (triangle ritual construct – gives proper energy). Take 4 pieces of parchment. In black, draw triangles on three and a circle on the fourth. Arrange them as such – one triangle at the top, the circle below it, and a triangle on the right and left of the circle. All the while – envision yourself or your unemployed family member or friend having a job. Now, draw the sigil of Belphagore in each of the triangles in green ink. Take three green candles (in candle holders) anointed with Belphagore oleum and place them in on top of the parchments, inside the triangles. In the circle, draw the sigil of Belphagore, the name of the person to be employed (along with a drop of blood after their name), and the word EMPLOYMENT. Put a green stone or piece of glass in the circle. Place also in the circle the brown candle anointed with Belphagore oleum, but also engraved with the name of the person to be employed. Burn an incense of cloves and mint (or Belphagore or something comparable). Let the candles burn down. Have the unemployed person carry the stone/glass with them. Repeat this ritual every three days until employment is achieved, though usually the ritual only needs to be done once.

Cause Change

A Generic Zagam Rite

Zagam or Zagon, is a Daemon said to change things into their opposite. So it makes sense that Zagam is the Daemon that is called upon when you want to cause change in your life. Whether you wish to get your crap together or turn a bad situation into something positive, the Zagam ritual is perhaps one of the more popular Daemonolatry specific rituals for change.

Invoke a triangle of Nine to construct the ritual space. Using a personal sigil (or sigil of Zagam, personal is better) on parchment invoke Zagam with the following Enn:

Enri Laris Zagam Antu.

Hold the sigil above you and vibrate:

Enra can on ca remi.

Kneel at the southern most point of the triangle, sigil held between your palms and recite:

Ana Zagam vindu ashan.

Stand and return to the altar. Spill your blood onto the parchment (a drop is enough). Say any prayers for change that you wish to recite over the sigil. Burn the parchment in the offering bowl. Close the ritual opposite how you opened it.

Close an Astral Portal

Most people may not realize that sometimes supernatural activity is a direct result of an open portal. So the first step to closing a portal is for the magician to learn to identify one that's open. Do not use this ritual lightly. It is very strong and is meant to close giant, gaping holes that lead from the physical realm to the astral realm. The reason you'd want to close a portal is usually because of the metaphysical havoc including haunting and poltergeist activity that open portals often encourage.

Signs of Open Portal Activity:
- A place where more than one entity or spirit dwells.
- Poltergeist activity
- Inanimate objects moving on their own.
- Disembodied voices
- Physical harassment of physical beings by otherworldly ones.
- Feelings of severe dread (check for high EMF and bad wiring first) or panic
- All of this centered around a single location (i.e. one spot).
- You will actually be able to feel the swirling energy of an open portal. It will push against you from up to ten feet from the actual opening epicenter.

Sure, this could also be a haunting. However, you'll know if it is just a haunting if the closing ritual doesn't work. In which case you might move onto a full out banishing or space cleansing ritual. A Daemonic exorcism (not to exorcise Daemons, but rather human and "other" spirits) **as a last resort**. For this, contact Daemonolatry clergy who can instruct you on the safe conduction and practical application of that particular ritual. For all intents and purposes, this ritual should be performed by gate keepers (preferred), walkers (second choice) or lastly - adepts. Gate keepers are actually people who live their entire lives in the presence of portals and understand their contents quite intimately. They are actually attracted to portals and will find themselves in the presence of one most their lives. Walkers (people who live between worlds) are people who can exist in a portal environment comfortably and are equally comfortable in both the astral and the physical realms. Finally, the adept being someone who can tell a portal from your standard haunting and can work successful magick to close it. Beginners and intermediate magicians can perform this ritual, it just may not properly work if you are not adept with energy work.

This ritual works in three parts. First - you banish everything back into the portal via fumigation. Don't worry - Demons may use portals for entry, however the most common entities that come through portals are "Others" so when you do this, don't worry about offending a Demonic force. Second you'll be closing the portal and sealing it via energy fusing, and finally, you'll perform a second fumigation to make sure you remove everything from the space.

So first you'll want to make the initial fumigation incense. The fumigation incense consists of a simple blend of equal parts of white sandalwood and frankincense (crushed if possible). You will need one of those incense burners on a chain so you can swing it around. Swinging the incense clockwise, fumigate the entire area surrounding the portal paying special attention to areas with heavy activity (this may be a specific room in a house if that's where the portal is). While doing this, recite the incantation (with FORCE and conviction!) for sending all things back into the portal:

"In the name of Satan [or your highest Daemonic Force] I banish all back from whence it came! You are not welcome here! Leave us in peace!"

You may also vibrate the Enns of any Demons you wish to fill the space with. Demonic energy will naturally deter and abolish the energy of lesser spirits.

Now - don't stop here or you could end up with more problems. Sometimes this ritual pisses non-Demonic "Others" off. You may experience, at first, increased activity (especially if the rest of the ritual is not performed properly or the person performing it doesn't have the necessary "ability" to close the portal). You may have to re-do the entire ritual a second time. Don't be surprised if everything you used in the ritual turns up missing or is scattered around the house as if it was thrown in anger. If this happens - lather, rinse, repeat.

Now comes the part where the astral portal is fused. The person performing the fusing should, in the very least, be able to feel the portal. Someone who can actually 'see' the portal is even better (and your results are more apt to be successful). If you must, you can travel to the astral to perform this part of the ritual. In your minds eye, see the portal opening. Using your own energy, encompass the portal and begin squeezing it shut, matching end to end. Once you bring all the edges together, use your own energy (you may invoke Daemonic force in Lucifuge Rofocal or Amducius using their Enns in order to draw from an outside energy source) to fuse the ends together, thus shutting the portal. As a final fusing, I like to add a "patch" over the opening in the form of a brilliant purple light that covers where the opening once was.

Communicate with Spirits

Workings of Necromancy can be, by far, some of the most dangerous workings out there because some spirits (notice I say 'some') are strong enough to cause the magician harm. If you are using a ouija/spirit board to contact the dead, be sure you have a strong banishing ritual handy just in case things get out of hand. See the divination section of this book to learn what to do if a nasty spirit attaches itself to your board and won't leave. Now onto communication with the dead. One way to keep oneself 'safe' from harm during a session of necromancy is to work with the Daemons Ba'alberith, Baba'al, or Eurynomous/Euronymous in a structured ritual space. You may invoke them in a triangle if you wish, or in conjunction with the elements in an elemental circle construct if you imbalance easily. Use their Enns to invoke them as is standard in Demonolatry rites.

First, you need to make a Tincture of Ba'alberith (Mullein Tincture). You can use a spagyric tincture making method (described earlier in this book) using the mullein leaves, or you can simply put Mullein leaves in some vodka and let them steep in a dark container for about a week. One part Mullein to two parts alcohol should do it. This tincture will be used to anoint the divination device and your third eye and wrist pulse points.

Keep your divination/communication device in your prepared ritual space. You should prepare your divination devices beforehand. Do not use divination devices dedicated specifically to Daemonic communication as human spirits cannot be channeled through them once they are consecrated to Daemonic communication. So keep your regular and Demonic devices separate. Your regular devices should be cleaned regularly. The Demonic ones won't need cleansing as frequently if at all.

There is no standard method to necessarily call forth a spirit of the dead. Most necromancers are natural mediums by their very nature and can contact the dead simply by calling on who they want to speak to such as:

"I call upon you [departed's name] to come forth and speak with me/us!"

Note that not being specific in who you're calling is more likely to lead to something nasty attaching itself to your communication device.

Some people say that timing for necromancy is very important. Three a.m. is allegedly when the veil between the worlds is said to be thinnest. Others insist that October 31 - November 1 is the best time of year to contact the dead. The reality is that if your medium is strong enough - (s)he should be able to perform a necromantic working at any time. For those who are still feeling their way around their own mediumship abilities, look up hourly and planetary correspondences and apply them to the timing of your necromantic work to see if it enhances your results.

Discover Things Hidden

I often use this ritual when I need to see the whole picture or if I feel I've been left out of the loop on something. There are a good number of uses for a ritual like this.

To discover untapped wisdom, to find out what people really think about you, to find out what's going on without your knowledge, to learn about plots against you or loved ones, or to find a missing item. So really - this rite can be a useful part of your magickal arsenal. First off, before asking for answers make sure you're prepared for the truth. Sometimes things are hidden from us for a reason. For example -- what someone really thinks of you. If you know that someone's opinion matters a great deal to you, you perform the ritual, and learn they don't really think that highly of you -- you could find yourself terribly disappointed, angry, and even vengeful. So seriously consider this and be prepared to accept all the consequences for your magick.

The easiest method to discover what is hidden - invoke a circle of water (the element of intuition) around your bed. Invoke Dagon from the North, Oroborous from the East, Egyn from the South, and Leviathan from the West. You may substitute if you choose. Put the sigils of Leviathan, Luithian, or Azlyn beneath your mattress. Anoint your temples and third eye with a salve made from lavender and calamus root. Before sleeping, write down a detailed account of what you would like to learn. Put this beneath your pillow. Focus on what you want to know as you're falling asleep. All will be revealed during sleep through a dream (so keep your dream notebook handy), or you will wake up knowing what you need to know. Those who are too grounded in the physical may have to repeat this ritual for a few nights before getting results.

This work can also be performed astrally, but I've found the dream method is less apt to be as influenced by your own worries or preconceived notions.

*A more advanced method is to simply slip into ascension and ask your mentors or patron for the answer.

Divination

See the divination section of this book to learn to prepare divination devices. To amplify your divination results, perform your divination in a circle, triangle, or hexagon constructed to Azlyn and Ashtaroth (or one of them if you so choose). To do this, simply invoke each Daemon of divination from each of the quarters or points. Sit in the center of the ritual space with your divination device and work as you normally would. Some say that anointing your temples and third eye with a salve made of Ashtaroth oleum and tiger balm helps with focus and opening up to the higher self and the Daemonic.

Draw New Friends

You will need:

- Oleum of Ashtaroth (made with equal parts of lemon, sunflower, and vanilla)
- Lapis lazuli stone (this can be in the form of jewelry but it's not necessary)

Anoint the stone with the oleum. Using a pillar rite, charge the stone with your desire to meet new people and make new friends. Keep the stone on the altar charging for seven days and nights (using a standard pillar rite) then carry the stone with you. You should recharge for seven days after every fourteen days it's used.

Dreamwork & Dream Walking

Dream work relies heavily on the ability to work astrally. Working in the astral temple will strengthen your psychic muscles and will naturally carry over into the astral's more difficult cousin, dream walking. Dream work is, essentially, the ability to go to the astral at will while in REM sleep and perform the work you intend to perform, waking to remember what you did, and still feeling refreshed and rested. It may sound simple, but it often isn't. I've had students who could Dreamwalk easily but had a hell of a time going into the astral while conscious while others can astral travel at will and have a harder time with Dreamwalking.

The best curative I can give for strengthening your dreamwork sessions and, in the very least, increasing your chances for success, is to anoint the temples with an oil consisting of camphor and mint, focusing on leaving the body, making it a point to know exactly where you're going before sleep, then doing it. When you fail, try again. Practice, in this sense, is going to improve your chances of success. There are numerous shamanistic techniques and treatises on this subject. I suggest those who wish to learn Dreamwalking/Dream Work research and practice astral travel and meditation as prerequisites to attempting their first Dreamwalk.

Now onto the uses of dream work. Being able to travel out of your body during sleep can be used for everything from seducing a lover, terrorizing enemies, conversing with the Daemonic Divine, discovering rituals and pathwork, and even checking in on loved ones in far off places to make sure they're okay. I know several skilled Necromancers who have developed methods to use Dream Walking as a means to speak with the dead. As a magician, you will undoubtedly find a million and one uses for this skill.

There is no prescribed ritual for this simply because different things work for different people. Some insist you should keep sigils of Ronove under the mattress or hanging on the wall above the bed. If you are doing the work for divination, Amon. Or, insert your Demon of purpose (for the work).

Emotional Balance

Emotional imbalance can often be a symptom of too much fire or water. In other instances it can be a symptom of hormonal surges or chemical imbalances in the brain. Firstly, if you feel emotionally imbalanced, you should seek the professional help of a trained and licensed physician. Secondly, you may find a typical balancing ritual like this one can help you. For a full elemental balancing ritual, please see the section earlier in this book.

Since emotional imbalance tends to be a sign of too much fire (anger/frustration) or water (weepiness/despair) you must first determine which of these elements you have too much of. Once this is determined – in an elementally balanced ritual space (using a standard elemental circle construction) sit at the circle's center facing West (water) or South (fire) or Southwest (for both). Imagine the excess element coming off of you in either blue or red hues (depending on which you have too much of – purple if both). Seat your palms firmly on the ground in front of you. Imagine that excess elemental energy leaving your body and surging into the ground.

For those who are more advanced, standard elemental balancing may seem too primitive. Instead – ascend and merge with the element you have excess of. Become one with the element then draw yourself away, leaving the excess behind. You can be more specific and merge with the energy or Daemonic Force that better represents your excess. After all, Leviathan may be a catch all for water, but there are many aspects of water that may be more specifically suited to your individual imbalance. Consider this and act accordingly.

Expose False Friends

No, this is not paranoid magick, but rather preventative. For some folks, a healthy relationship maintenance program requires a regular evaluation of friendships and a regular "life cleaning". As callous as that may sound.

False friends are those folks who may be using you or who are in constant competition with you. Some people will have no need for this ritual because they have a few good friends and that's it. Others may have large groups of friends and may wish to use this ritual to cull the herd. This ritual is for the latter folks. Perform this ritual during a Full Moon.

Construct a ritual space in honor of the Daemon Ashtaroth (invoke her from all the points). In the center of the ritual space, place a medium size mirror on the floor. Around it, set five white candles anointed with oleum of Ashtaroth or Astarte. On the back of the mirror, tape a piece of parchment with the names of all those friends close to you. On the front of the mirror (I find grease pens, erasable marker, or lipstick works well and will wash right off with some Dawn dishwashing liquid) draw the sigil of Ashtaroth. Light the candles. Circle the candles and mirror three times clockwise chanting, "Eylan ana Ashataroth". Then circle the candles and mirror three times counter clockwise chanting, "Remove them who are false".

Let the candles burn down. If you have carpets or hardwood flooring in your ritual space, you may wish to set down a hard surface or use a small table to set the mirror and candles on so wax will not spill. As long as you can walk around it, it will work. Close the rite as usual, thanking Ashtaroth for her presence. When the full moon comes around again, you'll find that certain people may have dropped out of your life.

Warning – do not perform this ritual if you expect to not have any strife or problems in your social life. Oftentimes this ritual works by causing problems between you and those with whom the relationship should be severed. This is how false friends are revealed.

If you experience no problems and no persons disappear from your life, then the friends you have are faithful to you.

External Beauty (Succubus/Incubus of the Self)

In their masculine form they are called incubi (incubus in the singular), and in a feminine form, they are called succubi (succubus in the singular). There are a lot of things to consider with regard to Incubi and Succubi. Firstly - they can be created as thought forms and sent to terrorize others. They can be created as thought forms to be used as sexual companions in the sense that they're a masturbatory device. To create Incubi or Succubi as thought forms, follow the instructions for thought form creation earlier in this book.

Finally - *they can be evoked from within the self* to make the self more desirable to the opposite sex. This particular rite is meant to do just this. It's a rite of seduction. So for external beauty or to become as an Incubus or Succubus, here is the ritual:

- Incense of Jasmine
- Rose Water
- Rose Petals
- Mirror (regular or Skrying)
- Red Candles

You may choose to do a self-cleansing ritual before the beginning of this rite and you can perform the rite before attending any social gathering where you want to be seductive. First, sprinkle the rose petals in the ritual space (you'll have to vacuum or sweep afterward). Sit completely naked in your constructed ritual space (choose your own construction here, I prefer to do this ritual in the name of Asmodeous and Rosier). Burn the Jasmine incense and anoint yourself with Rose Water. Reach into yourself and find your image of you at your most attractive physically. Place this image over yourself. Now think of the person(s) you would like to seduce. Imagine your physical self-seducing these people (specific people if you have them in mind.) Look into the mirror and SEE the image of you as the seductress (or seductor if male). The important thing is to evoke the feeling of beauty and seduction from within yourself and carry it with you from the ritual. It is important to note that you may be tempted to masturbate during such a ritual. However – don't. Part of the nature of the ritual is the sexual tension created by it.

Also note that if you're looking for long-term relationships or love DO NOT, I repeat DO NOT perform lust or seduction magick. Seduction and lust magick are about sex, not love. You may find yourself sorely disappointed at the results if your intention is to seduce someone you want a relationship with. The other person may only want a one-night stand. If you're seeking a lasting relationship or love, perform a ritual for such. Remember – always be specific.

Fertility

There are a number of magickal remedies for infertility. For example, some old spells suggest women should carry 3 hazelnuts, grow Jasmine or use Jasmine essential oil as a perfume. For men, an old charm is to carry a piece of mandrake root at all times (note that mandrake root contains poison so carrying it in a plastic bag is advisable if you are going to do it.) Other remedies still suggest men and women suffering infertility eat cucumbers, apples, basil, hazel and myrtle. Some books say the infertile couple should place an amulet of a bull beneath their bed or wear an amulet of a unicorn or fish. And finally, it is believed carrying the stone tanzanite (or wearing jewelry with the stone in it) will cure infertility, too

First, let's define infertility. Infertility is the inability to conceive children. I in no way endorse using just magick to work out infertility problems. There may be a genuine medical reason (and curable or manageable at that) that will help the infertile conceive. However, for those who have a diagnosed unexplained infertility, or an infertile part of land (test the soil first), or who want a good harvest, or who are battling an infertile imagination – this ritual may either **lend insight** or **help spur fertility** to those areas of your life. Or, if you're undergoing infertility treatments, this rite might help you take the treatments better. Remember, magick is not a substitute for proper medical care or science. It should be used in conjunction with medical care as merely a part of the healing process.

Infertility of any type can be heart breaking and frustrating. The main component of this ritual is to relax and focus on your goal without pressure or judgment. It's this relaxation process that opens us up to solutions or just opens us up.

You will need:
- Swatch of green cloth
- Green thread
- Lavender
- A diaper pin
- Lavender Oil
- Light green candle

This ritual should be performed to Unsere on a Monday (or during a new moon).

Take the lavender and the diaper pin (if you want a child – choose another object better suited if you're working with a different kind of infertility) and put them in the swatch of green cloth. Pull all the ends together and tie it closed with the green thread. Take your time. Anoint the candle and sachet you've just made with the lavender oil. Sit in front of the candle and sachet. Light the candle. Hold the sachet.

For physical infertility, imagine growing pregnant. Feel yourself healed and relaxed. All of your anxiety and worry should be discarded each time you perform this ritual (perform it as necessary).

For other types of infertility (imagination, land etc...) imagine the beautiful paintings you will and can produce. Imagine the books you've written, imagine the finished crafts you've made. Or – simply imagine a bountiful harvest. Always imagine the finished project and the relaxation that comes with being "finished".

Light the candle and sit quietly with the imagery **as needed**. If you need it five times a day – so be it. Carry the sachet with you and hold it when you start feeling stressed or hopeless with regard to your infertility. The soothing scent of the lavender will help you relax.

Note that Unsere is often seen as the great mother, whereas Lilith is the maiden, and Hecate the crone in TG Daemonolatry with regards to a "goddess" trinity. This isn't gospel, just suggestion based on what others have done with the imagery. The point being you can invoke other Daemonic forms if you are uncomfortable with Unsere.

Financial Help

Financial windfalls are something we all can use at one time or another. To gain financial help first (outdoors) create a circle of stones about one foot wide. In the circle of stones carve the sigil of Belphagore or Ba'al Peor into the ground. Start the ritual by invoking Belphagore by employing his enn *Lyan Ramec Catya Ganen Belphegore*, then spilling a few drops of your blood in the center of the circle.

Next, place one drop of blood on a dollar bill. Put this above the main door of your house. Next, on a piece of parchment, draw the sigil of Belphagore. Around it, write specifically that you need a financial windfall and how you would like it to happen if you know. Burn this in the offering bowl while reciting Belphagore's enn. Take the ashes of the burnt offering to your stone circle and leave them there.

Repeat this ritual for nine days straight. This will produce a financial windfall in a month's time.

Please note that if you are unspecific about what kind of windfall you'd like, that the windfall could happen in unsuspected ways. Such as a beloved relative dying. Or you may have an opportunity to sell something you love dearly at top dollar. So consider this when allowing the Daemonic Divine choose the method of your financial help for you.

Find Lover

Use this ritual in instances where you are seeking a sexual partner but you don't have a specific person in mind. DO NOT use this ritual if you are actually seeking a long term relationship or love because the chances of either manifesting due to this particular ritual is slim to none.

- Cedar
- Alcohol
- Rose Petals
- Bergamot
- One Red Candle
- Oil of Asmodeus

Construct a Heptameron circle in honor of Asmodeus and Venus. Employ the Enn of Asmodeus to construct the space.

In a brown glass vessel mix alcohol, cedar, rose petals, and bergamot along with two drops of your blood. Let it sit upon the altar. Using the oil of Asmodeus, anoint your penis (if male) or clitoris (if female) and begin masturbating, bringing yourself to climax. For males, catch your semen in a earthenware bowl. For females, it is easier to gently use the unlit candle as a dildo while stimulating the clitoris until climax is achieved and then using the fingers, spread your sexual fluids across the candle and into the brown glass vessel on the altar. For males, anoint the candle with semen and add some semen to the brown glass vessel on the altar. Light the candle

Lay naked on your back in the circle, close your eyes and thrust your pelvis in the air.

"Anayat Asmo At, Asmodai, bring me the lover I seek."

Repeat this for five minutes. Masturbate again if necessary. You may add more sexual fluid to the brown glass vessel.

Once you have successfully released all your sexual desire and are spent, close the ritual and place a tight lid on the brown glass vessel, gently shaking every fifteen minutes until the candle has burnt completely down. You can perform this last bit over a few days time.

Into a spray bottle, place some distilled water, some of the mixture from your brown glass vessel, and some of your favorite perfume or cologne. Use it as a body spray when going out. This mixture will help draw a lover to you.

(Also see the Incubi/Succubi Rite earlier in this section that can be done right before attending any social situation.)

Yes – we are aware we're including rituals to help people get laid. Here's the thing – it would be an unfortunate disgrace to write a book about magick without attention to more controversial rituals including rituals for sex.

Find Soul Mate

This is the ritual you'll want to perform if you are seeking a long-term relationship. You will not specify the name or an image of the person you're seeking. At this point, the purpose of the ritual is to attract the right person to you – not the person you **think** is right for you. Cleanse yourself using a self-purification ritual.

Place on pink candle anointed with oleum of Ashtaroth in each corner of your ritual space and light. In the center of the ritual space invoke Ashtaroth using her sigil and enn. A fifth prepared pink candle will be sitting on the altar at the center of the ritual space. Beneath that should be her sigil on parchment. On another piece of parchment write your name, the sigil of Ashtaroth, and your desire for a soul mate.

Imagine your own internal light extending out from you to fill the room. It reaches into the astral and seeks out a distant light the same as your own. It finds it and merges with it, making it whole.

Perform this visualization ritual and then forget about it for two months. If you are not in a relationship when the end of the second month comes around, perform the ritual again.

Focus

To learn focus one must learn visualization. Learning effective meditation skills is a key component to this. Those with a short attention span will soon learn that focus is essential to effective magick. Focus can be accomplished in one of several ways. Some choose to place a bit of oleum or oil on the third eye (between the eyes) with a compound such as camphor added so that the physical sensation of the camphor will bring the person's attention to that area of the forehead.

Others choose to stare at objects representative of what they're focusing on.

By invoking Ronove/Ronwe during any ritual, it will help you focus on your intended goal or outcome.

Kaymen Vefa Ronwe

Practice concentration by staring at a candle flame and vibrating the enn of Ronwe.

Gathering of the Will

Gathering the will is another exercise in meditation and visualization. Imagine your will as a bright light encompassing you. Pull it all into a ball between your palms until the energy is palpable. Focus, then direct the energy to the appropriate mental or physical representative image. We have found that invoking your own words of power during this process (via chanting and vibration) is, perhaps, one of the best magickal methods to effectively gather your will as a palpable energy source that can be utilized for effective magick. Experiment with this at your own leisure.

Harmony (Home or Work)

In the home...

A harmonious home is an essential part of a balanced life. Now by harmonious I don't mean boring, but rather free of stress and constant calamity. Any effective magician should be able to, in the very least, keep a harmonious household. That isn't to say you're never going to have problems or mishaps in the home, or that you and your spouse or children or parents or other housemates will never argue. Instead, a harmonious home has a smooth energy flow to it, it is welcoming, it exists in Daemonic presence, it is balanced, it is safe, and arguments and calamity caused by other human companions (or you) are at a minimum. There are several steps to creating harmony.

Firstly - perform a thorough space cleansing or blessing of your choice and establish your wards.

Secondly, invoke all the elementals at each of the corners in every room of the house, allowing them to come and go in their own time.

To keep things harmonious put sachets of sage, lavender and rose on doors (I generally hang them on door knobs) in the main areas of the house and inscribe or anoint the sigils of Unsere and Satan (or your head masculine and feminine deities of choice) over entrance ways. When tension builds, burn lavender to relax the home's occupants. Remember that when making sachets, always do so with your intent and focus clear on the end result. It may help to chant the enn of a Daemonic force you find soothing as you are putting together sachets.

In the workplace...

Keep a sachet of Lavender, Cinnamon, Roses, and sage in your desk or office (or your vehicle if you work on the road). Occasionally spritz a lavender spray in the air, especially before a meeting with hostile co-workers or bosses. For women, wearing a perfume with a lavender undertone will help. Lavender, as you may have guessed, is just very calming and balancing and can be used via therapeutic aromatherapy to help stress, insomnia, meditation, and focus. Carry the sigils of Satan or Unsere (or your heads of pantheon) with you.

Healing (Body)

Please Note: No ritual should be used as a substitute for professional medical care. Rituals and magick are a complimentary therapy and should be used in conjunction with regular medical care and science to get the best results. If you have a diagnosed illness, seek professional medical help and be careful to only used balanced magick. Certain ritual constructs can actually aggravate certain physical conditions including, but not limited to, chronic fatigue and arthritis.

This ritual best done skyclad (nude) or in robes with nothing underneath.

Prepare yourself using a self-purification ritual.

On a full moon, in the morning, after invoking Verrier, Verrine, and/or Buer (within an elementally balanced ritual construct is best), in a clean cauldron over a flame (do this outdoors if you can) boil 1 teaspoon of valerian root, 1/4 cup of hibiscus flowers and 1/8-cup mint in three cups of clean water.

Please have the proper implements ready including heat safe dishes, potholders, etc...

Strain the mixture through cheesecloth into a cup. Hold the cup above you - *"Adra enat misa Verrier et Verrine et Buer"*.

Drink the contents of the cup (carefully). Refill the cup and repeat until all of the mixture has been drank.

In an oleum or ink of dragon's blood, draw the sigil of Verrine on each thigh, on the stomach, and the breast.

Healing (Emotional)

Please Note: No ritual should be used as a substitute for professional medical care (including psychological). Rituals and magick are a complimentary therapy and should be used in conjunction with regular medical care and science to get the best results. If you have a diagnosed psychological condition including depression, seek professional help and be careful of using magick as magick can actually aggravate certain psychological conditions including depression and manic/bi-polar disorders.

Emotional healing requires an outburst, so it's suggested you do this ritual when you are home alone. Invoke at a single point of entry. That is - you invoke one Daemon into the space and that's that. I prefer to invoke Leviathan for this. Others prefer Verrine or Verrier or even Buer or Orias. It's important that for any emotional healing you identify the emotions you're feeling. Anger and Sadness are usually the offenders, but guilt and fear can sometimes be components, too. This is, more or less, a ceremony of letting go and moving on.

Once in your ritual space, write down how you really feel on a piece of parchment. If you have a lot of feelings, bring a lot of parchment and a good ballpoint pen. Take your time. Get it out. Cry, scream, and yell to get the emotions out. Imbue the paper with these painful feelings.

Then, sit in the center of your ritual space and take the Daemonic force invoked into you. Take deep, cleansing breaths. Imagine yourself happy, unafraid, healthy, strong, and decisive. Now burn all the sheets of parchment harboring your painful emotions.

Close the ritual space by thanking the Daemonic force invoked.

Repeat this ritual as necessary.

If you find yourself needing this ritual often, consider seeking professional psychiatric help or consider looking at the areas of your life that are causing the calamity and working on those areas.

Hecate's Curse
B. Morlan

Items needed -
- 1 pink candle with victims name inscribed on it
- a few drops of your blood
- parchment
- fruit of any kind

To begin this curse, go to a wooded area, and cast a circle as you normally would. Take the parchment and write the name Hecate on it and place on it, an inverted pentagram. Ask Her in your own words to bless your working and carry out this curse upon your victim. Or use the following:

All encompassing Mother, I ask you to be here with me to bring your blessings upon my rite, and send your destruction and vengeance out to <name>.

Place 3 or so drops of your own blood on the parchment, and place the pink candle in the center of the parchment and light it. Meditate on your victim, envisioning them as clearly as you can and see their demise, see them entering the fruit you have with you. Let the candle burn down completely. Thank Hecate and the other Daemons for their aid and leave the fruit in the woods so the animals can devour the victim. Close the rite as you would normally.

Hecate's Vision
B. Morlan

Items needed -
- a black bowl
- water
- a black candle
- a few drops of blood
- incense – Sandalwood or other woody scent

This rite is best done between the hours of 3 and 4am. Cast an elemental circle, calling Hecate from the center in your own words. Place the bowl in the center of the ritual space, and pour the water into the bowl. Next, prick your finger and place a few drops of blood into the water. Light the incense and a black candle and place the candle so that the flame is caught on the surface of the water. Draw with your finger, a sigil of Hecate (I have made 2, one from a magick square, one from a rose cross or you can use one of your own design) on top of the surface of the water and say:

Hecate of night with your bright light,
Come to me, and grant to me your sight!

Repeat this 9 times, gazing into the image of the candle flame on the surface of the water. Clear your mind and see what is to see.

After you are finished, close the circle as normal, thanking everyone present. Keep a small amount of the now Hecate infused water in a small jar. When you have need to see, follow the above, and add a small amount of this water with the new and it will grow even stronger.

Ignite the Fire Within

This is a ritual for creativity or call to action. It can be performed when you feel dead inside, unmotivated, or uninspired.

In the ritual space place three red candles in a straight line about 1-3 feet from each other. If you're working on carpet, get yourself several pieces of wood to put the candles on (for stability) or use tables.

Invoke Asmoday, Asmodeous, and Amducious as follows.

At the first candle, use the ZD sigil to invoke Asmoday by employing the enn, "*Alan Typan Asmoday*". Light the candle.

Go to the second candle and invoke, "*An Ayer on ca Asmodeus!*" Light the candle.

Go to the third candle and invoke, "*Secore myasa icar Amducious!*" Light the candle.

Go back to the first candle and lift your hands above your head. "*I seek inspiration!*" Bring your hands to your temples. "*This is to see!*"

Go to the second candle and lift your hands above your head and declare, *"I seek passion!"* Bring your hands to your heart and say, *"This is to feel!"*

Go to the third candle and lift your hands above your head and say, *"I seek action!"*

Bring your hands to your sides and say, *"This is to move!"*

Circle the candles three times clockwise. During each round chant, *"By Asmoday, Asmodeus, and Amducious may the fire within ignite!"*

Finally, write on a piece of parchment what you desire to achieve (be specific). Then burn it in the offering bowl. Close the ritual.

Repeat this for three nights.

Influence People or Situations

To influence others wear an oleum made of equal parts clary sage oil, rose water, your favorite perfume or cologne, and 2 drops of blood. Properly charge the oil in the name of your Patron/Matron. To do this, use a standard pillar rite. Wear the oleum to the meeting with those you wish to influence. When you first meet another person you'd like to influence, take their hand in a firm handshake, index finger touching their wrist, and look them straight in the eye. This will cause them to remember you.

Invoke Companionship

Some people call this ritual a Soul Mate ritual (very similar to the Find a Soul mate work included earlier in this section). In a ritual space invoking Ashtaroth and Rosier (for friendship and love).

Need:

- 2 Pink Candles

- Pink thread or Ribbon

- 2 drops of blood

- 1 piece of parchment

- Rosier oleum and incense

(use Ashtaroth Oleum and Incense if you are seeking just friends)

Start the incense.

On one candle carve your name.

Leave the second candle blank and without a face. PLEASE do not perform this ritual by inscribing a specific name on the second candle. This is a ritual meant to attract THE RIGHT person to you. Not the person you THINK is right for you.

Anoint both candles.

After invoking Rosier and Ashtaroth, light both candles. With the pink thread or ribbon, bind the candles together at the base. While doing this, imagine a compatible companion coming into your life. Write down on the parchment exactly what you seek. Add the sigils of Rosier and Ashtaroth and add two drops of your blood and burn it in the offering bowl. Let the candles burn down. Carry the ashes and wax remnants in a vial with you for one full lunar cycle.

This ritual can be repeated monthly if necessary.

Invoke Creativity

(for musicians, artists, and writers)

Perform this ritual with phones off, by adequate candle or soft lamplight, and in a place you will not be interrupted for at least an hour. Consider moon phases and hours for your operation to make it that much more "special".

In a circle wherein Ronove, Leviathan, Astaroth, and Flaros/Flereous have been invoked, sit with your devices of creativity (i.e. instrument, pen, computer, paint brushes, etc...). Draw several drops of blood and anoint your device with it. Take 10 deep cleansing breaths.

While still in the circle, begin using your creative device. Yes, this means that writers will need paper or the computer, artists will need paper or canvas and their medium of choice, and musicians may need paper and pen in addition to their instrument. Imagine your creativity as a violet light within you. Extend it outward to your creative device and allow the creativity to flow. Do not judge it or stifle it. Even if you think the ideas that come are silly or stupid, keep going. Write, paint, draw, sing, or play what comes to you. Continue what this magickal exercise invokes for as long as possible. Repeat the ritual as needed or as a simple creativity exercise whenever you experience a block or lack of motivation.

Learning

This ritual is dedicated to Ronove or Ronwe, the Daemon of learning and higher knowledge.

- Ronove Amulet
- Ronove Oleum
- 1-2 Drops of your own Blood

Create a clay talisman of Ronove's sigil (you can use the Ronwe Dukante sigil if you want) before this ritual (see creating amulets and talismans) and take it into the ritual chamber/space with you.

Invoke Ronove/Ronwe by employing his Enn *"Kaymen vefa Ronove/Ronwe."*

Anoint the amulet with the oleum. Anoint the amulet with 1-2 drops of your own blood.

Charge the amulet between your palms for 10 minutes, imbuing it with the energy of concentration and retention. Chant the enn over it if it helps you to focus.

Carry the amulet with you. When studying, pull out the amulet and every time you feel your attention wander, focus on it for at least ten cleansing breaths. Some people will wear Ronove/Ronwe oleum when studying or during an exam, and will say prayers to Ronove/Ronwe before study sessions to maximize retention and recovery of the material being learned.

Legal Success

In cases where you are undergoing a legal battle, before any court appearances or meetings with lawyers, invoke Leviathan and wear his oleum infused with your own blood.

For a more extensive legal working, invoke Leviathan (as he is wisdom and justice).

Choose one word to sum up your legal battle and inscribe this word on a black candle, anoint with Oleum of Leviathan.

On parchment write the EXACT outcome you wish to obtain from this legal proceeding. Seal with your name, Leviathan's sigil, and 1-2 drops of your own blood. Burn this in the offering bowl. Keep the ashes in a small container and powder them. Then mix in a small bit of Leviathan oleum infused with your blood.

Before any legal meetings or court appearances do a self-purification ritual. Then, on the soles of your feet, draw or paint the sigil of Leviathan using the ash/oleum mixture. Allow to dry, then dress normally.

Meditation Ease

Some tips for helping meditation:

- Take deep, even, relaxed breaths

- Focus on your third eye, a tarot card, a sigil, a candle flame, or another object.

- Use tiger balm or something with mint and camphor oil on your third eye (between the eyes). Be careful not to get any IN your eyes.

- Remember that meditation is not about clearing your mind of everything until nothing is left.

- Observe thoughts without judgment or reaction

- Keep distractions to minimum.

In an elementally balanced and charged ritual space, sit in the center of the room and follow your breath. Consider your breath and each element and relax. You've just meditated. There, wasn't that easy? Now simply repeat this and see if you can stay in ritual circle longer and longer each time you do it. Challenge yourself to beat your own times (if you're the competitive type), or simply stay in the circle for as long as it takes for you to feel relaxed, calm, and refreshed.

Motivation

Stuck in a pattern of procrastination? This ritual will get your motivation running again. Of course you first have to be motivated enough to do the ritual, right?

- 6 Red Candles

- Parchment

- Writing device

- 1-2 Drops of Blood

First, take six red or orange candles (symbolic of fire) and place one at each directional point of your ritual space and two on your altar. Light them. From the South invoke Flereous using his enn, *Ganic Tasa Fubin Flereous*. From the East invoke Amducious *Denyen valocur avage secore Amducious*, From the North invoke Amon *Avage Secore Ammon ninan* , and from the West invoke Agares *Rean ganen ayar da Agares*. Above the altar invoke Abigor, *Aylan Abigor tasa uan on ca.*

On the parchment write down all the things you'd do with motivation. Seal with your blood, and burn in the offering bowl.

Offering/Request Pots
Brid Delaney

Choose several earthenware jars with lids. During a rite constructed in a balanced space and overseen by either the Elementals or the Nine, paint on each jar the sigil of a Daemon you associate with (one of each) Blessings, Cursing, Prosperity, and Health. On an altar or shelf, keep these pots. Whenever you are angry with someone, concerned about health, needing additional funds, or are feeling particularly grateful or warm towards another, write it down on a square of parchment and toss it into the appropriate pot. Once a month, during the full moon, construct a ritual in honor of the Daemons of your choice (usually one for each pot) and empty the pots, burning all of the requests within them. Then begin again with the new moon cycle. This keeps your pots clear. Some people will wait longer to burn the requests and only burn them during solstices or equinoxes or the closest full moon to these dates.

Open Portals

You might be questioning why one would open an astral portal to begin with. Portals (also called gates) contain a great deal of energy. If opened properly, an opened portal can funnel massive amounts of energy into a ritual working. There are specific gates that can be opened, or a general portal can be opened. Sometimes portals are opened to make it easier to communicate with spirits or otherworldly entities.

Sometimes portals can be opened to make astral work more productive. Regardless your purpose for opening a portal, you must always be sure to close the portal once you've finished with it. Never leave a gaping hole leading into the astral world because you will open your ritual space to anything passing through. I've known people who opened portals, never closed them and who were sorry afterward because they weren't able to later close them. These people experienced severe and terrifying supernatural phenomena. See closing portals for more information.

To Open a General Portal

Invoke the Daemonic elements via their Enns, above and below, then conjure the image of the astral plane. Imagine the barrier between worlds thinning out. Make sure you are forcing your energy toward this task and NOT internalizing it, or you could end up accidentally opening yourself up to possession (non-Daemonic), imbalance, and illness. Using the ritual blade, gently slice through the veil between this world and the next. Imagine the portal opening. At this point you should be able to *feel* the open portal. It will be cool and cause the air to move slightly as if a soft breeze is present. You may even experience a cold burst of air or a quick wind. Some may even be able to *see* the portal.

To close the portal when finished, follow the instructions for closing the portal earlier in this section.

Passage (To Help a Spirit Cross Over)

This ritual is specifically to help a "stranded" or resistant human spirit cross over. This can happen if the death is a suicide, violent, or sudden and unexpected. Or if the spirit just wasn't ready to cross. Keep in mind that not all trapped spirits will haunt a place or produce paranormal activity. However, a medium may still feel their presence. This particular passage ritual is a very gentle nudging to the other side. For a more forcible ritual (usually needed with more resistant or negative spirits), use an actual banishing or cleansing or contact the clergy for help. Additionally - you can modify this ritual to something stronger of your own devise.

Within a ritual space wherein is invoked Ba'alberith and Eurynomous/Euronymous by employing their enns. All those participating will carry with them one white candle and one black candle anointed with a Eurynomous oleum. The medium should be an adept magician. The medium should make contact with the spirit.

After the Daemonic forces are invoked, the medium should be able to see or feel the spirits more strongly. (S)He should then say, *"Come close to me as I lead you to Eurynomous so that he can guide you to the other side."*

The astral portal to the death realm is opened with the ZD and the invocative Enn, *"Asee Cha On Ca Ba'alberith. Anat Eurynomous!"*

389

Those present repeat, *"Asee Cha On Ca Ba'alberith. Anat Eurynomous!"*

The medium raises her hands above her head, *"Cross over and be at peace."*

Those present repeat, *"Cross over and be at peace."*

Once the spirit crosses the portal is sealed (see portal closing for more information). The white and black candles are left in honor of the recently departed dead at the closed portal and left to burn down. The Daemonic is not asked to leave but allowed to depart in its own time.

Physical Manifestation (to bring about)

That is not to invoke or evoke a Daemon to physical manifestation but rather to cause the physical manifestation of our will to come to fruition.

Need:

- Wax (bar)

- Hot Water

- 1-2 Drops of your own Blood

- Oleum of Satan (or your All)

This rite is easiest to perform in the kitchen sink with hot water. Not boiling! Please be careful to only work with hottest water your bare hands can handle without burning yourself. Invoke Satan, "*Tasa Remy Laris Satan*" or your "All" and then fill the sink with the hottest water you can stand to touch. You can go a bit hotter and allow it to naturally cool off before submerging your hands.

Put your hands in the water and, thinking of what you want to manifest, allow your hands to begin forming the wax into a shape symbolic of the manifestation you want. When the water becomes too cool, reheat it. This can take an hour or more. Once your wax has reached a shape that pleases you and you have manipulated it with your own hands into the shape of your manifestation, take the wax from the sink and pat it dry. Then, anoint with the oleum and two drops of your blood and keep it on your altar or in a prominent place in your home. Once the manifestation has come to pass you can melt the wax for use in candles.

Pillar Ritual (standard)

Use this ritual to charge any talisman or amulet (or object). Pillar rites are rituals (of various construction) wherein you make pillars of energy within which the object to be charged is encased. The easiest method for this is to place 5 candles in a circle on the altar, and place the object inside the circle. The candles are lit and the circle of candles acts as the perimeter of the pillar of energy. Visualizing a pillar of light and fast moving energy that extends from the ground to the sky creates the pillar. Usually pillar rites are done for several days up to a month at a time to properly infuse items with the required energies. Charging amulets can be done in conjunction with any offering or religious rituals as well as during an actual magickal work. You just need to have the space to do both.

First, choose the appropriate color for the work. Then choose 5 candles of that color (or combination of colors). Choose 1-5 Daemonic forces to associate with the work. On the candles, carve the Daemonic sigil(s) and anoint with Daemonic oleum(s) of the chosen Daemons (with your blood added). Put the item on the center of the altar. Surround it with the five prepared and dressed candles. Invoke the Daemonic forces over the candles. Raise and project the energy onto the pillar, imagining its light extending from floor to ceiling running through the candles and the object you are charging. Let the candles burn down completely and then either use the item or start over with new candles and continue charging.

Positive Outcomes

This is a general ritual for a positive outcome in any situation whether it be an argument with a co-worker, or a good experience visiting your mother-in-law.

In a balanced ritual space arm yourself with a piece of aventurine, a piece of parchment, a pen, a green candle, some blood, and green thread. Next to you have a clay pot with a lid. Invoke your Patron/Matron with his or her Enn. On the parchment draw your Patron's sigil, then draw your personal sigil (join or combine them if you can).

Specify what you would like the outcome of the situation to be. Give the parchment a drop or two of your blood.

Carve both you and your patron's personal sigil combined onto the candle. Anoint the candle with a drop of your blood.

Next, wrap the piece of Aventurine with the parchment. Tie it closed with the green thread (wrap it up like a little package). Tie this to the base of the candle while it's in the candleholder. Light the candle and focus on your desired outcome. Build the energy and release it.

Once the candle has burnt down completely place your bundle into the clay pot. Set your clay pot up on a shelf out of the way until the situation is resolved. Later, after you no longer need the influence, you may burn the parchment (sending it back to all that is) and clear the stone for re-use at a later time. Keep one piece of aventurine for this particular type of work. The more you use it, the more potent it will become. This seems to be the case for reusable stones and roots.

Proclamation of Anger

Some Demonolater's we talked to were uncomfortable with curses and said they would prefer another method of getting rid of one's anger. This ritual is an alternative to cursing and will help the magician get rid of negative feelings.

You will need:
- 1 Black Candle
- Parchment
- Writing Utensil (fountain pens are just awesome for ritual)
- Burnt Offering Bowl
- Lucifuge Oleum
- Lucifuge Incense

Construct your ritual space to Lucifuge and invite him with his Enn. *Eyen tasa valocur Lucifuge Rofocale.*

Carve his sigil into the candle and dress it with the oleum. Anoint yourself with the oleum. Ignite the incense. Write down all of your negative, hurtful, angry feelings onto the paper.

Hold the paper above your head and say:
"In the name of Lucifuge I command and condemn this which I have written! I am incensed with the situation that has brought me here. This is my crossroads and I am choosing to let it go! In the name of Lucifuge, most Holy King of Darkness – so be it!"

With a heavy, dark ink, draw the sigil of Lucifuge OVER all you have written. Focus all of your anger into that piece of paper. Now burn it in the offering bowl. Close the ritual and walk away. Repeat as necessary.

Purification/Cleansing of Temple, Home, or Personal Space
Courtesy S. Connolly

You Need:
◊ A Temple Incense – something with a base of Frankincense, Myrrh, White Sage, Clary Sage or Calamus (or you can use a Sage smudge stick if you choose)
◊ A Sprayer Full of Salt Water mixed with 10 Drops of Water Oleum (Leviathan, Luithian or other water Daemon)
◊ A Purification/Water based Oleum of your choice

This ritual is a modern modification of an old ritual. To do it the old way – don't mix your salt water and oleum in a sprayer. Instead – mix it in a chalice and use your athame to sprinkle it using the standard hand/athame movement of "As Above, So Below" as demonstrated by your Priest(ess). When mixing the water and salt in the sprayer (chalice) with the oleum, intone, "Talot Pasa Oida Belial Et Leviathan". This vibration should be within the range of your normal speaking voice. If you are using a chalice, mix the mixture with the Athame. If you are using a sprayer – simply shake. Or – you can mix in the chalice with the Athame and then pour it into the sprayer.

Sprayer vs. Chalice. While the chalice may be the old school method of doing things, I discovered I didn't like huge droplets of water splattered in my ritual chamber falling onto my nice wooden tables and the paintings and linens. So I found that using a sprayer released the formula into the air, or the mist is so fine it dissipates before landing on my ritual implements. You can still use the movement "As Above So Below." Just squeeze the pump during the motion. (If you don't understand "As Above So Below", don't worry about it – ignore that part)

Using your athame (i.e. ritual dagger) invoke the Daemonic (using DZ) into your ritual space or the area to be purified. If you are a beginner, a standard elemental circle construct (at each directional point of the space – if this is a house, it's easier to go outside and circle the house as a whole) is acceptable. If you are beyond this – a ritual construct of your choosing is fine. I personally prefer a pentagram construct invoking a Water Daemon due North (Leviathan), Air Daemon Northeast (Lucifer), Fire Daemon Southeast (Flereous or Amdu), Spirit Daemon Southwest (Atem or Satan), and Earth Daemon Northwest (Belial or Ba'al) (choose your own Daemonic forces for this or use those suggestions provided). The purpose of this step is to **balance** the space completely.

Step Two: Either light the incense in the thurible (I like one of the swinging ones for this) or light the smudge stick. I prefer walking in a clockwise direction, swinging the incense counterclockwise (if using a sage stick for smudging, circle it counterclockwise) around the space. While doing this – imagine an overpowering silver light emanating from you and the incense and pushing outward (outside the constructed balanced space) all unwanted influences and energies from the area or space. Then – walk through the space, spreading the smoke from the incense, properly fumigating each room, corner, etc… Imagine the area free and clear.

Step Three: Using the oleum, approach each doorframe and window and apply Daemonic sigils for purification (choose a Daemon you would use for purification) or your wards (see warding for more information).

Step Four: Thank all Daemons present and bid them farewell.

Note: Candles and darkness are not necessary for this ritual, nor desired. To add to this, perform this ritual at mid-day during the springtime after a thorough cleaning of the space and open all the windows and doors while performing this ritual. Even better – right after a morning spring rain.

Purification of the Self (Also for Balancing)
Courtesy S. Connolly

Mix sea salt with the oleum of a mentor or Daemonic force of purification into a warm bath.

Bathe yourself completely.

Drink an 8-ounce glass of cold water (symbolic of internal purification).

Enter the ritual space nude or wearing white robes or clothing.

Invoke an elemental circle (for balance).

Anoint yourself with sage oil and burn sage incense.

During this meditation imagine breathing in silver light and exhaling dark smoke. Do this for 15 minutes. Press your hands firmly into the ground, releasing any thick, black, astral sludge back into the earth. Feel yourself balanced, calm, and purified.

Repeat as necessary. When you are ready, thank all Daemons present and bid them farewell.

Reconcile Friendships

One main thing really ought to be considered before performing the reconciliation of friendship rite. That is – do both parties truly wish for reconciliation? Do not attempt to reconcile with someone who truly wants nothing to do with you. This ritual will not work if the friendship was not meant to be.

On a new moon mix equal parts of Hibiscus and Sage in water drawn from a running river or stream and add 2 drops of your blood. Let it sit within a pillar of Ashtaroth (see pillar rites for more information) for a full moon cycle. On the pillar candles, inscribe your name and your friend's name on each one and anoint with Ashtaroth oil.

Mix the wax and mixture and on the following new moon, take the mixture to your friend's house and pour it on their property or where you know they'll walk. If the friendship is meant to be, you will reconcile within the month. If not, you will grow further apart.

This ritual can be done astrally for distance friendships but may not be nearly as effective.

Rite of Making (Wands/Blasting Rods)
Lisa P.

Select a branch of oak. At its top set in a clear or white crystal to focus power. 1/3 down the shaft tie a piece of leather infused with a sigil of protection. 1/3 down from that, set in a black tourmaline. Just above the tourmaline tie a thin swath of cloth. You may also carve the demonic sigils into the wand. Place the wand/rod on the altar and surround it with 5 white candles in the shape of an inverse pentagram. With red thread or yarn, make the pentagram. The wand should sit at its center. Call Tezrian, Amducius, Ba'al, and Dagon with their enns to infuse the wand with their protection and energy and to attune the wand to you. It must sit for 9 days and nights with the infusion and attunement done each night in the 20th hour. After the ninth day you may use the wand. When depleted or if it feels imbalanced, repeat this process.

Rite of Renewal
By Gavin Bradshaw

Perform this rite at the beginning of an endeavor, at the end of a bad relationship, or whenever you need to feel renewed.

You will need:
- 1 Hot Cup of Hibiscus Tea
- The Name of Anubis in Hieroglyphs on parchment as such:

- A drop of blood.
- An incense made of Myrrh and Hibiscus

Perform a self-purification before this ritual. Just before sunrise, step outside, nude if possible, with the cup of tea and the parchment. Draw a drop of blood and place it on your third eye. Sit comfortably outside (if nude be sure the neighbors can't see or you could end up with an indecent exposure charge). Wait for the sun to rise and drink the tea. Once the sun comes up over the horizon stand and lift your hands into the air saying: *Nuc per Amen, Ami-ab, per-ab ami kshat. Anksh-a em, t'ett'a-a.*

Don't just say it, feel it.

Place your hands over your eyes: *This is to see.*
Place your hands over your heart: *This is to feel.*
Place your hands in front of you palms up: *This is to be.*

I AM.

Safety for Yourself & Others

On your vehicle (in an appropriate oleum), on parchment with a magical ink, or as a clay amulet, draw the sigil of your All. The highest Deity of your personal pantheon. Invoke this Daemonic force by employing its Enn or by using a personal invocation created by you. After you have finished the invocation, over this sigil say (keeping a strong mental image of those who you mean to keep safe):

I surround this vehicle/object/person with a shield of protection invoked by {Daemonic Name}. Stand as a wall against danger. Stand as a wall against negative influence. Stand as a wall against ill health. Send away all harm that all forces shall be friendly unto me/him/her/them. In the name of {Daemonic Name}, So be it!

If the sigil is on parchment or an amulet, give it to the person needing safety or protection that they may carry it with them.

You can charge such amulets and talismans in pillar rites as well then give them as gifts. You can also disguise protective talismans as bonded objects if the person you seek to protect isn't open minded to wearing or carrying sigils. See the execration chapter for more information.

See Clearly

This ritual means to help you see things clearly. Whether it be what's in your Skrying mirror, or what's going on in your life. Perform this ritual right before bed, in the bedroom if possible.

Place the sigil of Lucifer, Wadjet, Leviathan, or Dagon beneath your bed. Then, after employing the Enns or invocations of whichever Daemonic force(s) you choose for Wisdom and Seeing, kneel at the bedside with your hands above your head, palms upward.

"It is by your enlightenment and wisdom that I come forth seeking your guidance and counsel that I may see clearly my situation and those things which are hidden unto me."

Stand and press your palms into your eyes gently.

"Open my eyes that I may see far and wide, without judgment or guilt."

Remove your hands and open your eyes.

"I see all before me with clear vision and an open heart. I seek the truth of all before me. In the name of {Daemonic Force}, so be it."

Place a drop of your blood on the sigil, then go to bed. When you awake you will have insight into your situation. The sigil should be disposed of by burning it in the offering bowl with a prayer of thanks. Some may choose to use a Skrying mirror or crystal during this ritual and perform it in the temple instead of the bedroom (depending on what the work is for).

Self Esteem

Clear yourself using the Self Purification ritual.

You can perform this one of two ways, you can either enter the ritual chamber nude, or you can enter it clothed in your best ritual robes.

Use 2 parts sandalwood, 1 part myrrh, and 1 part frankincense to make the incense. Burn this during your ritual.

Enter the ritual space (suggested ritual construct, Heptameron configuration with consideration to the Sun, Sunday, Ra, and Lucifer) and carefully draw Lucifer's sigil onto a piece of parchment, all the while vibrating his Enn:

Renich Tasa Uberaca Biasa Icar Lucifer.

Go to the East-most point of the room and place the sigil there. Repeat the Enn. On bended knee lift your hands into the air, palms upward.

"I am worthy of your audience. I am respected. I am loved. There are many things I do well. Of you, Lord Lucifer, I ask this - let me see my self worth as those who adore me do. Let me see myself as a divine being as you see me."

Stand, fumigate the entire ritual chamber and the self. Take a few moments of quiet contemplation. Retrieve the sigil from where it sits. Place a drop of your blood as offering upon it. Kiss the sigil and burn it in the offering bowl, sending it to Lucifer. Say any prayers of thanks and close the ritual as normal.

Self Reflection

On the back of a Skrying mirror draw the sigils of Azlyn and Leviathan. Anoint your third eye with an oleum of the same mixed with blood.

In a standard ritual space, invoke these two Daemonic forces and sit within the circle gazing into the mirror. Two candles should flank the mirror. Take several measured breaths. Gaze, without expectation or thought into the mirror.

Vibrate: *Ana mana esta tae. Rena esta oran tae.*

Repeat as necessary. Let your mind go, stay completely relaxed. Eventually the mirror will clear and shapes - images will begin to appear within it.

Let the mirror reveal to you your true self. This experience may be jarring and occasionally and Daemonic force will show up and speak to you. Expect this as a possibility before you begin so you are not surprised.

If the magician is not a medium, this ritual may not be as effective or may not work at all. In the case of poor mediumship ability, you may choose to work with a medium. You as the operator (the one who performs the ritual and does all the invocation and vibration) and the medium as a mere conduit between the Daemonic Force in the mirror and you. When choosing a medium be sure to choose someone you trust.

Send Away

To send away someone you dislike (this is a great ritual to get rid of an annoying neighbor).

In a jar place black mustard seed, pepper, and graveyard dirt. Add urine. Mix well by putting the lid on the jar and shaking. Bring this closed jar with you to the ritual chamber. Set the Jar on the altar. Light a standard temple incense.

Invoke Valefor upon Focalor with their vibrated Enns. (This means you combine their energies and you can join their sigils. For more information about this see M. Delaney's *Sanctus Quattuordecim*) Construct their sigils on 3 x 3 pieces of parchment (if you make your own paper you can imbue it with corresponding energy).

Draw a triangle at the center of the ritual space (a wooden triangle or cloth triangle will suffice). Place the jar inside it. Place the sigils on either side of the jar. Either put a taglock or personal item of the person you want to leave on top of the jar, or create an effigy of this person in the form of a drawing or symbol. Place a brown candle with Valefor upon Focalor's sigil carved into it, upon the taglock, item, or effigy on top of the jar. Let the candle burn down.

As it burns, build negative, putrid energy between your palms and "give it" to the jar and candle. Take two drops of your own blood and give the blood to the sigils. Once the candle is out, take any leftover wax and add it to the jar. Place one of the sigils in the jar, re-cap, and shake, mixing well. Close the ritual as normal then take the remaining sigil and the jar to the property of the person you want to leave. Pour the contents of the jar onto their property. Then take the second sigil and leave it where you know they will walk.

In instances where you want to get rid of a co-worker or another annoying person you would still commit the contents of the jar to the ground, you'd just dispose of it someplace close to your workplace, at your workplace, or the person's home (if you know where they live). Then, you'd leave the sigil beneath the person's desk, under their chair, in their locker, under their car bumper etc... It's probably a good idea to keep it hidden. If you attach a piece of tape to the sigil you can easily walk by a desk and tape it underneath without anyone noticing.

Send Good Fortune

Sending good fortune can be as simple as creating a bonded object and giving it to someone you care about (see execration chapter), or you can actually perform a ritual like this one for them.

Into the ritual chamber, wherein you will invoke Belial, Belphagore, and Bael, take with you a green candle, a staff, and a wand. Inscribe onto the candle the name of the person to whom you wish to send good fortune. Anoint the candle with a drop or two of your blood. Also inscribe into the candle the sigils of Belial, Belphagore and Bael.

Vibrate the three Enns over the candle until you feel a palpable energy and can see, in your minds eye, the energy encircling the candle. Walk around the altar with the staff and circle the candle/altar three times clockwise. Tap the staff on the ground twice. Retrieve the wand. Point the wand at the candle and the energy compiling there and direct it toward the person you are sending good fortune to. Make sure you have a clear mental image of the person. If necessary, use a picture or personal items of the person in question to help you focus on them.

Close the ritual as usual and allow the candle to burn down completely.

This ritual can be used for execration and love magick as well.

Strength

Use this ritual whenever you need to infuse yourself with strength and resolve, before competitions, before surgery, or before any situation or event requiring strength of mind, body, and/or spirit. You may need to construct some items for this ritual beforehand. Or, alternatively you can construct them during the ritual. That is up to you.

- 2 Black Candles
- 1-2 Drops of your blood
- Sigil of Satanchia
- Parchment
- Black ink and a writing implement
- Knife for carving the candle
- Amulet of Satanchia
- Oleum of Satanchia (orris root, devil's claw, and marjoram)
- Incense of Satanchia

Wear black robes or dark clothing for this ritual. Enter the circle from the North carrying two black candles. Place the candles on the altar. Construct the ritual space invoking Satanchia from the South, Flaros from the East, Bathim from the West, and Orias from the North (in that order and using their Enns, see appendices). This gives the ritual construct sort of a zigzag. Carve the sigil of Satanchia into both black candles and anoint them with the Oleum. Anoint yourself with the oleum and light the incense. Place the sigil of Satanchia in a prominent place where it can be seen. Build energy between your palms, a strength like no other. Vibrate Satanchia's Enn. Feel Satanchia's strength draw yours outward - unyielding, unmoving, strong and forceful. Feel your will, solid and fortified. When you feel Satanchia, draw from him. Take into yourself his energy, seeing your own 'light' grow stronger and stronger until there is no darkness in your ritual chamber or beyond and your own energy fills every crack and crevice.

Add one drop of blood to the amulet. Charge the amulet with this Daemonic force. Now write your name three times on the parchment. Over each recitation of your name, write STRENGTH. Over that draw the sigil of Satanchia while vibrating his enn. Next, add a drop of your blood to the parchment as your "signature". Burn this in the offering bowl with prayers of thanks.

Finally, place the amulet around your neck and close the ritual. Extinguish the candles and reuse them during any repetition of this or any other ritual in honor of Satanchia.

Transform the Self

Use this working to help break bad habits, minimize negative traits, and to enhance positive traits.

You will need:
- White face paint
- A Mask
- A Washcloth
- A Prepared Mirror
- A bowl of water
- A Drop of your own blood
- Parchment

First prepare your mirror. On the reverse of the mirror draw the sigil of Zagam for minimizing bad traits, Ashtaroth to enhance positive traits, or Lucifuge to break bad habits. Depending on what you're using this work for, you'll work with a different Daemon. This also means you'll be using their specific enn during the work. Invoke the Daemon of the work at each of the four points of the ritual space utilizing its enn. Then sit comfortable in the center of the circle, still vibrating the Enn of the Daemon you are working with. In front of the mirror begin painting your face white. This is symbolic of the trait or habit you want to minimize, or the veil hiding the trait you want to enhance. You can use the paint to draw appropriate sigils on your face and then slowly cover them until most of your face is covered. Next, put on the mask, symbolic of the various layers of change you wish to effect. Now, on the parchment, write down exactly what you want to change and why. Sign this with your personal seal and the seal of the Daemon you're working with. Add a drop of your blood to the parchment. Put into this paper all of your desire and want for change. Allow any emotions to come forward during this process and if you need to cry (some people do), do so. Get it out. Next, burn the parchment in the offering bowl with a prayer of thanks to the Daemon you're working with.

Next, sit down in front of the mirror again. Look at yourself long and hard. Finally, remove the mask. Stare at yourself again. When you're ready, start revealing the new you. Imagine the person you WANT to be, free of the bad trait or habit, or with the enhanced trait you desire. Now, begin slowly removing the face paint by dipping the cloth into the water and washing a small part of your face at a time. As you reveal more and more skin, imagine you are revealing the new you.

This is a very empowering ritual and can be performed at regular intervals during the additional self-work you're doing to effect this change in yourself.

True Intent

Sometimes our true intent can be hidden so deeply that we don't understand why a working didn't manifest results or won't manifest results. Sometimes what we think we want is really symptomatic of something deeper that is our true intent. For example, if you really don't want to hurt a person, a curse on them may not work. The pure want, desire, and intent needs to be present for magick to manifest to its full potential. The reason you may not be winning the lottery is because in reality you really have no true desire to be wealthy, just comfortable and not plagued by money worries. Chances are you don't really want to be famous, but rather shown respect and loved by those you care about. However – sometimes our true intent doesn't show its face until long after the fact. Hindsight is 20/20 after all.

If you are having difficulty with your magickal work manifesting, this working is going to help you discover your true intent. I wouldn't be surprised if it didn't also help you discover a few other things as well. The Daemonic always has a way of shoving that little extra piece of wisdom in there for us to chew on. Such things often happen with this ritual. Epiphanies abound.

The Beginner Method:

During this ritual you are going to need a divination device that works for you. If none do, you are going to need a medium to help you perform the work. You may even be able to find a medium online to help you with this ritual. Yes, I said online, as in over the internet. Sometimes Daemonolaters are so far removed from one another that the closest magickal partner you'll be able to find will be two states away.

So you have your prepared divination device (see the divination section) that works for you (or your medium who will either be present to use the divination device or who will use it at the same time from another location for you) and you will take it to your ritual chamber and invoke your Patron/Matron or current Mentor. Relax yourself completely and chant or vibrate the enn of the Daemon you're working with until you feel the presence. At this point you need to ask outright that you are seeking help to discover your true intent (or anything else you're seeking if you're modifying). Let go of your own thoughts and preconceived notions. Begin using your divination device. Let the Daemon "talk". Listen. When finished or tired, close the ritual as normal and go about your business. You will have a revelation during the ritual or within 24 hours of performing it.

The Advanced Method:

In a prepared ritual space (so you aren't interrupted by other astral entities) go into ascension and find your Patron/Matron or current Mentor. Merge with them and seek your truth and any wisdom they have to offer you. A regular ascension practice will reveal your true intent to you more frequently and help guide you along your spiritual and magickal path. This sounds easier, but it takes someone well versed in ascension practice to perform this. Do not stay connected too long or you could end up imbalanced or ill.

Weight Loss

Perform a self-purification ritual beforehand. Burn a standard temple incense for the duration of the following ritual (unless you have severe allergies in which case you can skip incense altogether). Or you can make an Asafoetida incense. It's entirely up to you.

Mix mint, lavender, and rose oil in Water of Asafoetida. Construct a ritual space of your own devise invoking Daemonic forces you associate with weight loss and the physical body. Also invoke Asafoetida (the Daemonic Force, not the plant). Stand naked in the prepared ritual space.

In a dragons blood ink mixed with a drop of your blood, draw the sigils of the Daemons invoked on your body. You can use a paintbrush if a quill pen is too sharp. Then, imagine your personal energy radiating from you in all directions encompassing the circle. Bring this energy back into yourself and see your body change before you. See your body the way you want it to look. Invoke the Daemons again, vibrating their enns as you repeat the visualization.

You may also choose to make an amulet or talisman for weight loss at this time using clay or wooden disks and incorporating sigils of the Daemons you are working with. Anoint it with your blood for this purpose along with appropriate oleums. If you can go into ascension and ask the Daemons to give you the symbols for the amulet or talisman, all the better because it will be specific to you. Anoint and charge these items with appropriate pillar or charging rituals. After the ritual you can either keep the drawn sigils on your person until your next bath/shower, or you can shower again directly after the ritual. I prefer the former when doing any physical "body" work whether it be healing or physical self-transformation. Wear any amulets made or carry any talismans made and cleanse them nightly on the altar. Repeat this ritual monthly until you reach your weight loss goals. Other Daemons helpful in this particular area are Asmodeus, Orias, Buer, Verrine, Verrier, and Ashtaroth.

Appendices:
Enn Reference

Dukante Hierarchy

Family 1 :

Satan - King : *Tasa reme laris Satan - Ave Satanis*
Unsere - Fertility and Sorcery : *Unsere tasa lirach on ca ayar*
Satanchia - Grand General (War) : *Furca na alle laris Satanchia*
Agaliarept - Assistant Grand General (War) : *On ca Agaliarept agna*
Lucifage - High Command (Control) : *Eyen tasa valocur Lucifuge Rofocale*
Flereous - Fire Elemental : *Ganic Tasa Fubin Flereous*
Lucifer - Air Elemental : *Renich Tasa Uberaca Biasa Icar Lucifer*
Beelzebuth - Lord of insects : *Adey vocar avage Beelzebuth*
Belphegore - Master of Weaponry- gain : *Lyan Ramec Catya Ganen Belphegore*
Mesphito - Keeper of the book of death : *Mesphito ramec viasa on ca*
Delepitoré- Daemoness of magick. : *Deyen pretore ramec Delepitore on ca*
Belial - Earth Elemental : *Lirach Tasa Vefa Wehlc Belial*

Family 2
Luithian - Advisor : *Deyan anay tasa Luithian*
Leviathan - Water Elemental : *Jaden Tasa Hoet Naca Leviathan*
Sonnelion - Daemoness of hate : *Ayer Serpente Sonnillion*

417

Family 3
Abbadon - Advisor : *Es na ayer Abbadon avage*
Ammon - Daemon of domination : *Avage Secore Ammon ninan*
Mammon - Daemon of Avarice : *Tasa Mammon on ca lirach*

Family 4
Rosier - Daemon of love : *Serena Alora Rosier Aken*
Astarte - Daemoness of love : *Serena Alora Astarte Aken*
Ashtaroth - Priestess of friendship : *Tasa Alora foren Ashtaroth*
Astarot - Matters concerning the heart : *Serena Alora Astartot Aken*
Amducious - The destroyer : *Denyen valocur avage secore Amducious*
Asmodeus - Daemon of Lust : *Ayer avage Aloren Asmodeus aken*

Family 5
Eurynomous - Daemon of Death : *Ayar Secore on ca Eurynomous*
Balberith - Prince of dying : *Avage Secoré on ca Baalberith*
Babeal - Keeper of Graves : *Alan Secore on ca Babeal*

Family 6
Verrine - Daemon of Health : *Elan Typan Verrine*
Verrier - Daemoness of herbal knowledge : *Elit Rayesta Verrier*
Ronwe - Daemon of Knowledge : *Kaymen Vefa Ronwe*

Family 7
Svengali - Daemon of Vengeance : *Desa on Svengali ayer*
Tezrian - Priestess of battle : *Ezyr ramec ganen Tezrian*

Family 8
Asafoetida - Daemoness of feminine attributes : *Asana nanay on ca Asafoetida*
Rashoon - Priestess of seduction: *Taran Rashoon nanay*
Taroon - Priestess of Desire: *Taroon an ca nanay*

Family 9
Berith: *Hoath redar ganabal Berith*
Agares: *Rean ganen ayar da Agares*
Abigor: *Aylan Abigor tasa uan on ca*
Lilith: *Renich viasa avage lilith lirach*

Goetia

Goetic Daemon Enns compiled by Valerie Corban
Bael – Ayer Secore On Ca Ba'al
Agares – Rean ganen ayar da Agares
Vassago – Keyan vefa jedan tasa Vassago
Samigina (also Gamigin) – Esta ta et tasa Gamigin
Marbas - Renich tasa uberace biasa icar Marbas
Valefor – Keyman vefa tasa Valefor
Amon - Avage Secore Amon ninan
Barbatos – Eveta fubin Barbatos
Paimon – Linan tasa jedan Paimon.
Buer - Erato on ca Buer anon
Gusion – Secore vesa anet Gusion
Sitri – Lirach Alora vefa Sitri
Beleth – Lirach tasa vefa wehl Beleth.
Leraje (also Leraikha)- Caymen vefa Leraje.
Eligos – Jedan on ca Eligos inan.
Zepar – Lyan Ramec catya Zepar
Botis – Jedan hoesta noc ra Botis.
Bathin - Dyen Pretore on ca Bathin
Sallos (also Saleos) - Serena Alora Sallos Aken
Purson – Ana jecore on ca Purson
Marax (also Narax) - Kaymen Vefa Marax

419

Ipos – Desa an Ipos Ayer
Aim – Ayer avage secore Aim.
Naberius – Eyan tasa volocur Naberius
Glasya-Labolas – Elan tepar secore on ca Glasya-Lobolas.
Bune (also Bime) – Wehl melan avage Bune Tasa.
Ronove – Kaymen vefa ronove
Berith – Hoath redar ganabal Berith
Astaroth – Tasa Alora Foren Astaroth
Forneus – Senan okat ena Forneus ayer.
Foras – Kaymen vefa Foras
Asmoday – Ayer avage Aloren Asmoday aken
Gaap – Deyan Anay Tasa Gaap
Furfur – Ganen menach tasa Furfur
Marchosias – Es na ayer Marchosias Secore.
Stolas (also Stolos)– Stolos Ramec viasa on ca.
Phenex (also Pheynix)– Ef enay Phenex ayer.
Halphas – Erato Halphas on ca secore
Malphas– Lirach tasa Malphas ayer
Raum – Furca na alle laris Raum
Focalor – En Jedan on ca Focalor
Vepar – On ca Vepar Ag Na
Sabnock – Tasa Sabnock on ca Lirach
Shax – Ayer Avage Shax aken
Vine – Eyesta nas Vine ca laris
Bifrons – Avage secore Bifrons remie tasa
Uvall (also Vual or Voval)– As ana nany on ca Uvall.
Haagenti – Haaventi on ca Lirach
Crocell – Jedan tasa Crocell on ca
Furcas – Secore on ca Furcas remie
Balam – Lirach tasa vefa wehl Balam
Alloces – Typan efna Alloces met tasa
Camio (also Caim) – Tasa on ca Caim renich
Murmur (also Murmus)- Vefa mena Murmur ayer
Orobas – Jedan tasa hoet naca Orobas
Gremory (also Gemory or Gamori) – An tasa shi Gremory
on ca

Ose (also Voso or Oso) – Ayer serpente Ose.
Amy (also Avnas) – Tu Fubin Amy secore
Oriax (also Orias) – Lirach mena Orias Anay na
Vapula (also Naphula) – Renich secore Vapula typan
Zagan – Anay on ca secore Zagan tasa
Volac (also Valak, Valac, or Valu)– Avage Secore on ca
Volac
Andras – Entey ama Andras anay.
Haures (also Flauros, Haurus, or Havres) – Ganic tasa fubin
Flauros.
Andrealphus - Mena Andrealphus tasa ramec ayer
Cimejes (also Cimeies or Kimaris) – Ayer avage secore
Cimejes
Amdusias (also Amdukias)– Denyen valocur avage secore
Amdusias
Belial – Lirach Tasa Vefa Wehl Belial
Decarabia – Hoesta noc ra Decarabia secore
Seere (also Sear or Seir)- Jeden et Renich Seere tu tasa
Dantalion – Avage ayer Dantalion on ca
Andromalius – Tasa fubin Andromalius on ca

A note about the Enns: If you are looking for
Enns not included in this book, an ascension session should
provide you with one. Personal invocations can also be
used. If you have friends who are Daemonolaters, they may
be able to provide you with Enns as well.

Sigil Reference

Dukante Sigil Art courtesy Kenneth Betts

Abbadon

Abigor

Agaliarept

Amducius

Ammon

Asafoetida

Ashtaroth

Asmodeus

Astaroth/Astarot

Astarte

Ba'al

Ba'alberith

Balandax/Ba'alandax/Dax

Beehamoth/Behamot

Baelzebuth

Belial (Ba'al El)

Belphegore

Boragas

Delepitore/Delepitorae

Eurynomous

Flereous

Hecate

Leviathan

Lilith

Lucifer

Lucifuge

Luithian

Mammon

Mesphito

Rashoon

Ronwe/Ronove

Rosier

Satan

Satancha

Sonnillion

Svenagali

Taroon

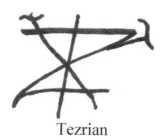

Tezrian

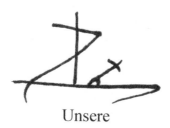

Unsere

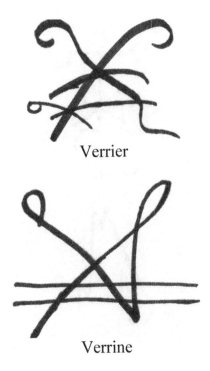

Verrier

Verrine

This invocation sigil can also be used to represent Satan, The All or any of the Nine Divinities. See the section on Invocation to learn more about the invocation sigil.

The Daemonolater's Guide to Daemonic Magick

Goetic Hierarchy Sigils

Bael

Agares

Vassago

Gamigin

Marbas

Valefor

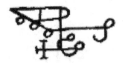

Amon

Barbatos

Paimon

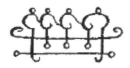

Buer

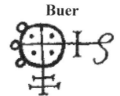

Gusion

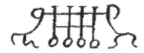

Sitri/Sytry

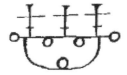

Beleth

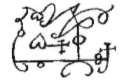

Leraje

Elgios

Zepar

Botis

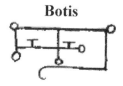

Bathin

Sallos

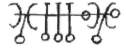

Purson

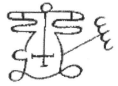

Marax

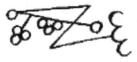

Ipos

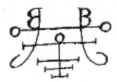

Aim

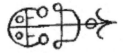

Naberius

Glasya-Labolas

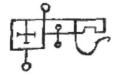

Bune

Ronove

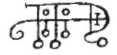

Berith

Astaroth

Forneus

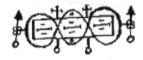

Foras

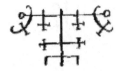

Asmoday

Gaap

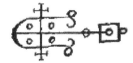

Furfur

Marchosias

Stolas

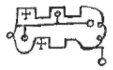

Phenex

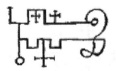

Halphas

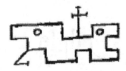

Malphas

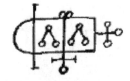

Raum

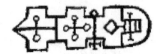

Focalor

Vepar

Sabnock

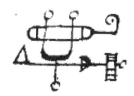

Shax

Vine

Bifrons

Uvall

Haagenti

Crocell

Furcus

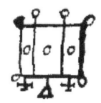

Balam

Alloces

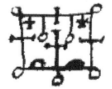

Caim

Murmur

Orobas

Gremory

Ose

Amy

Orias

Vapula

Zagan

Volac

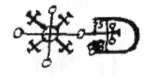

Andras

Haures

Andrealphus

Cimejes

Amducious.

Belial

Decarabia

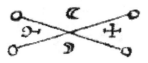

Seere

Dantalion

Andromalius

Daemonic Correspondences

Dukanté Hierarchy

Note: The correspondences of the Nine Daemonic Divinities came from Richard Dukanté's grimoires. The rest are personal correspondences from the authors including S. Connolly, S. Dukante-Mallory, Valerie Corban, and Brid Delaney. If these do not work for you, feel free to use your own.

The Nine Daemonic Divinities

Belial – Earth elemental.

- Colors: Green, brown, black.
- Direction: North.
- Holy Day: December 21st.
- Month: December.
- Season: Winter.
- Ritual: Initiation, new beginnings, winter solstice.
- Herb: Patchouli.
- Element: Earth.

Lucifer – Air elemental.

- Colors: Yellow, white.
- Direction: East.
- Holy Days: March 21st and November 13th.
- Month: March.
- Season: Spring.
- Ritual: Enlightenment, spring equinox, initiations.
- Herb: Lemon Balm or Lemons.
- Element: Air.

Flereous – Fire elemental.

- Colors: Red, orange.
- Direction: South.
- Holy Day: June 21st.
- Month: June.
- Season: Summer.
- Ritual: Baptism, love, action, solstice.
- Herb: Sandalwood, Sage.
- Element: Fire.

Leviathan – Water elemental.

- Colors: Blue, grey.
- Direction: West.
- Holy Days: May 1st and September 21st.
- Month: September.
- Season: Autumn.
- Ritual: Emotions, initiation, equinox, healing, fertility.
- Herb: Calamus.
- Element: Water.

Satan – The All is One (*I gohed I gohed*).

- <u>Colors:</u> All.
- <u>Directions</u>: All.
- <u>Holy Days</u>: All.
- <u>Months</u>: All.
- <u>Season</u>: All.
- <u>Ritual</u>: All.
- <u>Herb</u>: All.
- <u>Element:</u> Spirit (Fifth Element).

Verrine – Positive polarity (healing).

- <u>Colors:</u> Blue, white.
- <u>Direction</u>: Northwest.
- <u>Month</u>: November.
- <u>Season:</u> Late autumn.
- <u>Ritual:</u> Healing.
- <u>Herb:</u> All
- <u>Element</u>: Earthy part of Water.

Amducious – Negative polarity (destroying).

- <u>Colors</u>: Orange or Red.
- <u>Direction</u>: Southeast.
- <u>Month</u>: May and August.
- <u>Season</u>: Late spring, Late Summer.
- <u>Ritual:</u> War, action, dispelling negativity, demands.
- <u>Herb:</u> Black mustard and Saffron.
- <u>Element:</u> Airy part of fire.

Unseré – Fertility and sorcery.

- <u>Colors</u>: Green, white.
- <u>Direction</u>: Northeast.
- <u>Month</u>: February.
- <u>Season</u>: Late winter.
- <u>Ritual</u>: Understanding, patience, motherhood.
- <u>Herb</u>: Sage and Mugwort.
- <u>Element</u>: Airy part of earth.

Eurynomous – Daemon of death.

- <u>Colors</u>: Black
- <u>Direction</u>: Northeast.
- <u>Holy Day</u>: October 31st.
- <u>Month</u>: October.
- <u>Season</u>: Late autumn.
- <u>Ritual</u>: New beginnings, death, rebirth, celebration of death, Halloween.
- <u>Herb</u>: Mullein.
- <u>Element</u>: Earth.

Other Daemons of the Dukanté Hierarchy:

Abaddon – Advisor, hatred, vengeance, war.

- <u>Color</u>: Red.
- <u>Direction</u>: South.
- <u>Ritual</u>: Cursing, binding, bidding.
- <u>Herb</u>: Hemlock and Black peppercorn.
- <u>Element</u>: Fire.

Ammon – Daemon of domination.

- Color: Pink.
- Direction: Southeast.
- Ritual: Binding, compelling.
- Herbs: High John.
- Element: Fire part of Air.

Ashtaroth – Priestess of friendship and divination.

- Color: Aqua
- Ritual: Finding friends, divination
- Herb: Cassia or Clary Sage
- Element: Watery Fire.

Asmodeus – Daemon of lust.

- Color: Crimson or Red.
- Direction: South.
- Ritual: Lust workings, sexual magic.
- Herb: Myrrh and Cinnamon
- Element: Fire

Astarte – Daemoness of love

- Color: Maroon
- Direction: Southwest.
- Ritual: Love relationships, soul mates
- Herbs: Jasmine and roses
- Element: Watery part of Fire

457

Azlyn – Weaves the threads of things to come, future, divination.

- <u>Color</u>: Light Blue.
- <u>Direction</u>: West.
- <u>Ritual</u>: Divination.
- <u>Herb</u>: Water Lily or Camphor
- <u>Element</u>: Water.

Baalberith – Prince of dying.

- <u>Color</u>: Black, gray.
- <u>Direction</u>: North.
- <u>Holy Day</u>: October 31st.
- <u>Ritual</u>: Death, rebirth, protection of the dead.
- <u>Herb</u>: Solomon's Seal, Mandrake, Mullein
- <u>Element</u>: Earth.

Babeal – Keeper of graves.

- <u>Color</u>: Gray.
- <u>Direction</u>: All.
- <u>Holy Day</u>: October 31st.
- <u>Ritual</u>: Death, rebirth, protection of cemeteries.
- <u>Herb</u>: Sage, Myrrh
- <u>Element</u>: Earth.

Beelzebuth – Lord of Lords.

- <u>Color</u>: Brown.
- <u>Direction</u>: Northeast.
- <u>Season</u>: Autumn.
- <u>Ritual</u>: Money, prosperity, luck.
- <u>Herb</u>: yarrow
- <u>Element</u>: Earthy part of air.

Belphegore – Mastery, gain, money, armor

- <u>Color</u>: Green.
- <u>Direction</u>: North.
- <u>Holy Days</u>: March 31st, April 9th, and May 13th.
- <u>Season</u>: Spring.
- <u>Ritual</u>: Gain, money, jobs, shielding
- <u>Herb</u>: Mint
- <u>Element</u>: Earth.

Delepitoré – Daemoness of magic, divination, ascension.

- <u>Color</u>: Violet
- <u>Direction</u>: Southwest
- <u>Season</u>: Spring.
- <u>Ritual</u>: Magic/sorcery, divination, ascension onto the Daemonic plane.
- <u>Herb</u>: Frankincense and Clary Sage.
- <u>Element</u>: Fire part of water.

459

Lilith – Feminine mystique, power.

- <u>Colors</u>: White
- <u>Direction</u>: East
- <u>Ritual</u>: Wisdom, motherhood, feminine
- <u>Herb</u>: Angelica Root.
- <u>Element</u>: Air.

Mesphito – Keeper of the book of death.

- <u>Colors</u>: Black and gray.
- <u>Direction</u>: Northwest.
- <u>Ritual</u>: Knowledge, secrets, sorcery.
- <u>Herb</u>: Mandrake and Frankincense.
- <u>Element</u>: Watery part of Earth.

Ronwe – Daemon of knowledge.

- <u>Color</u>: Yellow or White.
- <u>Direction</u>: East.
- <u>Ritual</u>: Knowledge, creativity, learning, enlightenment, inspiration.
- <u>Herb</u>: White Sandalwood.
- <u>Element</u>: Air

Rosier – Daemon of love.

- <u>Colors</u>: Pink.
- <u>Direction</u>: Southwest.
- <u>Ritual</u>: Long-term relationships, love, self-love.
- <u>Herbs</u>: Roses and Cardamom
- <u>Element</u>: Watery part of Fire.

Sonnillion – Daemoness of hate.

- <u>Color</u>: Crimson
- <u>Direction</u>: Southwest.
- <u>Month</u>: July.
- <u>Season</u>: Midsummer.
- <u>Ritual</u>: Letting go of anger, cursing, balancing, focus.
- <u>Herb</u>: Cinnamon
- <u>Element</u>: Firey part of water.

Svengali – Daemon of vengeance.

- <u>Colors</u>: Bronze
- <u>Direction</u>: Southeast.
- <u>Ritual</u>: Cursing, hatred, vengeance, Protection
- <u>Herb</u>: Coriander.
- <u>Element</u>: Fire of air

Tezrian – Priestess of battle.

- <u>Color</u>: Gold or Yellow.
- <u>Direction</u>: Southeast.
- <u>Ritual</u>: Cursing, wisdom/power.
- <u>Herb</u>: Devils Claw
- <u>Element</u>: Fire part of air.

Verrier – Daemoness of herbal knowledge, healing.

- <u>Color</u>: Light green.
- <u>Direction</u>: Northwest.
- <u>Month</u>: November.
- <u>Season</u>: Early Spring & Late autumn.
- <u>Ritual</u>: Healing, earth, knowledge of herbalism.
- <u>Herb</u>: All
- <u>Element</u>: Earthy part of water.

Goetic Hierarchy:

Kings –

- Color: Yellow.
- Incense: Frankincense.
- Metal: Gold.
- Planet: Sun.

Bael (Fire)
Vine (Water)
Paymon/Paimon (Water)
Balam (Earth)
Belial (Fire)
Zagan (Earth)
Asmoday (Air)
Purson (Earth)
Beleth (Earth)

Dukes –
- Color: Green.
- Incense: Sandalwood.
- Metal: Copper.
- Planet: Venus.

Agares (Earth)
Barbatos (Fire)
Gusoin (Water)
Zepar (Earth)
Aim (Fire)
Bune (Earth)
Astaroth (Earth)
Berith (Fire)
Focalor (Water)
Vapula (Air)
Amducious (Air)
Vepar (Water)
Uvall (Water)
Crocell (Water)
Alloces (Fire)
Murmur (Fire)
Gremory (Water)
Haures (Fire)
Dantalion (Water)
Bathin (Earth)
Sallos (Earth)
Elgios (Water)
Valfar/Valfor (Earth)

Marquis –
- <u>Color</u>: Violet.
- <u>Incense</u>: Jasmine.
- <u>Metal</u>: Silver.
- <u>Planet</u>: Moon.

Decarabia (Air)
Cimejes (Earth)
Andrealphus (Air)
Andras (Fire)
Amon (Water)
Naberius (Fire)
Ronove (Air)
Forneus (Water)
Marchosias (Fire)
Phenex (Fire)
Sabnock (Fire)
Shax (Air)
Leraje (Fire)
Oriax (Air)

Princes –

- Color: Blue.
- Incense: Cedar.
- Metal: Tin.
- Planet: Jupiter.

Vassago (Water)
Sitri (Earth)
Ipos (Water)
Stolas (Air)
Orobas (Water)
Seere (Fire)

Presidents –

- <u>Color</u>: Orange.
- <u>Incense</u>: Storax.
- <u>Metal</u>: Mercury.
- <u>Planet</u>: Mercury.

Gamigin (Water)
Marbas (Air)
Buer (Fire)
Botis (Water)
Marax (Earth)
Glasya-Labolas (Fire)
Foras (Earth)
Gaap (Air)
Haagenti (Earth)
Caim (Air)
Ose (Air)
Amy (Fire)
Volac (Earth)
Malphas (Air)

Earls –
- Color: Red.
- Incense: Dragon's Blood.
- Metal: Copper or silver.
- Planet: Mars.

Furfur (Fire)
Halphas (Air)
Raum (Air)
Bifrons (Earth)
Andromalius (Fire)

Knights –
- Color: Black.
- Incense: Myrrh.
- Metal: Lead.
- Planet: Saturn.

Furcus (Air)

Daemons Listed By Purpose

By S. Connolly

Love -- Lust -- Relationships --Compassion

Rosier
Astarte
Ashtaroth
Astaroth
Asmodeous
Agrat-bat-mahlaht
Eisheth Zenunim
Lilith
Naamah
Asafoetida
Rashoone
Taroone

Hatrid -- Vengeance -- Anger -- War

Amducious
Andras
Merihim
Abbadon
Satanchia
Lucifuge Rofocale
Agaliarept
Feurety
Sargatanas
Nebiros
Baal
Sonnilion
Tezrian
Olivier
Mephestophiles
Dumah
Proserpine
Belphegore
Svengali

Life -- Healing

Unsere
Verrine
Verrier
Belial

Death

Eurynomous
Baalberith
Babael

Nature

Belial
Lucifer
Satan
Flereous
Leviathan
Rimmon
Dagon
Rahab
Seriel

Money -- Prosperity -- Luck

Behemoth
Belphegore
Asmodeous
Astaroth
Oeillet
Olivier
Beelzebub
Mammon

Knowledge -- Secrets -- Sorcery

Ronwe
Pytho
Lucifer
Leviathan
Baalberith
Unsere
Delepitorae
Mesphito
Luithian
Abbadon
Verrier

Magickal Scripts & Languages

A book about magick would be incomplete if we didn't include something in the appendices about magickal script and languages. Oftentimes the inexperienced magician will complain, "Why do something in a language or script other than your native tongue? It will lose its meaning! Why do all that work to translate?"

There are reasons. First – translating invocations into Enochian, for example, will ensure you've put a proper amount of thought and effort into your intent. Since you initially wrote your invocation in English (or whatever your native tongue is), chances are you understand it quite well. The use of a different language, or requests written in a magickal script and burnt, for example, is that in the act of translating and 'creating' as it were – you are actually fine tuning your intent. Or, you might use different languages or scripts to keep your magickal work secret from prying eyes. The following pages contain some of the more popular magickal scripts for your reference. Additionally, I suggest the book *The Magician's Companion* by Bill Whitcomb for a more thorough encyclopedia of magickal correspondences, alphabets, and symbolism. For those interested in Enochian, a good Enochian dictionary is in order.

473

Enochian Script

⚡ A	ꓶ I	ꓷ S			
V B	ⅽ L	⁄ T			
ꓮ C	Ɛ M	ꓒ U			
ꓫ D	Ɔ N	ꓒ V			
ꓶ E	⌐ O	ꓒꓒ W			
ꓙ F	Ω P	ꓦ X			
ꓭ G	Ⴗ Q	ꓶ Y			
ꓳ H	ꓮ R	Ⴔ Z			

Ogham Script

┼	A	╪	I	╡	S
┤	B	╡	L	╞	T
╞	C	┼	M	╪	U
╠	D	╡	N	╪	Z
╪	E	┼	O	✳	ea
╡	F	╪	P	◇	oi
╪	G	╠	Q	ꝗ	ui
├	H	╪	R	✕	ia

Runic Script

ᚠ	A	ᛋ	J	ᚱ	R
ᛒ	B	ᚲ	K	ᛋ	S
ᛞ	D	ᛚ	L	ᛏ	T
ᛖ	E	ᛗ	M	ᚢ	U
ᚠ	F	ᚾ	N	ᚹ	W
ᚷ	G	◇	ng	ᛉ	Z
ᚺ	H	ᛟ	O		
ǀ	I	ᛈ	P		

Theban Script

ᚦ	A	ᚦ	I	ᚦ	Q
ᚦ	B	ᚦ	J	ᚦ	R
ᚦ	C	ᚦ	K	ᚦ	S
ᚦ	D	ᚦ	L	ᚦ	T
ᚦ	E	ᚦ	M	ᚦ	U
ᚦ	F	ᚦ	N	ᚦ	V
ᚦ	G	ᚦ	O	ᚦ	W
ᚦ	H	ᚦ	P	ᚦ	X
				ᚦ	Y
				ᚦ	Z

INDEX

E

Earls
  of goetic hierarchy,
    338
Effigies, 80
Egypt, 263
Elemental Alchemical
  Properties, 202
elemental balancing
  identifying imbalance,
    99
Elemental Balancing, 98
elemental balancing
  ritual, 102
Elemental Circle, 39
elemental herbs, 334
Elemental Magick, 97
Elements, 97
Elgios, 336, 436
Emerald Tablet, 134
Energy work, 276
enn reference, 419
Enochian, 18, 21, 22,
  196, 197, 198, 204,
  213, 216, 249, 251,
  252, 473, 474
Eurynomous, 164
Evocation, 41
execration magicks, 283.
  See curses

F

fasting, 73
Fertility, 360
Financial Magick, 363

Fire Base, 334
Flereous, 164, 334
Focalor, 336, 443
focus energy, 279
Foras, 338, 440
Formulary, 326
Forneus, 337
Four Worlds, 254, 268
Frankincense, 335
friendship magick, 399
Furcus, 338, 445
Furfur, 338, 441

G

Gaap, 338, 441
Gamigin, 338, 433
Gematria, 196, 198, 200,
  201, 204
Glasya-Labolas, 338, 439
Goap, 334
Goetia Elementals, 38
Goetic Demonic
  Hierarchy, 334
Gremory, 336, 446
grimoires, 18, 20, 31, 64,
  258
Group Magick, 70
Gusion, 336, 435

H

Haagenti, 338, 444
Halphas, 338, 442
harmony magick, 369
Haures, 336, 448

Presidents
  of goetic hierarchy,
    338
Priesthood, 223
Princes
  of goetic hierarchy,
    337
Prometheus, 53
Psychic Attack, 295
Psychic Self Defense, 292
psychic vampires, 310
Purification, 395, 398
Purson, 335, 437

Q

Qabbalah, 21, 134, 196,
  225, 249, 254, 268,
  269, 270, 488
Qlippoth, 255, 267
quantum physics, 60

R

raise energy, 277
Raum, 338, 442
residual energy, 241
Rite of Making, 400
Ritual Construction
  various forms of, 45
Ritual Constructs
  basic elemental circle,
    39
Ritual oils, 116
Ronove, 337, 439
Rue, 334

S

Sabnock, 337, 443
Sallos, 336, 437
Salves, 119
Sandalwood, 334, 336,
  338
Satan, 164
Sator square, 226
Seduction, 359
Seere, 337, 450
Selinda's Favorite Base,
  334
Sending energy, 280
sephira, 220, 254, 267
Servitors, 234, 281
Sex magick, 230, 231
Shax, 337, 443
sigil, 38, 54, 82, 137, 139,
  141, 142, 144, 171,
  179, 180, 193, 194,
  232, 234, 236, 237,
  238, 240, 242, 243,
  287, 288, 290, 295,
  305, 306, 308, 315,
  340, 342, 343, 356,
  363, 366, 371, 375,
  376, 382, 383, 384,
  386, 392, 393, 394,
  400, 402, 403, 404,
  406, 407, 409, 410, 411
  goetic, 433
  invocaton, 432
sigil magick, 238
sigil reference, 422
Sitri, 337, 435

ABOUT THE AUTHORS

S. Connolly

Ms. Connolly has devoted her entire life to the study of magick and the occult. She has been a practicing Daemonolatress since 1988, and a practicing magician since 1984. She is the author of Modern Demonolatry, Lessons in Demonolatry, The Complete Book of Demonolatry, and The Art of Creative Magick. She edited and contributed to Ater Votum: Daemonolatry Prayer, and Demonolatry Rites. Her forthcoming work includes The Daemonolatry Goetia (co-author), and The Kasdeya Rite of Ba'al. A practicing soft-polytheist pantheistic Daemonolatress and working magician, she was taken on as a student of Selinda Dukanté at the age of 16. She was formally initiated into the family sect tradition of Traditional Khemetic/Canaanite based Daemonolatry in 1990, and is a traditionally ordained priestess. She is currently the Reverend High Priestess of the Daemonolatry sect Ordo Flammeus Serpens. She maintains memberships and degrees in several initiatory organizations that aren't "religious" per se, but that do compliment her "occult" philosophies, beliefs, and practices.

Valerie Corban

Valerie Corban is Beloved of Valefor. She met her husband (a raised generational Daemonolater) in 1984 and immediately converted. They were married in 1985. Prior to that, she was a practicing ceremonial/goetic magician (since 1978). She is a former degree-holding member of the OTO.

Bridgette Delaney

Brid Delaney is a first generation Daemonolatress and was raised with Daemonolatry as her religious belief. She has been working with Goetic and Semitic Daemons since the late 60's (as long as she can remember) and has been practicing Daemonic Magick since the late 70's. She is the mother of two and is married to a Generational Daemonolater.

OTHER CONTRIBUTORS

Anjie Anon – Is a Khemetic Daemonolatress and Vampyre who has been practicing since the late 1980's. She is beloved of Bast and a Keeper of the Path of Ptah.

M. Delaney – M. Delaney is a generational Daemonolater whose family traditions have been traced back to the 1500's. He has been working with Daemons and practicing Daemonic Magick for as long as he can remember. He is the author of *Sanctus Quattuordecim,* a book about Traditional Daemonolatry Sigil Magick.

Selinda T. Dukanté. – Ms. Dukanté is a second generation Traditional Daemonolatress. Her father, Richard Dukanté, put together a popular, largely Western Semitic Daemonic hierarchy in the 1960's. He was a renowned magician (in the Daemonolatry community) who spent the bulk of his career seeking to discover the mysteries of both known and unfound Daemons and their correspondences. He, unfortunately, passed on before his work or his hierarchy were even close to being complete. Ms. Dukanté's experience with Daemonolatry and Daemonic Magick extends back into her childhood, but took off in the 1970's.

D. Mallory - D. is a convert to Traditional Daemonolatry from Golden Dawn where he was a degree-holding member. He is well versed in Hermetics, and Rosicrucianism (AMORC) and has been practicing ceremonial magick and Daemonic Magick since the late 1970's.

Brad Morlan – Brad Morlan is a blended Generational Daemonolater and Traditional Witch. He was ordained as a High Priest in both traditions by his late Grandfather. His family Matron is Hecate, who still holds a great presence in his life, even though his Patron Demon is Lucifer. Hecate gave Brad the magical name of Merwyyn when he was a young child.

Ellen Purswell – Ellen Purswell has been a practicing Goetic Magician for over 50 years, and a Daemonolatress for over 40 years. She married into Traditional Daemonolatry and is the author of the book *Goetic Daemonolatry.*

Lisa P. – Lisa is a Generational Traditional Daemonolatress and a Priestess of Ba'al. She has been practicing Daemonic Magick since the late 1970's and has a strong background in Canaanite practices and Qabbalah.

Kelly Schneider – Kelly is a recent convert to Daemonolatry. However, she has been a practicing magician since the mid-eighties and has experience in witchcraft, ceremonial magick, and Khemetic magick.

Nick Schneider (GoeticNick) – GoeticNick is a first generation Traditional Daemonolater and practicing magician who has spent his entire life working with the

Goetic hierarchy. He is also the co-author of the book *The Daemonolatry Goetia.*

THE PINEAPPLE

Made in the USA
Coppell, TX
21 September 2020